Talking with Dementia

Reconsidering Dementia Series Editors: Dr Keith Oliver and Professor Dawn Brooker MBE

Talking with Dementia

*Keith Oliver, Reinhard Guss
and Ruth Bartlett*

Open University Press

Open University Press
McGraw Hill
Unit 4
Foundation Park
Roxborough Way
Maidenhead
SL6 3UD

Email: emea_uk_ireland@mheducation.com
World wide web: www.mheducation.co.uk

Commissioning Editor: Sam Crowe
Editorial Assistant: Hannah Jones
Production Manager: Ben King
Marketing Manager: Suzzy Bailey
Cover Design: Adam Renvoize
Cover Art: Keith Oliver
Logo Design: Julia Heron
Content Product Manager: Graham Jones

British Library Cataloguing in Publication Data

A catalogue record of this book is available from the British Library

ISBN-13: 978-0-3352-5128-5
ISBN-10: 0335251285
eISBN: 978-0-3352-5129-2

Typeset by Transforma Pvt. Ltd., Chennai, India
Printed and bound by CPI Group (UK) Ltd, Croydon, CR0 4YY

Praise Page

"An important addition to the lexicon and discourse around dementia. It made me reflect on how much advocacy of dementia has developed in the last 30 years. The voice of lived experience is ever growing and without doubt we should never miss an opportunity like this to listen, capture and learn from it."

Paola Barbarino, CEO, Alzheimer's Disease International

"Keith Oliver continues to be amazing and this latest book will help so many people - those with dementia and their loved ones."

Victoria Derbyshire, British Journalist, Newsreader and Broadcaster

"This book gives a voice to those living with dementia. It shares their experiences, shows their reality and highlights the difference that seeing the person, and not the dementia, has. It showcases so clearly that whilst there are common threads in this lived experience, all wish to be seen for who they are. It reminds us that whilst dementia can alter a person, who they are is still there at the core."

John Suchet OBE and Nula Suchet, Ambassadors for
Alzheimer's Society and Dementia UK

*"*Talking with Dementia, Reconsidered *is an engaging work of dementia activism that draws inspiration from both heart and head. It builds on interviews with a wide range of people with dementia to argue - convincingly - that personhood and Kitwood's famous flower endure as key lenses to understanding the lived experience. Accessibly co-produced, authentic and enlightening,* Talking with Dementia, Reconsidered *comes highly recommended."*

Kate Lee, Chief Executive Officer, Alzheimer's Society, UK

"This book successfully uses Kitwood's flower of needs to guide interviews with 15 people living with dementia. These voices so eloquently detail not only what it is like to live with dementia, but more importantly how they have adapted and what is important to live life as well as possible. A key theme running through the book is how peer support, and a focus on strengths and what can be done, has helped each person navigate through some difficulties along the way. I found Part 2 of the book really enlightening and would strongly advise all health and social care professionals to read this and rethink what they "know" about dementia."

Dr Hilda Hayo Chief Admiral Nurse and CEO Dementia UK

"Keith, Ruth and Reinhard's book, Talking with Dementia, Reconsidered *provides another contribution to the narrative of people who themselves are diagnosed with dementia, from the perspectives of people based in the UK. It references a few of the pioneer advocates, and also draws on the expertise of others. Whilst the changing narrative is important, it is yet to contribute to significant change such as reducing the numbers of human rights breaches experienced by people with dementia, and I hope this book contributes to a growing global voice of people with and without dementia, campaigning collectively, albeit in different ways, for the much needed change. Congratulations to the authors and contributors."*

Kate Swaffer, Author, Researcher and Co-founder,
Dementia Alliance International

"This is a wonderful and creative book, packed full of people, stories, perspectives, hopes, wishes, expectations and deep philosophical reflections on what it is and means to live with dementia. 'The Fifteen' are at the heart of this book–fifteen diverse people with dementia supported to reflect on identity, occupation, inclusion, attachment, comfort and love in their experiences of living with dementia. These are multiple stories of connection, collaboration and belonging that provide a backdrop to explore the power of Tom Kitwood's work and enduring legacy, skilfully analysed by the book authors. There is a depth to this book which will stay with me for a long time."

Rachael Litherland, Co-Director of Innovations in Dementia

"This fascinating book is almost like two books in one, or perhaps an 18-part motet. There are 15 voices of selected dementia activists, mostly known well by the authors. They are interviewed based on the components of the 'Kitwood flower' – identity, occupation, inclusion, attachment, comfort and love. The varied and individual impacts of dementia upon people's lives emerge strongly and authentically. Loss and frustration, yes, but also growth and personal development. Interactions with people, families and peer group especially, are crucial though even activists need to withdraw and recharge at times.

The other three voices are the authors, who provide a helpful thread of commentary, but there's also a supporting cast of students and partners who have helped bring this unique project together. And the second book within the book? That consists of the detailed explanation of how to approach writing a book of this kind, which must be required reading for any successors looking to amplify and broadcast dementia voices. Talking with Dementia, Reconsidered *is a landmark, which will inspire professionals, researchers and the upcoming cohort of people whose lives are affected by dementia."*

Tom Dening, Professor of Dementia Research,
School of Medicine, University of Nottingham, UK

"It is heart-warming to see such a change in the way people can learn about dementia care. When I began research in this field 25 years ago, we often failed to ask people with dementia what they thought or felt, many undermining the subjectivity of their judgement. 'One door will close but another one will open', quoted by author Keith Oliver upon his diagnosis of Alzheimer's; is to me a summary of the book as well as the direction that his life has taken. This inspiring book takes the philosophy and ideas of Tom Kitwood, written nearly three decades ago; to the next step. Each 'petal of his flower' is reflected upon by 'The Fifteen', fifteen individuals all with their unique stories of life with dementia; as well as professionals though discussion of its current application in staff training and clinical formulation. These are the perspectives that really matter.

The test for us all now is to apply the fundamental messages portrayed in this book into practice. I would highly recommend this as essential reading for anyone working, studying or living with dementia."

Aimee Spector, Professor of Clinical Psychology of Ageing,
University College London, UK

"The best books tell an important story and **Talking with Dementia, Reconsidered** *certainly does that- fifteen of them in fact! It takes the seminal thinking and ideology of Tom Kitwood, expert and activist, bringing it to life through the very different stories of fifteen very different people united by their experience of living with the condition. A dementia diagnosis is earth shattering but this book shows it can also be the start of a journey not its end. By combining theory with authentic voices, we see that dementia cannot and should not ever be the person. This is an important message for those with lived experience or working professionally in the field. It is a seminal message for our times."*

Debbie Hicks MBE, Creative Director, The Reading Agency, UK

This book is dedicated to the Fifteen – Agnes Houston, Chris Maddocks, Chris Norris, Chris Roberts, Dianne Campbell, Frances Isaacs, Gail Gregory, George Rook, Jennifer Bute, Jim McNee, Julie Hayden, Keith Day (Cam), Masood Ahmed Qureshi (Maq), Nigel Hullah and Tracey Shorthouse, together with Lara Stembridge and Ellie Warman, and all those who provided inspiration along the way. This one is for all of you.

Contents

About the authors

Keith Oliver: Soon after his diagnosis of Alzheimer's disease, Keith Oliver was forced to retire in April 2011 from his career as a primary school headteacher and local authority education advisor alongside abandoning a master's course at his local university. After a period of adjustment and inertia, he met and befriended clinical psychologist Reinhard Guss and embarked upon creating a new teaching role for himself as an advocate, activist, ambassador and envoy within the world of dementia. He has written or contributed to six books: *Walk the Walk, Talk the Talk* (2016), *Welcome to Our World* (2014), *Dear Alzheimer's* (2019), *Time and Place: An Anthology of Poetry* (2021), *The Forget Me Nots* (2022) and chapter 5 of *Dementia Reconsidered, Revisited* (2019), the latter with Reinhard Guss. Keith is the co-editor with Professor Dawn Brooker of the *Reconsidering Dementia Series* in which this book sits. He has co-written many published articles, served on many dementia research project advisory groups, featured often on radio and television, has spoken widely at conferences in the UK and at Alzheimer's Disease International in Chicago, USA, and addressed the United Nations commission representing the rights of people with disabilities in Geneva. His work was honoured in November 2021 with a doctorate from Canterbury Christchurch University. Keith is married with three grown-up children, three grandchildren and lives in Canterbury, Kent.

Reinhard Guss: While studying Clinical Psychology with Gerontology in Germany, Reinhard came to the UK to complete his dissertation research project and stayed to specialise in working in mental health services for older people. In over 30 years of clinical practice as a clinical psychologist and neuropsychologist in the NHS, Reinhard has been involved in working with people with dementia, their families and carers, in diagnostic memory clinics, providing psychological therapies, teaching and training, and service development. Given the scarcity of Psychology resources, he has worked to support the systems and policies that improve quality and accessibility of services for people with dementia. He has worked with the Alzheimer's Society and Young Dementia UK in developing early services for younger people with dementia, with Dementia UK in the support of Admiral Nursing services, and with the Dementia Engagement and Empowerment Project (DEEP) in setting up involvement groups for people with a dementia diagnosis. Reinhard has served as chair of the Faculty of the Psychology of Older People (FPOP) in the British Psychological Society (BPS), and has been their dementia workstream lead for many years. He is Deputy Chair of the Memory Services National Accreditation Project (MSNAP), hosted by the Royal College of Psychiatrists. Reinhard is the BPS/UK representative on the European Standing Committee for Geropsychology of the European Federation of Psychology Associations (EFPA), which he currently chairs.

Ruth Bartlett: Ruth began her career as a mental health nurse. For the last 20 years, she has been working as an academic, researching and teaching subjects related to dementia care and citizenship. Ruth is interested in social justice and the power dynamics of dementia care and has been instrumental in bringing a citizenship lens to the field of dementia studies. She has published over 60 peer-reviewed research articles, three books, as well as editorials, essays and thought pieces for mainstream media. Her most cited work is 'From personhood to citizenship: broadening the conceptual base for dementia practice and research', written with Deborah O'Connor and published in the *Journal of Aging Studies* in 2007. In 2018, Ruth was invited to become editor of the journal *Dementia: The International Journal of Social Research and Practice*, a role she fulfilled with Elaine Weirsma for a 4-year term until December 2022. Ruth writes and collaborates with a wide range of people, including academics, experts by experience, artists, nurses and allied health professionals. Ruth has received funding from the Economic and Social Research Council, Alzheimer's Society, and National Institute for Health and Care Research (NIHR) to advance understanding of the needs and rights of citizens with dementia. She is currently leading a NIHR-funded project that aims to find out about access to social farms for people with dementia. Ruth currently lives and works in Southampton.

Foreword

To see the list of friends whose thoughts and experiences contributed to this book was such a joy.

All those friends from different backgrounds and different locations, yet brought together by a single diagnosis of dementia. Not a diagnosis anyone would wish to have but I see it as a gift bestowed on us, the ribbon that ties us loosely altogether and makes our voices stronger.

We all had talents before a diagnosis of dementia and we continue to use those talents to the best of our abilities. Keith, a headteacher in his previous life, continues, in this book, to lead the writing with the help of his academic allies.

As this book shows, we all had lives before a diagnosis of dementia and those life experiences contribute to the people we have become today

I am sure this book will be a valuable addition to the *Reconsidering Dementia Series*.

Wendy Mitchell, author and person living with dementia

The Reconsidering Dementia Series

The dementia field has developed rapidly in its scope and practice over the past 25 years. Many thousands of people are newly diagnosed each year. World-wide, the trend is that people are being diagnosed at much earlier stages. In addition, families and friends increasingly provide support to those affected by dementia over a prolonged period. Many people, both those diagnosed with dementia and those who support them, have an appetite to understand their condition. Care professionals and civic society also need an in-depth and nuanced understanding of how to support people living with dementia within their communities over the long term. The *Reconsidering Dementia* book series sets out to address this need. It takes its inspiration from the late Professor Tom Kitwood's seminal text *Dementia Reconsidered* published in 1997, which, at the time, revolutionised how dementia care was conceptualised.

The book series is jointly commissioned and edited by Professor Dawn Brooker MBE and by Dr Keith Oliver. Dawn has been active in the field of dementia care since the 1980s as a clinician and an academic. She draws on her experience and international networks to bring together a series of books on the most pertinent issues in the field. Keith is one of the foremost international advocates for those living with dementia. He also brings an insightful perspective of his own and others' experience of what it means to live with dementia gained since his diagnosis of Alzheimer's Disease in 2010.

Dawn and Keith have been professional colleagues for many years. They worked together on the second edition of Kitwood's book entitled *Dementia Reconsidered, Revisited: The Person Still Comes First*. This 2019 publication was a reprint of the original text by Tom Kitwood alongside contemporary commentaries for each chapter written by current experts. Many topics in the field of dementia care, however, were simply unheard of in Kitwood's lifetime. When Open University Press approached Dawn and Keith with the idea of developing a book series dedicated to dementia, they were very pleased to accept. The subsequent titles in this series are cutting-edge scholarly texts that challenge and engage readers to think deeply. They draw on theoretical under-standings, contemporary research and experience to critically reflect on their topic in great depth.

This does not mean, however, that they are not applicable to improving the care and support of those affected by dementia. As well as the scholarly text, all books have a 'So what?' thread that unpacks what this means for people living with dementia, their families, people working in dementia care, policy-makers, professionals, community activists and so on. Too many books either focus on an academic audience OR a practitioner audience OR a student audience OR a lived experience audience. In this series, the aim is to try to address these perspectives in the round. The *Reconsidering Dementia* book series brings together the perspectives of professional practice, scholarship and the lived experience as they pertain to the key topics in the field of dementia studies. All the books aim to help us to think afresh, to reconsider our standpoint and to ultimately improve the experience of those affected by dementia for years to come.

Preface

The *Reconsidering Dementia* book series is co-edited by myself and Keith Oliver. This book has been a different editorial experience in that Keith has also been the lead author. And so I find myself writing the editors' preface on my own.

All books in the series take the inclusion of the perspective of those living with dementia very seriously. However, most are led by authors who are highly experienced clinicians or academics in their field. When Keith and I were discussing potential titles that we thought were important to include in our series, we both knew that we wanted a book that was primarily authored by people living with dementia. Keith was keen to take a direct lead on this and was in an excellent position to do so, given his extensive networks and his considerable success in writing books and chapters to date. Keith had talked on many occasions about how important the Kitwood flower model had been to him in making sense of his dementia and he suggested this could be a good structure for a book through which other people could also share their insights.

I have to admit, when he first talked about this, I was rather taken aback. Kitwood developed the flower model in an era when most people were not diagnosed till late stage, if at all. During the 1990s, the prevailing wisdom was that people with dementia could not provide reliable accounts of their own experience. As a clinical psychologist working in that era originally, I had utilised the flower model of psychological needs primarily to understand why people might be experiencing distress, agitation and depression. Understanding which psychological needs were not being met, and how this could be remedied, was my day-to day work. To my mind, the flower model was something that I used clinically to help me understand the needs of people living with complex needs in later-stage dementia. When Keith started talking about it in the context of his life as someone living with dementia (but very able to articulate his feelings), I had a 'light-bulb' moment of insight. I realised that these psychological needs are universal and dementia has a direct impact on them from its earliest stages. Would it be possible that these concepts developed by Kitwood nearly 30 years ago, resonated with people today speaking about their lives? This idea bloomed into the book that you are reading today.

In many respects, discussions about what it is like to live with dementia are a million miles away from the discussions that took place during Kitwood's lifetime. He could not envisage that people living with dementia would be active players in shaping government and international policy; work as educators and motivational speakers; edit book series; create books, poetry and art that people would pay for; be social media experts and activists; or run conferences and undertake research. What Kitwood did recognise, however, was that personhood is a deep issue in the humanity of all of us. He recognised the vital importance of ensuring that the key psychological needs of Inclusion, Attachment, Comfort, Occupation and Identity are met. Moreover, Kitwood articulated that it is the wellspring of Love for our fellow human beings that has to remain at the heart of all our endeavours collectively and individually. Dementia sets up barriers to this but it does not defeat us.

Of all the books in the *Reconsidering Dementia* series, it is this one which is the most radical and authentically co-produced. The friendship between Keith and Reinhard enables them to bring their unique perspectives on personhood to bear on their conversations with fifteen remarkable people. The Fifteen share their insights with breath-taking honesty, wisdom and humour. Many times in reading their accounts I found myself choked up with emotion despite my many years spent working directly with those affected by dementia. There is something uniquely powerful in the space provided by Keith and Reinhard that enables people to express how they feel. The conversations bring us all to witness the heart of the human condition. Ruth also joins with Keith and Reinhard to explore what this means for our contemporary and future understandings of dementia. This book is truly Kitwood Reconsidered in the twenty-first century.

Series Editor: Professor Dawn Brooker MBE

Acknowledgements

Whilst this book is not in any shape 'ghost written', it is fair to say that without the help of a number of people there is no way that we could have successfully completed this project. First and foremost, Professor Dawn Brooker, while also being a tremendous editor alongside Keith for this book series, has always been steadfast, encouraging and supportive with her wisdom and good humour throughout. Next, Hannah Jones and Sam Crowe, alongside their team at Open University Press, have been so helpful and affirming, and never once have they failed to answer our questions or come up with a solution that worked well for everyone.

There have been occasions when we did wonder if, and when, the book would be completed. Central to overcoming these worries and doubts were the diligent and conscientious undergraduate psychology students who stepped into the breech and did so much to help. They shared the typing of transcripts, formulated thematic analyses from the transcripts, joined and took diligent notes during deep philosophical conversations between Reinhard and Keith about Kitwood and Buber, and crucially did a lot of the typing, referencing and organising of the text. The initial group included Theo Chan, Jonah Desalesa, Heather Winch and Adam Reid, whose conscientious transcribing of the audio interviews was used by Ellie Warman, Lara Stembridge and Millie Godfrey, joined later by Abigail Lugg, to produce the thematic analyses. Initially, all of the students were on placement with Kent and Medway NHS Social Care Partnership Trust (KMPT); after their placement finished, Ellie, Lara, Millie and Abigail continued as volunteers. All four were amazing in their commitment, enthusiasm and skills despite the pressures of their NHS placement followed by their final year as undergraduates back at the University of Kent. Indeed, Lara and Ellie went the extra mile when writing thoughtful contributions to Chapters 2 and 16. As the book progressed, the baton was shared with Mia Drury and Ashley Maina who were on placement with KMPT during 2022–23, and they too brought patience and fervency to the project. No one could have given more to this book than these ten outstanding young adults who we know will go on to successful careers.

We were absolutely delighted when Ruth Bartlett agreed to join our writing team, and Ruth has brought an academic perspective based upon wisdom and experience which enriches the understanding of the issues we have explored elsewhere in the book.

Thank you Wendy for your most thoughtful foreword, we know of no one better placed to do this. It was with great sadness that we learnt of Wendy's death in February 2024, shortly before the publication of this book. This makes her words in her foreword even more special. We are both immensely sad to think that you will not be with us to continue to talk about dementia and life in general, but what you have left behind will continue to speak to many and for many for years to come.

The life and world of an author is seldom easy, and those closest to us often share the highs and the lows that writing sometimes generates. So, heartfelt thanks to Rosemary and Wendy for your understanding and patience, without which the book would not have materialised.

Although sadly he is no longer alive to read this, it is important to acknowledge the work of Tom Kitwood and the place he still occupies in the dementia world. This book has his presence throughout, and one often wonders what he would think of people with dementia not just expressing themselves as the people in this book do, but also that a person with dementia is the lead author of the book. Maybe, just maybe, his legacy is part of the reason for this.

Finally, and without whom there would be no book, sincere thanks to the Fifteen, who freely opened up to us about their lives. What was abundantly clear in our conversations with you all was that you are holding on to, and in many cases actively enhancing, your personhood despite the challenges which each of your dementias confronts you with. We are proud to travel this pathway with you and let's hope for a long and smooth road ahead.

Sincere thanks to everyone.

Keith Oliver and Reinhard Guss

Glossary of terms

3 Nations Dementia Working Group: The 3NDWG is a working group of people living with dementia across England, Northern Ireland and Wales who can lead and participate in national and regional projects.

Action on Living Well: Asking You (ALWAYs Network): A group of people living with dementia and family carers who advise on different aspects of the IDEAL study based on their personal experience, skills and expertise.

Alzheimer's Research UK: A charity whose purpose is to conduct research into Alzheimer's disease and other forms of dementia.

Alzheimer's Society: The largest charity in the UK supporting people with dementia and family carers.

Ashford Phoenix group: An NHS-supported service user group that meets to give hope to people with dementia about the future.

Beth Johnson Foundation: A charity whose goal is to stimulate / facilitate change to enhance the quality of life and experience of the ageing process for older people. Currently, there are four programmes of work – Advocacy, Health, Intergenerational Practice and Midlife – to influence policy-makers / funders to have increasing focus on effective measures to increase people's wellbeing and health as they age.

British Heart Foundation: A charity founded in 1961 by medical professionals to raise funds for research into heart and circulatory diseases.

Certificate of Secondary Education (CSE): This was a subject-specific qualification family awarded in both academic and vocational fields in England, Wales and Northern Ireland.

Clinical commissioning groups (CCG) / Integrated care systems (ICS): Clinical commissioning groups (CCGs) were created as part of the 2012 Health and Social Care Act, and replaced primary care trusts on 1 April 2013. They were clinically-led statutory NHS bodies responsible for the planning and commissioning of healthcare services for their local area. Dissolved in July 2022, their duties were taken on by the new integrated care systems (ICSs).

Cruse: A bereavement charity that provides campaigning, support and information for people experiencing bereavement.

Dementia:
- **Alzheimer's disease:** A physical illness that damages a person's brain, eventually leading to dementia. Alzheimer's disease is the most common cause of dementia.
- **Dementia with Lewy bodies (DLB):** A type of dementia caused by Lewy bodies, which are clumps of protein in the cells of the brain.
- **Frontotemporal dementia (FTD):** Also called Pick's disease or frontal lobe dementia, FTD is one of the less common types of dementia. The first noticeable FTD symptoms are changes to personality and behaviour and / or difficulties with language.
- **Vascular dementia:** The second most common type of dementia, it is a condition caused by poor blood flow in the brain, resulting in symptoms that include memory loss, confusion and thinking difficulties. Symptoms vary depending on the person, the cause and the areas of the brain that are affected.

Dementia Action Alliance: Where people came together to connect, form friendships, exchange ideas, learn and create a better community in which to live with dementia. It added the word National to avoid confusion with local alliances. It was an alliance for organisations across England to connect, act on dementia and work together to contribute towards building dementia-friendly communities.

Dementia Alliance International (DAI): A group of individuals diagnosed with dementia that provides a unified voice of strength, advocacy and support in the fight for individual autonomy for people with dementia.

Dementia Engagement and Empowerment Project (DEEP): A network of dementia voices in the UK, DEEP consists of around 80+ groups of people with dementia – groups that want to change things for the better for those living with dementia.

Dementia Envoys: People living with dementia in Kent who assist with the development of the healthcare service through being a source of knowledge, advice and consultation.

Dementia Friends: Dementia Friends are part of an Alzheimer's Society initiative. They learn about dementia so they can help their community.

Dementia UK: A charity that provides Admiral Nurses for families affected by dementia.

European Dementia Working Group (EDWG): The EDWG is a member-led campaigning group.

European Federation of Psychological Associations (EFPA): EFPA actively participates in mental health advocacy throughout Europe and, alongside its collaborators, internationally.

Faculty of the Psychology of Older People (FPOP): A faculty of the Division of Clinical Psychology within the BPS providing a forum for psychologists specialising in working with older people, later life and dementia.

Forget-me-nots (FMNs): A group of people with different diagnoses of dementia based in Canterbury, Kent who are not willing to sit back and let life pass them by.

General Certificate of Secondary Education (GCSE): An academic qualification usually awarded at the age of 16 in a range of subjects, taken in England, Wales and Northern Ireland.

General practitioners (GPs): They are doctors who treat all common medical conditions and refer patients to hospitals and other medical services for urgent and specialist treatment.

Healthy Generation Approach: This is an approach that is rooted in evidence-based best practices for creating school environments that promote learning and support the physical, mental, and social and emotional health of students and staff.

IDEAL Project: This project is the largest study of living well with dementia in Great Britain. The evidence will enable the development of new policy, interventions and initiatives to transform the lives of people with dementia and their carers. It has run in two parts from 2014 – 2023.

Improvement Cymru: This is an improvement service for NHS Wales.

Kent and Medway NHS and Social Care Partnership Trust (KMPT): A service that provides a range of adult mental health and learning disability for their local population.

Lewy Body Society: This is the first charity in Europe exclusively concerned with dementia with Lewy Bodies (DLB). The charity's mission is to raise awareness of DLB for the general public and educate those in the medical profession and decision-making positions about all aspects of the disease and to support research into the disease.

Malignant Social Psychology: Was the term Kitwood used to describe the collective impact of certain behaviours and traits in the care deliverer which led to an overall pervasion and erosion of the person with dementia's personhood.

MBE: This is the third highest ranking Order of the British Empire Award.

Memory Services National Accreditation Programme (MSNAP): A quality improvement and accreditation network for services that assess, diagnose and treat dementia in the UK.

National Activity Providers Association (NAPA): This is the UK's leading activity and engagement charity, usually focusing upon creative arts and often working in the care home sector.

National Association of Care Caterers (NACC): This is recognised as a respected source of information and opinion for the dynamic and growing area of care catering in the UK sector.

National Care Forum (NCF): This is a membership organisation for not-for-profit organisations in the care and support sector. They ensure the members interests are represented at all levels and are in constant contact with government departments, politicians and the media to ensure your message gets across.

National Children and Adult Social Care Conference (NCASC): This is a 3-day conference for elected members and senior leaders in local authorities with responsibility for, or an interest in, the delivery of effective services and opportunities for children, young people and adults.

National Dementia Action Alliance: Where people came together to connect, form friendships, exchange ideas, learn and create a better community in which to live with dementia. It added National to avoid confusion with local alliances. It was an alliance for organisations across England to connect, act on dementia and work together to contribute towards building Dementia Friendly Communities.

National Health Service (NHS): The NHS is a publicly funded national healthcare systems of the United Kingdom (UK).

National Institute of Health and Care Research (NIHR): British government's major funder of clinical, public health, social care and translational research.

National Institute for Health and Care Excellence (NICE): This is an executive non-departmental public body of the Department of Health and Social Care in England. They balance the best care with value for money across the NHS and social care, to deliver for both individuals and society as a whole.

NHS Midlands Steering Group: This is a group that meets every 2 months to ensure the principles and duties of safeguarding are delivered by Trust principles and duties of safeguarding are delivered by clinical commissioning groups across the NHS system in Midlands and East.

Open University Press (Open UP): A trusted social science publisher specialising in education, nursing, health and social work, research and study skills, psychology, counselling and psychotherapy, and coaching.

Person affected by dementia: Is a label initially introduced by the Alzheimer's Society to encompass both the person with a diagnosis and family caregiver.

Picture This Project: Picture This Project is a project facilitated by Bright Shadow to teach people with dementia how to take interesting photographs and to make better use of cameras.

Posterior Cortical Atrophy (PCA): Posterior cortical atrophy causes the loss of brain cells at the back of the brain. This changes a person's ability to process visual and spatial information.

Post Traumatic Stress Disorder (PTSD): It is a mental health condition that's triggered by a terrifying event – either experiencing it or witnessing it.

Royal College of Nursing (RCN): The RCN is the world's largest nursing union and professional body.

Salzburg Global Fellow: Salzburg Global Fellow are members of the Salzburg Global Seminar, which is an independent non-profit organisation founded in 1947 with a mission to challenge current and future leaders to shape a better world.

Scottish Dementia Alumni: The Scottish Dementia Alumni is a group of friends with various diagnoses of dementia, one diagnosed in 1999, giving the group over 60 collective years of lived experience of dementia. They partake in project and campaigners that actively fight for the rights of people living with dementia.

Scottish Dementia Working Group (SDWG): The SDWG is a national, member led campaigning and awareness raising group, for people living with a diagnosis of dementia in Scotland.

SUNshiners: A friendly, relaxed, all-inclusive group of people in the early stages of dementia based in the Dover, Deal and the Shepway area in Kent.

Time & Place poetry project: A project run in 2020 for 15 people with dementia across the UK by Keith Oliver, Jess Shaw and Liz Jennings, inspired by living through the pandemic and lockdown in one's own home.

Together In Dementia Everyday (TIDE): A collective of unpaid carers of people with dementia with the advocacy skills, knowledge and passion for making positive change for everyone impacted by dementia.

Tree of Life: An approach based on Narrative Therapy which uses the metaphor of a tree for a person's life to help people with telling their preferred stories in ways that make them stronger.

UNISON: This is a union that represents members (who work in a range of public services and utilities), negotiate and bargain on their behalf, campaign for better working conditions and pay and for public services.

United Nations (CRPD): Convention on the Rights of Persons with Disabilities. Based in Geneva.

University of Kent (UKC): University of Kent is a semi-collegiate public research university based in Kent, United Kingdom.

Winston Churchill Memorial Trust: A national network of 3,800 dynamic individuals who are inspiring change in every part of UK life. Their mission is to develop new solutions for today's key challenges, based on learning from the world.

Young Onset Dementia: When a person develops dementia or whose symptoms started before the age of 65, this is known as 'young-onset'.

Part 1

Drawing Together

Perspectives on our motivations

Keith Oliver, Reinhard Guss and Ruth Bartlett

Keith's perspective

For Reinhard and me, the starting point for writing this book was an invitation to contribute to *Dementia Reconsidered, Revisited* (2019). This book took the original, seminal text by Tom Kitwood, published as *Dementia Reconsidered* (1997), and with contemporary commentaries written in 2018–19, updated it for the twenty-first century. Being a part of the writing team made us realise that we both had important perspectives to contribute, alongside other academics and authors. While our friendship extended back to 2011, we had not previously written a book contribution. Writing the commentary to chapter 5, 'The experience of dementia', motivated us to work on a bigger project which, over time, after conversations and cups of coffee in our respective gardens, transformed into *Talking with Dementia*.

The *Reconsidering Dementia* book series arose initially through discussions between Professor Dawn Brooker and Sam Crowe and his colleagues at Open University Press and was inspired by the 2019 book. Knowing how the work of Kitwood has influenced my life with dementia since my diagnosis with Alzheimer's disease aged 55 in December 2010, Dawn approached me early in the series project to invite me to collaborate closely and equally with her as joint series editors. Recognising this honour – but also the challenge – I thought about it for 5 minutes before saying yes! Soon after, I discussed with Dawn my desire to write one of the books in the series so I could stand alongside other authors within the series with my head held high.

With the start of the COVID-19 pandemic as a background, a few ideas were floated between Dawn and myself as I, like many others, felt isolated. The government directive to stay socially distanced was affecting me quite badly and I said to Dawn, better to be socially connected but physically distanced. I then took this seed of an initial idea to one of the 'catch-up and coffees' that Reinhard Guss and I have enjoyed for the 12 years we have known each other, and which we were able to resume in July 2020. Reinhard listened as always to my outpouring of ideas, some half – and others more fully – baked! He explained that he had for a little while thought of documenting the authentic words of people with dementia, especially those who like me put their heads above the parapet as activists, advocates, ambassadors, DEEP (Dementia Engagement and Empowerment Project) group members or Dementia Envoys. I really liked this idea and in Chapter 2 we explain how we went about making this happen.

I had already written or contributed to books to raise money for dementia charities, including *Welcome to Our World* (Jennings 2014), a book of life writing with seven other people with dementia and *Walk the Walk, Talk the Talk* (Oliver 2016), a snapshot of my life past and present. In 2019, I wrote *Dear Alzheimer's*, an Alan Bennett inspired book combining a diary of living with dementia for 7 years alongside a short 10-minute film script with letters to Alzheimer's lurking deep in my own psyche. I also contributed to leading and writing *Time and Place* (Jennings et al. 2021), a poetry anthology involving 10 people with dementia. I was excited by the concept of providing a platform for other people living with dementia through the 'lens' of the Kitwood flower model, and then with Reinhard to consider closely what we heard and analyse it in the context of Kitwood and people's lives in the 2020s. Kitwood's flower is a model I hold dear, a photo of which I have carried in my diary for each of the past 8 years. If I had a tattoo, then that is the one I would have, as I think it captures everything that life holds for me, and maybe for others too. I was delighted when we, as an editorial team, decided to adopt the flower as the logo for this book series, and have it boldly centred on each title using the image taken from *Dementia Reconsidered, Revisited* (2019).

We felt that this book would contribute to the lasting legacy of Kitwood, and raise greater awareness of his work, not through professionals and academics, important and valid though that is, but from the perspective of people living with dementia. I was pretty sure that this had never been done before in a book, and knew that if we succeeded, it would add something rather different to the growing body of knowledge about dementia, some of which is penned by others like me with real lived experience (Bryden 2005, 2012, 2018; Swaffer 2016; Mitchell 2018, 2022, 2023). We also felt our book would sit comfortably alongside, but offer something different to, *Watching the Leaves Dance* (Stokes 2017) and *People with Dementia Speak Out* (Whitman 2016), both of which I wrote pieces in. From the outset, Reinhard and I were determined that the book would be written in a conversational, journalistic style, because after all we are 'Talking Dementia' rather than writing academically in an academic manner with a solely academic focus.

While I have been fortunate to listen to and to read the wise and knowledgeable words of professionals and academics on the subject of dementia, there is no substitute for the authentic, honest words of lived experience of those who spend each day affected by their dementia to varying degrees. It was my absolute priority and desire to do the right thing with the words of the fifteen people who had so willingly shared their innermost thoughts with us. Because I am not aware of anyone with dementia taking on this role before, I felt – and continue to feel writing this – a heavy sense of responsibility which, thankfully, is balanced by the excitement of the challenge.

I had suggested that maybe we could talk to people with dementia from around the UK using Kitwood's flower (page 92 in *Dementia Reconsidered, Revisited*) as the loose structure of those conversations. As we were still living in very uncertain times during the summer of 2020, the conversations were conducted by Zoom mainly with a few face-to-face meetings with those living near to Reinhard and I in East Kent. In Chapter 3, we explain in more detail how the fifteen participants were chosen to provide a wide range of experience, geography, age, ethnicity, gender and different types of dementia. Most had not contributed to a book before, and I did ask myself what was the motivation for them to take part. I concluded that it gave them an opportunity to have a voice, to help me and Reinhard in writing the book, and to inform readers about what living with dementia was like for them in a meaningful way as individuals. Because they all knew me, I felt that there was a bond of trust between us.

While Reinhard and I once considered ourselves to be 'professional friends' and collaborators, as his professional circumstances have changed, our friendship and collaborations have morphed and grown into a more personal relationship aided by lots of shared interests and points of view alongside living in the same suburb of Canterbury. So while I know Reinhard very well, the same cannot be said of Ruth, the other co-author of this book. We did work together on a peer-reviewed journal (Bartlett et al. 2017) in 2014/15, and we have chatted socially at one or two pre-pandemic conferences. I was very pleased when Dawn Brooker suggested Ruth join us in order to give a more academic perspective to the book, especially Part 3, which sits squarely in one of Ruth's many areas of expertise.

Alongside the words, every book in the series has a front cover designed and illustrated by a person with dementia which, in the case of this book, is me. When creating an image for the cover, I wanted to express the idea of people with dementia talking openly in a semi-structured conversation and to pay tribute to Kitwood's flower, which is the basis of Part 2 of this book. My original design, which now appears on page 17, was also inspired by the album cover of Sergeant Pepper's Lonely Heart Club Band – an album much loved by those of my generation both with and without dementia. I deliberately used the same turquoise as on the cover of *Dementia Reconsidered, Revisited*, with six bubbles representing the six elements of Kitwood's flower, which are the basis of the six chapters in Part 2 of this book. I then added forget-me-nots to the bubbles, a flower often associated with dementia. I also wanted the speech bubbles to overlap because the conversations with the 'Fifteen' (as our contributors are known collectively), while all were unique and different, revealed elements of common ground. Finally, I wanted to bring the various elements together to make a whole and to showcase another flower with six petals. I actually worked on the cover during a period when I was struggling with the organisation and writing of the text, and being creative with colour really helped restore my confidence in the project. I have always tried to maintain a 'can do' approach including when teaching. I would like to think I instilled this in my staff and the pupils I taught or was headteacher of. When our paths now cross, this is often confirmed, something of which I am very proud.

Reinhard's perspective

Keith has described our monthly or so catch-up meetings, where over the years we have enjoyed coffee and biscuits alongside wandering in our respective gardens, and held more in-depth conversations about our experiences, our work and our ideas around dementia services and policy development. Our collaboration on chapter 5 of *Dementia Reconsidered, Revisited* developed in this way, and was an encouraging experience of working together in a different way.

Dawn Brooker has been a peer, friend and much-admired colleague for almost as long as I have lived and worked in the UK. I have followed her work closely over the past decades, especially her move from a practising clinician in clinical psychology to the academic world, her time as Director of the Oxford Dementia Services Development Centre and eventually the professorship at the Association for Dementia Studies at the University of Worcester. Her academic work with its clinical focus has accompanied me over the years and often closed the gap between my practice base enthusiasm for service development and the need for sound science, models and evidence to underpin proposals and business cases. I considered it a great honour when asked to contribute to *Dementia Reconsidered, Revisited,* so the possibility of a larger project was very exciting.

Professionally, having taken early retirement from my NHS consultant post in a way that did not seem entirely voluntary, the time leading up to the COVID-19 pandemic was a period of reflection and re-grouping while working part-time in a purely clinical role and contemplating what semi-retirement might look like. Where would my accumulated experience be most useful, which of my various roles should be curbed in exchange for more retired time? And if I was to continue in posts that have little influence in the wider system, what would have an impact and keep frustrations at bay? In addition, the enforced pause of many outside activities as a result of the pandemic appeared to suggest many days of leisure stretching ahead, potentially to be spent on a larger writing project.

Perhaps the most exciting, satisfying and enjoyable aspect of my work over the past 10 years or so has been working with the increasing number of people with dementia who have started taking on activist roles, steadily making their way into the world of professional and academic conferences, NHS development and steering groups, Department of Health advisory bodies, and service user involvement in its varying guises. While I have always learnt from my clients and patients in a clinical context, here were the experts by experience in the world of service design, development and improvement, and more often than not we turned out to be natural allies. Many professional and increasingly personal friendships emerged from collaborations, joint travel and post-meeting de-briefings in cafes and pubs. One of the striking realisations was that almost all the activists seem to remain so much more well, able and active for so much longer than professionals would have expected at the outset. While I have some ideas of my own as to why that may be so, I thought how much more interesting it would be to hear from these pioneers of activism themselves.

The other thought on working with the dementia activists of the first or second generation was that, over time, people need more support in order to be able to continue this work, and at some point it will not be possible to hear their voices in the way we do now. While many of the activists publish material on a variety of platforms, for example in blogs, on Facebook, in the DEEP newsletter and, more recently, on dementia radio, there did not seem to be an anthology of their experience and wisdom available, one that combines their words with some of their background and life experience. Never having gained in my second language the ease, speed and confidence I used to have when writing in German, I find writing quite hard work, slow and laborious, so did not consider this a natural retirement activity for myself, though the thought that this would be a book worth writing lingered.

I will write more later about the prominent place that Tom Kitwood holds in the development of my clinical practice and in my thinking about dementia therapy and services. Suffice to say here that the idea of bringing together Kitwood-based ideas, models and philosophy with the voices of present-day dementia activists, developed over several socially distanced garden visits with Keith, encouraged by Dawn and eventually conceptualised in the book proposal, was an irresistible formula that I was only too happy to help progress.

As the project moved forward, supported by several generations of placement students, the biographies collected, conversations arranged, held, recorded and transcribed, the pandemic began to recede, life became much busier again, and with a professional change back into a part-time psychology lead and consultant role, it became more of a challenge to find space for the more time-consuming aspects of the project. I am grateful to Keith, Dawn, Hannah and Sam for their support and for applying the gentle but firm pressure of timelines and deadlines without which there would have been too many distractions for me to complete my parts!

Ruth's perspective

Dawn was one of my PhD supervisors and I have always admired her and the contribution she has made to the field of dementia care. So, when she first asked me if I would like to get involved in this writing project, I was (a) pleased to be invited, (b) welcome of the opportunity to work with Keith again and (c) keen to find ways to incorporate ideas on citizenship into the text. I know how powerful and useful the Kitwood flower model is for advancing thinking and practice, and I like how it has been used in this text to frame the interviews. It is novel: I am not aware of anyone doing this before. But for me, the Kitwood flower model does not go far enough. As I explain in the book I wrote with Deborah O'Connor, *Broadening the Dementia Debate: Towards Social Citizenship* (2010), it does not take account of wider social structures such as ageism and racism, or people's rights as equal citizens. It seemed to me that working on this project would allow me to air those ideas once again, and maybe develop some new ones. That is something I am keen to do, as we are planning to write a second edition of *Broadening the Dementia Debate* for publication in 2024.

Throughout my academic career, I have always found it difficult to say 'no' to invitations to write, especially when they come from people I know well and respect a great deal. I like writing. It is a skill I have always enjoyed developing and using as an academic. I like writing in different ways, with different people, and for different audiences. I think it helps one to stay sharp and relevant. Hence, I said 'yes' to getting involved in this writing project because it was unlike any other I have been involved in before. I understood my brief to be this: to write about the interviews in the context of social citizenship, and to bring an academic focus to the whole text. I know it can be challenging to engage with other people's writing, as everyone has their own style. However, I could see this project promised to result in an important and innovative book and I wanted to be a part of the writing team.

In sum, I am grateful for the opportunity to bring a social citizenship lens to this book, and to be able to contribute to the *Reconsidering Dementia* book series.

2 Multiple facets of collaboration

Keith Oliver, Lara Stembridge,
Ellie Warman and Reinhard Guss

As illustrated by the four authors of this chapter – Keith Oliver (person with dementia), Lara Stembridge (student), Ellie Warman (student) and Reinhard Guss (clinical psychologist) – this book is an example of collaborations on many levels. Beginning with Reinhard and me generating the initial concept, through to working on the book behind the scenes with Dawn, Hannah, Sam and the Open UP team. Then to recruiting and engaging with the fifteen key players who each have dementia and were so open, honest and passionate in what they shared with us in the recorded conversations, to bringing in and benefiting from the huge support given by the undergraduate students and to having Ruth involved to add an academic perspective.

Keith on collaboration

While Reinhard and I have collaborated on many projects over the past 12 years, we have not written a book together before. We both felt that this opportunity, while being challenging, would be a very worthwhile undertaking for us to share. We both, from different directions, share a passion for person-centred care, which has as one of its central elements the work of Tom Kitwood.

For me as a person with dementia, writing a book is an enormous challenge. I have never sought or used a ghost writer or writing collaborator but I do find a blank page or screen is now immensely intimidating and, in order to meet this challenge, I have been fortunate to seek the support of a number of diligent and enthusiastic undergraduate psychology students. Without their support, there is no doubt that we would not have been able to write this book together. The students involved were all introduced to us during a placement year with Kent and Medway NHS Social Care Partnership Trust (KMPT) as part of their 4-year degree. Most were studying at the University of Kent. Before having the confidence to engage with them in relation to the book, we built a connection, assurance and trust in each other, through attending our monthly service user group in Canterbury called the Forget Me Nots. We walked and talked together as part of my care plan; prepared for events; travelled to meetings and conferences in London and Birmingham after COVID-19; worked on dementia projects together; and spent time sharing intergenerational thinking with a coffee in Canterbury cafes.

During the summer of 2020, Reinhard and I conducted the fifteen semi-structured interviews with the participants, all of whom have dementia, either by Zoom or face-to-face. The conversations were recorded and the recordings either emailed in the case of Zoom, or given to students on a memory stick if conducted face-to-face. No students were present when the conversations took place because it was felt that this might discourage the participants from speaking openly and honestly in the presence of someone they did not know. Four students and an assistant psychologist working with Reinhard then typed up the transcripts and returned them to us. As each interview lasted approximately one hour this was a massive task, and the transcripts were each about 20 pages long. We left it to the students to decide how to present the typed transcripts, and all four of them did a fabulous job in making it easy for us to analyse and process them. Reinhard and I then read through the transcripts with the Kitwood flower model in mind devising a colour code to make highlights so that relevant parts of the conversation could be placed in the correct chapter (petal).

At this stage, there was a transition in the student support – Theo, Jonah, Heather and Adam needed to move away from the project to complete their studies, and the next cohort of students stepped into the breach.

Taking the colour highlighted transcripts, the next group of placement students – Ellie, Lara and Millie, joined later by Abigail – met with Reinhard and Keith on a number of occasions to begin the process of thematic analysis. Alongside this, the students, Reinhard and I spent a number of hours talking, and each of us actively listening. Having built trust and mutual respect within the group by Reinhard and I getting to know the students, we engaged in discussing dementia, Martin Buber, Tom Kitwood and psychology in general, some of which was noted at the time and then written up afterwards by the students for use within this book. I find it increasingly hard due to my dementia to read and remember what I have read, and holding onto conversations is also very difficult. Although the students did join the in-depth conversations, their main role was to make computer notes on the conversations we were having, which were then shared with us afterwards.

As typing is now a significant challenge for me, a key role for the students then became that of primarily typing up my thoughts and words, but their role was more than this because we would discuss each paragraph and they would help formulate my sometimes tentative ideas and contribute a different perspective, which I found most useful and encouraging. They took on the mantle of critical friend. It was usually a different combination of two from the four students, depending upon their university and other commitments, who would come to my house to work on the book with me every 2 or 3 weeks for about 2 hours each visit. On a number of occasions, I found the task of conveying what I wanted to share within the book quite overwhelming, and it was the students who came to my aid and helped me find a route through the fog so that I could see the task in front of me more clearly. We would exchange regular emails and

WhatsApp messages so lines of communication, which were so crucially important, were always open, encouraging, honest and conducted as quickly as possible to save any panic on my part. The students would make suggestions knowing that some would be accepted but perhaps others would not. This never stopped them from continuing to contribute.

Lara and Ellie on collaboration

As two of the students involved in the project, we think the experience and understanding of dementia we gained from working on this book is unparalleled and builds upon the general curriculum from our university. We definitely feel that this opportunity has allowed us to learn not only directly through working with Keith, but also indirectly when reading through the fascinating interviews of the fifteen people living with dementia in order to get an insight into their lives. As we joined the project midway through, it felt rewarding to carry on the previous placement students' great work and we benefited from the project having already been grounded. This meant we were able to offer the best possible support as the need for support had already been identified and we were easily able to provide it. Since we had all worked with Keith and each other previously during our placement year, we had a good idea of one another's strengths and were able to utilise them in order to tailor our support. We were therefore able to ensure the meetings with Reinhard and Keith were supported to the highest standard, allowing them to converse freely and in great depth about their ideas on the topic being focused upon, and hopefully we were able to capture this in a way that will inspire the readers of this book. These meetings covered a range of topics, where we were introduced to the teachings of Buber, key aspects of person-centred care and how attitudes towards dementia have evolved, influenced by key ideas from Kitwood's *Dementia Reconsidered* (1997).

It is important to note that the transition from the previous placement students wasn't the sole transition, as we transitioned from placement year into our final year of university while supporting this book during an inherently stressful time. However, it was continuously made clear to us that any support we were able to provide was well appreciated, as long as communication was maintained to ensure that all parties were on the same page. This alleviated our stress as our desire to help with this project was not dampened by our other commitments, allowing us to thrive in both settings – academic and volunteering. This intergenerational way of working is something that we were not aware of previously, and the benefits to all involved are so obviously evident. Consequently, we look forward to future opportunities in similar settings and advocating how beneficial this type of work can be.

We have gained such a rich experience from getting to know Keith and gaining insight into his life not just since diagnosis but from listening to him talk about his life in general and how he has, with support, taken on an activist role.

Among the group of students who have helped with this book, Theo, Lara, Millie and Abigail have all attended, supported and in a number of cases spoken alongside Keith at conferences. Through the fifteen people with dementia who contributed to the book, as well as the 10 students, he tells us he has gained better insight, not only into their world but his own. *Talking with Dementia* is an excellent example of intergenerational collaboration and we all hope that everyone will still be able to play a part in the story of this book once it is published.

Reinhard on collaboration

Collaboration has been a key part of this book project in multiple ways, as described by Keith and two of the student supporters above. Collaboration is also a theme that has featured prominently in my professional life, with the book project building on and extending past experience. Collaboration with Keith for over 12 years now is clearly the starting point and main feature, with the whole project informed and underpinned by our friendships and contacts in the world of dementia activism. There we have both collaborated and co-created – at times jointly, at others separately – with the Fifteen, enabling us to build on pre-existing relationships when holding our Kitwood-themed conversations on Zoom or in gardens in 2021.

Collaboration has been the foundation of the relationship Keith and I developed and was the starting point of our 'professional friendship'. In the early days, it was finding opportunities and opening doors for Keith to explore 'service user involvement' and 'awareness raising' and supporting a process of evaluating benefits and stresses arising from activism. We both learned from this for our joint projects of setting up DEEP groups in Kent and developing the Dementia Envoy roles within an NHS mental health trust. Collaboration quickly moved on to new territories when Keith became rapidly engaged in wider, national projects, while my role as Dementia Lead in the BPS Faculty of the Psychology of Older People meant that I often found myself representing psychology in forums where Keith was representing people living with dementia. With our often similar views and aims, we were able to discuss strategy and ensure that issues we both felt strongly about would not be left off the agenda.

Collaboration with Keith has also meant remaining mindful of my professional role and balancing this with a developing friendship, knowing when to support in practical or emotional ways, and when to step back, and ensuring that my enthusiasm for pursuing policy aims and service developments does not take undue advantage of Keith's willingness to help. This dynamic has also played out over the 3 years or so of this project, with a new dimension added for me as we moved from planning, discussing, conversing, analysing and conceptualising to completing, writing up, editing and finishing. During the earlier stages, it felt like my role was one of supporting Keith in developing his ideas and giving the project structure and method while keeping a clear view of the focus and limits of the content. With Keith's overall editorial role and responsibilities and my post-pandemic, much-increased professional responsibilities, and the renewed possibilities of travel to see family and friends in far-flung places (not to mention my general resistance to large-scale writing), meant that increasingly it was Keith structuring my time and ensuring that my contribution to the collaboration would remain on track.

Collaboration with Dawn is a particular honour and achievement for an NHS clinician of my generation, and like Keith described earlier, I also have to pinch myself at times to believe that my contribution in a series of Tom Kitwood related books is considered to be of interest and value in the illustrious academic company of the other contributors to the series. More used to publishing small practice-based articles in the less academic journals of the field, working on this project was a learning curve, much facilitated by Dawn and the helpful publishing team. I know how important meetings in person and timely email contact were for Keith over the course of this project, to provide reassurance and structure and mitigate obstacles imposed by dementia, but it should be noted that this was equally helpful to a practitioner inexperienced in the world of academic publishing.

Collaboration with the Fifteen was a particular highlight of the project for me. Learning more about people's lives from their short biographies, hearing their experiences of managing life with dementia in more depth in our conversations, and spending extensive time with the rich material they had shared with us built on what I had learnt from their talks and presentations at conferences, their online materials and discussions on various media, and continues to inform my clinical practice as well as my teaching and training activities. In this way, and by sharing their experience through this book project, the collaboration with the Fifteen extends well beyond our initial recorded conversations and will hopefully continue well into the future.

Collaboration with several cohorts of student supporters was essential to make this project possible, not only by supporting Keith, but also by undertaking much of the time-consuming work needed to transcribe recordings, group our colour-coded themes into documents for Keith and I to work from, keeping records of discussions and meetings, and contributing their thoughts and ideas. Having grown and co-ordinated the placement scheme for undergraduates in the local mental health trust while working there, and having set up the system of student support for Keith, the Dementia Envoys and the Kent DEEP groups, it is good to see that this continues to enthuse and inspire new generations of students more than 5 years after I left. Working with students and aspiring psychologists early on in their qualification journeys has always been important in the specialism of older people's psychology, and all the more so in working with dementia. These are not the specialisations foremost in young people's minds, and it has long been recognised that attracting psychologists to working with older people early in their career is key to attracting well-qualified and -motivated people into this area. In order to do this we have to provide opportunities to counter stereotypes, foster positive attitudes and find inspiration – all to be found in abundance in working with Keith, the Fifteen and the world of dementia activists.

Collaboration requires all participating parties to benefit from the joint working, and in a large multi-faceted project such as this, there will be different ways the participants can benefit according to their interests and motivations. When working with students on year-out placements, I am very aware that they are not paid by the NHS trusts where they are working, and this is brought into sharper focus when they leave placements, return to their final year at university and later are looking for employment, and yet continue to volunteer to support some of our work, projects or individual people. Offering some time to student volunteers to think about post-university work applications, reflective practice exercises to prepare for applications for clinical doctorate requirements and career planning seemed an important contribution to ensuring benefits for unpaid helpers in the project that made good use of my many years of experience in the field. In addition, the overall project also contains multiple aspects that can be linked to learning and study, for example in cognitive psychology, and the philosophical underpinning of care and psychotherapy. And while Keith and I have been clear that ours is not a PhD project using qualitative research methodology, but one based on a more journalistic and experiential approach, the project offered students experience in aspects of qualitative methods well suited to informing future qualitative research.

So what learning can we take from the Fifteen?

Keith: Person with dementia perspective

1 Support based upon trust, respect, clear communication, honesty and understanding the other person's perspective is crucial for collaborative working.
2 Give yourself time and space to think things through as well as to do things relating to projects.
3 Create a realistic time-related plan and then, while it can be amended, it should not be abandoned.

Lara: Student perspective

1 More meaningful learning and development of knowledge.
2 Ability to relate to the lives and rich experiences of people with dementia.
3 Dementia doesn't have to limit a person's ability to lead a quality life, as is so often shown by negative stereotypes.
4 Consistent, clear, two-way communication between the person(s) with dementia and the students supporting, benefits everyone involved.

Reinhard: Professional perspective

1 Working closely with people with dementia is of great benefit to professionals in their clinical learning as well as in the evaluation and development of service.

2   Getting to know individual people with dementia over time and collaborating on multiple projects grows and deepens relationships, in turn benefiting the collaboration.

3   Close collaboration between professionals and people with dementia challenges established notions of professional boundaries and requires thought and outside perspective from clinical supervision to manage the impact this can have for both.

4   Innovative projects with people with dementia are highly suited to provide positive experiences of specialist services alongside generic learning for motivated early years professionals.

3 Introducing the Fifteen

Keith Oliver

The participants

In choosing contributing participants to this book, we used the networks available to us, mainly the 3 Nations Dementia Working Group and the Dementia Engagement and Empowerment Project (DEEP), but also others including the Kent Forget-Me-Nots and Kent SUNshiners.* We wanted to harness a range of experience and backgrounds but also were mindful that most of the participants could be described as activists or advocates living with young-onset dementia. Although several have now lived with the condition for a number of years and are aged 65+, they could justifiably be referred to as in the mild-to-moderate stages of living with varying forms of dementia. The Fifteen come from different ethnic backgrounds and live in England, Wales or Scotland. We felt fifteen was a manageable number to give us a wide range of experience, diversity and perspectives on life. Only two people we invited failed to speak with us due to factors beyond everyone's control, so an additional two people, Ronald Ferguson and Martina Kane, readily stepped forward, each offering to write a lovely poem (these poems can be found in Part 2 of the book).

I knew all of the people with dementia we spoke with quite well, having become friends since my diagnosis, the exception being Jim McNee, who I had previously known when we were both teachers. In 1988, when Jim was head of science at a local high school and I was a primary deputy head and year 6 teacher, we worked on a joint project celebrating 400 years since the Spanish Armada. I reminded him of this recently and how we both set up science experiments. My class built cannons from scrap materials, elevating their cardboard barrels to varying angles before firing missiles across his laboratory and measuring the distance the projectiles travelled. Great fun and good learning! He later facilitated my class and I, using his school dark room to develop some black-and-white photographs my pupils took of the local area our two schools served and where the children lived. I guess I have always been a bit of an innovator as no one had done what Jim and I were doing back in those days.

---

* The 3 Nations Dementia Working Group [www.3ndementiawg.org/]; Dementia Engagement and Empowerment Project (DEEP) [www.dementiavoices.org.uk/]; Kent Forget-Me-Nots [www.kmpt.nhs.uk/get-involved/participation-and-involvement/living-with-dementia/forget-me-nots/]; Kent SUNshiners [https://www.kmpt.nhs.uk/get-involved/participation-and-involvement/living-with-dementia/sunshiners/].

Figure 3.1 The Talking with Dementia Team

In September 2021, soon after completing the interviews, I sent an email to each of the fifteen people with dementia asking them to write a biography for inclusion here, and they all responded promptly to my request.

We have not altered or edited the biographies in any way; they appear exactly as they were written. We felt this was important in enabling the participants to confidently express themselves in ways that worked for them. Some describe themselves at length, others are more succinct. Some describe themselves in the first person, others choose the more formal third person. There is no hierarchy among the Fifteen, and we introduce them in alphabetical order of their first name.

Within the flower in Figure 3.1 are the fifteen people with dementia we spoke with, while Kitwood features in the central heart. Around the speech bubble are those who listened and wrote – the authors and supporters of the book project.

Participant biographies

Agnes Houston

Agnes Houston MBE lives in Coatbridge, in the west of Scotland. She was diagnosed with early-onset dementia of the Alzheimer's type 15 years ago

*when working as a practice manager. She cares for her husband Alan, who
also lives with dementia. She enjoys gardening, yoga and crafting.*

*After receiving her own diagnosis, Agnes Houston was driven to push for
better information and resources for people experiencing dementia and sensory challenges. She has occupied many high-level policy and advisory roles
through which she has campaigned for improved dementia care.*

*She is former chair of the Scottish Dementia Working Group, founding
member and past vice-president of the European Dementia Working Group,
member of the Dementia Engagement and Empowerment Group and the Scottish Dementia Alumni.*

*Agnes' special focus is that Dementia is more than memory and she has
recently written the book Talking Sense – Sensory challenges and dementia
where she explored how ageing and dementia can create sensory challenges
and how to seek support or help.*

*In 2013 she was awarded a lifetime achievement award from Alzheimer's
Scotland. In 2015 she published a peer-to-peer information booklet 'Dementia
and Sensory Challenges' and was awarded an MBE for her work in the field.
In 2016 she was awarded a Churchill Fellowship which enabled her to travel
to Canada and Ireland to seek out examples of best practice relating to sensory
challenges and dementia and led to her publishing her book Talking Sense –
living with sensory changes and dementia and has recently been awarded a
second grant from the Winston Churchill Memorial Trust to further her work
in this field.*

Chris Maddocks

*In July 2016 I was diagnosed with Vascular Dementia when I was 60 years
old, this was following a couple of minor strokes. Previous to that I had been
working for the Environment Agency, having been a police officer for 30
years. I am an ambassador for Alzheimer's Society, Lewy ---Body Society and
National Activity Providers Association (NAPA). I am a steering group member of 3 Nations Dementia Working Group and an active member of the DEEP
network. I have spoken at national conferences for Dementia UK Admiral
nurses and also spoken with NAPA at the National Care Forum.*

*I am actively involved with the Alzheimer's Society, speaking at various
national conferences, such as the National Children and Adult Social Care
and the UK Dementia Congress (2018). I have chaired the National Dementia
Action Alliance conference, spoken at an International conference for Palliative Care and Dementia in Belfast in May 2019. I have participated in many
projects across the organisation including co-producing 'Bring Dementia
Out' to help LGBT+ (Lesbian, Gay, Bisexual and Transgender) people benefit
from dementia awareness and services – an innovation project which received
a People Award nomination. In my local area, I am currently taking the lead
with local organisations to create a number of Involvement groups giving
other people affected by dementia the opportunity to influence inclusion and
change locally.*

I would describe myself as a dementia activist giving talks and lectures to a variety of audiences to raise awareness of dementia.

I enjoy walking, gardening, taking walks by the sea and in the woods observing nature.

Chris Norris

I am married and have two grown up children. I was diagnosed with fronto-temporal dementia in December, 2012 when I was 58 years old. 6 months before this I had been diagnosed with M.E. (Chronic Fatigue Syndrome). I had been experiencing cognitive challenges for well over 2 years, but it took this long to reach my dementia diagnosis.

In the 1970's, I was an Army musician in the Mounted Band of HM Lifeguards. I had to be able to play my instrument whilst also riding a horse! Not an easy task!

On leaving the Army, I joined the Kent Police and spent most of my career as a village policeman. I continued my music and was a founder member of Kent Police Band in 1977. I still play in Brass Bands and most weekends throughout the Summer I can be found playing my Tenor Horn on a bandstand somewhere in Kent or further beyond.

On retiring from the police, I worked as a Driving Instructor and then became a Driving Examiner. I was forced to retire when I was diagnosed with my dementia.

About a year after my diagnosis, I joined the Kent Forget Me Nots. This is a proactive group of people, all with a diagnosis of dementia, that promote the understanding around the subject of dementia by talking at conferences and seminars to health organisations and their staff, and to the general public at large. I am also a founder member of the Ashford Phoenix Group which is similar to the Forget Me Nots.

Shortly after joining the Forget Me Nots, alongside seven other members of the group, I was involved in writing a book Welcome to Our World (2014). The book is an eclectic mix of stories and anecdotes from the eight authors about experiences in their lives prior to dementia and their journeys thus far through the weird and varied landscape of dementia.

I have subsequently taken up voluntary roles as an Alzheimer's Society Ambassador and a Kent and Medway Primary Trust Dementia Envoy.

I endeavour to live well with dementia and I have a daily mantra of 'I may have dementia but dementia does not have me! Dementia comes in CANS. We must focus on the things we CAN still do!'

Chris Roberts

I am married to Jayne Goodrick, we have five children and four grandchildren.

I have vast experience in an array of jobs from Coal Mining, Farming, Sales and retail to owning a Custom Motorcycle Shop to mention just a few.

We have a Property Rental business which is family run.

I am living with emphysema and mixed dementia, Vascular and Alzheimer's.

I spend a lot of my time raising awareness of dementia, its symptoms, services and support to dispel the stigma that is associated. I have spoken nationally & internationally wherever and whenever I can supported by my wife Jayne as far away as Australia and Japan.

Our lives were portrayed in a BBC Panorama Documentary titled Living With Dementia, Chris's Story and in a BBC Wales, Week In Week Out programme, titled Who Will Look After Mum, Dad or Me.

I'm very proud to part of Alzheimer Europe as Chair of the European Working Group of People With Dementia.

An Ambassador for Alzheimer's Society UK.

I am a Co-Founder & Member of the 3 Nations Dementia Working Group (England, Northern Ireland and Wales).

I was awarded an Honorary Fellowship & Honorary Lecturer in MSc Dementia Studies, School of Healthcare Sciences, Bangor University.

Salzburg Global Fellow (International Seminar 587).

An Ambassador for National Association of Care Caterers.

A long standing Member of Dementia Alliance International (DAI) & former Board Member.

I was a Member of the Expert Working Group for the Wales Dementia Action Plan 2018 and part of the NICE Clinical Guidance Dementia Review Committee.

A Champion of Join Dementia Research.

I was an Outstanding Contribution Award Finalist 2015 and a recipient in 2016 as part of the People Awards, Alzheimer Society.

I was a finalist and winner UK Dementia Care Awards.

I'm very honoured to have received a Wales St. David Award as a finalist 2018.

Dianne Campbell

I live on my own in north west London and first noticed problems with my memory in my mid 40s for example remembering when to pick up prescriptions from the chemist or spoiling food when I was cooking – I would often burn what was on the stove. I was quite lucky that my GP recognised my difficulties and referred me for a scan and memory tests which in the summer of 2013 resulted in a diagnosis of vascular dementia. Again although I try and stay independent and look after myself, it is not easy and I was lucky soon after that I was introduced to a lovely occupational therapist who helped me come to terms with my diagnosis and the depression I felt after the diagnosis. Her support continued and she helped me secure a paid position within a Dementia Support programme local to where I lived in London. This helped me as I was made redundant from my job when I was diagnosed with dementia.

I am so pleased to be able to help other people affected by dementia by talking with them and listening to their problems because I have found it difficult at times to find services which meet the needs of people like me. I have spoken at lots of conferences including one in Chicago supported by the Alzheimer's Society. It was at a conference for UNISON in London where I first met Keith since when we have become friends and a part of the ALWAYS group attached to the IDEAL project.

Life is getting harder but I try and stay positive and always enjoy a laugh with family and friends and although I benefit from some help and support I am determined to continue to try and help myself for as long as possible.

(Compiled by Keith based upon an article in *Living with Dementia* magazine published by the Alzheimer's Society, March 2015)

Frances Isaacs

Born: June 1946 in Hampstead, London
Education: St Christopher's Prep, The Downs [mid school], Montesano [senior], Aberystwyth University (current)
I attended a local prep school where the love of music and the arts was instilled into me. I listened to Schubert's Trout Quintet, watched as the music teacher wept at the death of a fabulous soprano of the day whilst playing her music, had my imagination stretched by a fabulous English teacher and learned the love of literature. No other schools I went to had as much influence. Next stop was an English girl's boarding school with strict rules, endless amounts of fresh air and sports. To say it toughened me up and taught me independence would be to under-exaggerate the resulting 'Frances'. Thereafter, I was sent to the relative freedom of a Swiss boarding school where no English was spoken so it didn't take long for me to become fluent in French.

Although a competent artist, I failed the exam to St Martin's School of Art. My father wasn't a great believer in education for girls and said I must learn to type. I got a job in a local School, University College School, Hampstead, where I wreaked havoc and earned myself £10 a week in 1962 which was pretty good.

My next career change was to become a very junior marketing manager for what is now Smith Kline Beecham Group. This is where I learned the marketing skills that would become so valuable in later years.

I didn't suffer with many social skills, to my mother's disgust. I secretly played my guitar and sang in local coffee bars. My mother had been a debutante in her day and had 'great hopes' for me all of which were to be dashed when in 1967 I married my husband, Barrow, Chartered Surveyor and love of my life and best friend.

Benjamin was born in 1969 and Edward 1972. I stayed home and enjoyed the two little boys. We went to museums and art galleries, concerts and all the tourist venues – everything London has to offer.

In the mid 1970s I trained in fundraising techniques. In those days, consultancy companies were run by former military, so I learned from bristling brigadiers and majors. Super efficiency at every turn, and a perfect grounding for my future.

After cutting my teeth on one huge fundraising campaign and further training, I began to run fundraising appeals for small charities. My interests turned to charitable taxation and strategic fundraising. I sat on a government consultancy on Gift Aid and together with a computer guru, we produced a fundraiser's management program. My consultancy grew and I became a favourite within the education sector. Wonderful days.

We moved to the Brecon Beacons in 1994, commuting back and forth for work for a further 6–7 years.

In retirement I spent much time doing local voluntary work with wonderful friends and since diagnosis with Posterior Cortical Atrophy [PCA] I have been helping people to learn to use watercolour paints. I decided to do a degree in Fine Arts (at long last!). I am doing it slowly through Aberystwyth University and I will be a 125 years old when I get my degree. Nowadays I spend a lot of time with our dog out on the Beacons which inspire me to write prose, poetry and to paint. Not a bad life!

Gail Sharon Gregory

My name is Gail ... Gail Sharon Gregory. My life began as Gail Sharon Brown when I was born in a small mill town in Lancashire.

I had a very happy childhood wanting for nothing, I was an only child, spoiled really.

I left high school at 15, the youngest in the school year.

I completed my GCSE and CSE exams.

I took a 12 month course on Textile and design at college for one day a week within my last year at school.

My best attributes were design and crafts, needlework, anything creative. One of the things I wasn't good at was Art, or so I was told by my art teacher. I was definitely more of a practical person rather than an academic, or so I was told!

When I left school, I studied hairdressing for 2 years at college, I suppose it was just another way of expressing my flare for design and crafts through cutting and styling hair. Unfortunately, this was not meant to be as I was made redundant 2 years into my employment.

A career change at 18 when I took a job in a weaving mill. Most of my family had worked in the mills, so when I started to work there we had 4 generations all working in the same factory.

Married at 19 well nearly 20. My first daughter before I was 21. Second daughter at 23. Young mum and now in a very unhappy marriage, I suffered from bouts of depression.

This is when I felt the urge to find out and understand more about depression. I signed up to study counselling, which I did for 3 years at my local college.

My marriage broke down when I was 26.

A new chapter began as a single parent.

When my daughters were old enough to start nursery, I applied for a position in Local Government. I was completely shocked when I was offered the position of Area supervisor. It was a great achievement, I was so proud. I worked for Local Government for 15 years.

Another career change came when a management opportunity arose in Manchester working with asylum seekers.

Age 39, I married a second time, life was good.

I was assaulted at work not long after I was married leaving me wary and uneasy about the kind of employment I was in.

The best was yet to come as me and hubby created Bears 4U, an online personalised teddy bear business which we ran successfully for 15 years.

Around 2016 All our children had left home and had families of their own.

In 2017 we decided to downsize and buy a property close to the sea, a place we had always loved, as we had a static caravan situated on the Fylde Coast for quite a number of years.

Just as things were looking good. I was diagnosed with Early Onset Alzheimer's 2019. I thought that was it!

No not me!

I'm enjoying living my life with my Hubby, my four legged friends, Art, Nature and of course family

George Rook

I was born in the early 1950s, in the time of Birmingham smogs, open back double-decker buses, and walking, yes walking, to and from school.

However, I was sent to board from 11, and had some unpleasant years at school. My family was a typical professional, middle class mess of rows and simmers.

After leaving school I trained as a Chartered Accountant, qualified, and immediately gave it up to study English at York University. I had grown a deep love of the written word and tried my hand at writing self indulgent verse.

After one more shot at accountancy, in a rural Shropshire practice, I decided to teach English. After 'training' at Manchester University I got my first job (13th interview) in Redditch, then developing as a new town. I soon loved it (the teaching) and returned to Shropshire.

Thus I progressed gently until I ran out of steam around my mid 40s. A hiccuppy 4 years followed, with several little part time jobs as I recovered strength, until I returned to school as a Business Manager, a new and evolving post in the late 90s.

I remember vividly the drive back from work on the afternoon of the 9/11 attacks in New York, followed by the wretched footage of the Towers falling.

I worked in Cheshire until 2008, surviving several illnesses and a cardiac bypass.

Around 2005 I began to notice little difficulties at work, and in some family situations. Decisions under pressure became hard. Remembering names had gone. My language and behaviour became a little uninhibited in social situations. I began to have to make copious notes of every conversation and meeting I had, so that I could check back when I needed.

In 2007 I floundered and again ran out of steam, but time away from work did not make any difference to my symptoms. I left my job, but a year later I found a local part time manager post with a major charity. I found it increasingly difficult to understand and retain explanations of systems and clients, and to deal with some of the less than helpful behaviours of some charity staff.

We parted company in 2013 and a year later I was diagnosed with vascular and Alzheimer's dementia. There is much scientific evidence (as well as personal experience where I live) that interventions can make a huge difference. It gives me such joy to help others understand how they can enrich people's lives while walking the path alongside others who live with dementia through improving the often non-existent support services post diagnosis. I developed several DEEP peer support groups in Shropshire market towns.

During lockdown I have loved making very, very good friendships through frequent zoom meetings, mostly through the DEEP Network.

My symptoms slowly developed. Now and then I suddenly realise that I cannot remember how to do something, or my balance gets worse. But keeping relaxed and calm, without pressure or noise, enables me to enjoy life, and to learn new skills, like carving and painting.

There's a fair bit of life left in this old dog.

Jennifer Bute

My life could well have been described as successful. I thrived in my career as a well-respected family doctor and was involved in medical education. I was married with three children and I had various commitments outside of work and the home. However, all that was about to change when I developed symptoms of dementia in my late 50s. My father had dementia and so I had seen something of how it affects families over the years. Then as a family doctor I had patients with dementia, so I thought I knew exactly how my life would be affected.

It started with not remembering how to find my way to places; I struggled to complete simple tasks like shopping or cooking; I couldn't remember who people were – but my colleagues didn't believe me because they weren't prepared to lose a good doctor. I still remember the terror of getting lost on the way to the surgery where I had worked for 25 years. One time I phoned my husband on the way home from work not knowing whether to turn left or right at a crossroads – and he, who loved me dearly, told me not to be so stupid. Not being believed was almost worse than being lost, but I knew that these situations could be seen as valuable learning experiences. My faith has taught me that nothing in life is wasted. When I was finally diagnosed in 2010 I was so relieved that at last I was believed!

After some time I could no longer run my own house and my cooking became rather bizarre! I did not recognise visitors or even guests staying (sometimes not even recognising my own husband). We moved to a dementia inclusive village in North Somerset as I wanted to stay as independent as possible (although there is always '24 hour care' available). My husband died quite unexpectedly soon after we arrived, so I have had much opportunity over the subsequent 10 years learning different ways to enable others. The true person remains to the end and my joy is to 'find them' and to enable people to talk again – even when in the final stages of dementia. Following opportunities to give talks about the why and how, I was persistently asked to write a book, so eventually with help it was done: Dementia from the Inside: A Doctor's Personal Journey of Hope (Bute and Morse 2018).

Medicine has changed a lot over the years. Previously when people had a stroke nothing was done. Now, with rehabilitation, there is always improvement – even complete recovery (although the damage is still there in the brain). So too, I believe we can improve quality of life for people with dementia. I have been able (with help) to make many videos explaining different aspects of dementia and coping strategies for various situations. all freely available on my website [www.gloriousopportunity.org] *and also a weekly blog illustrating practical ways to help others with dementia* [www.facebook. com/gloriousopportunity/].

Jim McNee

I was born in Shettleston, in the east end of Glasgow, in September 1949. Having gone to primary and secondary schools in Glasgow I completed my education at Glasgow University where I obtained an Honours Degree in Physics in 1971.

After leaving university and following a secondary teachers training course for 1 year I started teaching in a secondary school in the east end of the city in 1972.

In January 1975 I moved, with my wife, to West Germany to work for the British Forces Schools at a place called Rheindahlen, the Joint Headquarters of the British Forces in West Germany. Our first daughter was born there.

Life there was very good. During school holidays we travelled all over Europe for the next 11 years visiting many different countries.

My main hobby during this time was playing football and I played in a league consisting of army, RAF and civilian teams.

During my time there I progressed from being a teacher of Science to Head of Physics and finally Head of Science.

In 1987 we decided to return to UK and came to Kent when I obtained a position as Head of Science and Senior Teacher in a large secondary school in Canterbury. Our second daughter was born here in Kent.

I continued to work in the same school until I retired 2009, ending my career there as Deputy Head in charge of finance. During this time my main hobby continued to be football, finally retiring at the age of 58.

After retirement from both work and football my main pastimes became reading and playing golf, which l am not very good at despite having a son-in-law who is a golf pro.!

In May 2017 I was diagnosed with Alzheimer's disease.

After my diagnosis, I attended a 4-week course run for people who had recently been diagnosed with dementia. It was here that I heard about the

Forget Me Nots, and I joined them in September 2017, here I met Keith again who I had known when we had worked in the education system. I enjoy being a member of the Forget Me Nots as it offers an opportunity to meet and be involved with others with a similar problem as mine.

I decided to sign up for a clinical trial being held in London as I thought it might help others suffering from the disease. The final screening process for eligibility for the trial, however, was a PET scan and when the results of that came back I was turned down for the trial as there was no evidence of any plaques or tangles in my brain. My consultant in Kent then arranged for me to have a further PET scan which measured glucose uptake in the brain and the results for that were normal. As a result of the two PET scans my condition was re-diagnosed. At the moment no one can tell me what exactly is wrong with me! My symptoms have not changed. At the moment I have been diagnosed as having a developing neuro-degenerative disorder.

Julie Hayden

Hello, my name is Julie Hayden, and I was diagnosed over 5 years ago at the age of 54. I live alone in Halifax, West Yorkshire. Although this is my hometown, I have actually spent most of my adult life in the Greater London area and the home counties. My move South was just after I qualified as a general nurse, and I later specialised in respiratory medicine. After marrying I became mother to two girls and returned to full time education in my 40s to retrain as a social worker. I went on to work in older peoples' community services where most of my clients were living with a form of dementia.

On the personal front my family have a long experience of dementia. On my dad's side late-onset dementia has occurred in every generation, sometimes more than once. I also lost my mum to dementia. I am the first to develop young onset. Since my diagnosis I have developed a 3rd career for myself from the range of activism I become involved in, and I am grateful for that as it helps with my neuroplasticity. However, that doesn't mean that I am only about dementia. I remain essentially a parent, grandparent and enjoy spending as much time as possible with my friends. I have a lifelong love of the arts, particularly the theatre, and over the last couple of years have begun to write poetry. I have also always been interested in criminology and forensics.

Keith Day (Cam)

Hi, my name is Keith I am 72 years old. I live on the Isle of Sheppey Kent. I have been married now for 46 years. I have two children both married and have three grandchildren, two girls and a boy. I meet my wife when I was in the Royal Navy. I left the navy and we moved to Bradford Yorkshire. I was working for Yorkshire Water, but the pay was poor and my wife who was a career person and we talked about role reversal. We were a modern couple and after talking it over we decided to swap our roles I become the house husband and my wife went back to banking.

This worked well, as the children got older I joined the Citizens Advice Bureau in Yorkshire as a Volunteer which I enjoyed and I stayed with them for several years. A position came up for my wife which she worked for several years to achieve. We talked about the position as it meant a move from Yorkshire to the South of the country. Bradford where we lived were having riots and we wanted to move for the children's safety so we decided to move. When the children settled into their new schools, I volunteered to become a bereavement counsellor with CRUSE I did this becoming the only male children counsellor in the Swale area. I was working in schools and ran an adult's support group for about 5 years. By this time my children were in college, so I started to look around for more work. I was extremely fortunate and found employment as a residential social worker in a children's home for abused children. 7 weeks after starting work I had a stroke. I pushed myself to regain the ability to speak and to learn how to read and write again. I returned to work after about 3 months. I took the position of a counsellor because all the children had losses i.e., home, parents, and friends. I also took a role in anger management soon after becoming a shift leader, this entailed running the shift with 3 to 4 staff members. I remained there for 11 years until I retired.

In a way I look back and realize now I was struggling to do my work and give it 100 per cent. I started to have bouts of depression, and over 2 years this got worse and I starting to isolate myself. My wife and my daughter watched as my personality started to change. I was doing things that were out of the ordinary for me. My wife asked if I would go to the doctor's as she was worried. We talked to the doctor and my wife told him this is not the man I married. This was in September 2015, and he decided to refer me to the older person mental clinic and by April of 2016 I had a confirmed diagnosis of dementia. I was told that I had frontotemporal dementia (FTD). At that time, I went into denial but after a couple of months I noticed the changes in myself. I decided to investigate more about dementia and also joined a support group. It was the best thing I have ever done, I learnt so much from the group and I then decided that I HAVE DEMENTIA BUT I WON'T LET DEMENTIA HAVE ME. I became a dementia activist and my goal is to enlighten people about dementia, and help reduce the stigma that goes with dementia. Just because I have dementia it's not the end of life, I am still capable to understand and make good decisions. I also have a voice and want people to listen and not put me on the scrap heap.

Masood Ahmed Qureshi (Maq)

I was born in Pakistan, and did my basic education there up to High School level. I came to the UK in 1971 when I was 14 years old. I could not speak English and came at a time where racism in the community was challenging. I went to school and attended night school to learn English. Being a Muslim in a Christian country took a long time to adjust to. I went to a catholic school in Stoke on Trent and attended until after my C.S.E. exams. After passing these exams, I went to college to further my education up to A Levels. After that, I sought employment and was employed by the French Michelin Tyre company. 2 years later I was promoted and became a team leader and was employed there until the business moved to France. I now needed to begin job hunting.

Not having much luck I enrolled for a book keeping and accountancy course at the local college, which resulted eventually in me starting my own business as a bookkeeper. My office became a hub for the local Asian community and I started to provide other services for the community. Including travel arrangements, passport renewal, sending monies abroad, translating and general financial advice.

My wife passed away in 1989 and I found it difficult to look after our children while maintaining my business. I needed to find self-employed, part-time employment. In 2009 I was taken ill and had major heart surgery (triple bypass) and had to give up work.

After my heart surgery, I was diagnosed with frontal temporal dementia in 2010. While still recovering from the bypass it was like having surgery all over again. It took a long time to come to terms with the diagnosis, my confidence went completely and I detached myself from the outside world. Not having any knowledge of the condition and only knowing the last stage, I was terrified. The thought of having a disease that has no cure was frightening. Financially, physically, emotionally and psychologically I was a real mess. I had never claimed any benefits before and did not know my entitlement or where to go for help. I was fortunate to find Beth Johnson Foundation who are part of the DEEP Network and they acted as my advocate. The support of the foundation and DEEP was the backbone of my recovery and I started to get my self-esteem back.

We then started a peer support group and I am proud to be a founding member of the group that helped me and many others that joined us.

I have been part of quite a number of study programmes conducted by Keele, Leicester, Bradford and Manchester Universities. I have attended many conferences and made presentations to trainee doctors and nurses at those universities. I wrote articles in 'Dementia Together' magazine (April–May 2020), DEEP newsletter, 3 Nations Dementia Working Group newsletters and Beth Johnson Foundation Newsletter and the local newspaper. The lockdown put a stop to all of that, but I kept doing my bit for dementia awareness using Zoom and Teams. I became a regular panellist for Healthy Generation (Stoke on Trent) Approach, Change For You, Together In Dementia Everyday (TIDE), DEEP, Three Nations Dementia Working Group, Dementia Friends, Dementia Alliance International and NHS Midlands Steering Group. In 2021 I saw an advert for the Alzheimer's Society about Side By Side inviting people to volunteer to support others with dementia I stepped forward and became a companion caller. Alongside this, I offer support to people who are not familiar with zoom calls.

I am proud to be part of Beth Johnson Foundation, DEEP and the 3 Nations Working Group where I have met and gained friends for life.

Nigel Hullah

Homelife:
Nigel lives in the Peoples Republic of Townhill, Wales. He lives alone but is supported by 15–20 good friends who allow him to do all the things that are important to him and remain independent. He is bullied by two feral cats as is the rest of his neighbourhood. Nigel is blessed with strong non-clinical support from people who 'get him.'

Preferences:
Nigel enjoys a good malt whisky or aged Bourbon, enjoys fresh food and is not a fan of processed food. Nigel enjoys the company of people with opinions based on facts not bias even if they don't agree with him. Nigel is politically active and believes passionately in socialism so engage him in conversation about this at your peril. Nigel spends time with good friends particularly watching football and travelling.

What does Nigel believe/feel?
Nigel believes the aims of dementia care/support services must align with human rights values. This includes supporting people living with dementia.

Nigel is committed to supporting and working towards people affected by dementia having as much control as possible over their own lives care and treatment.

Nigel is passionate that all people affected by dementia must be treated with dignity and respect in all interactions with care agencies and all service providers. to live as independently as possible, for as long as possible.

Nigel supports the right of a person to determine their own identity and live accordingly irrespective of the presence of dementia or any other disability.

Nigel despises stigma, prejudice and marginalisation of any part of society.

Nigel knows that better literacy on Human Rights will inform better care planning, and using this approach is enabling, and allows for many light bulb moments turning decision making on its head.

Nigel is a believer that Human Rights must be premised on the inherent dignity of all, no matter what an individual's frailty or flaws.

Nigel lives by this quote 'To deny people their human rights is to challenge their very humanity.' Nelson Mandela

Tracey Shorthouse

I am 51 and have been living with dementia since I was diagnosed with Posterior Cortical Atrophy in 2015 at 45 years old. At the time, I was working as a Community Staff Nurse. Since being diagnosed, I have retired and stopped driving. Posterior Cortical Atrophy affects the perception of things, causes visual problems and basically the brain changes how the eyes see.

Since retiring, I have been involved in a variety of ventures and I speak at a range of events which I feel are important to me. They all help to educate and bring an understanding to members of the public and health professionals that dementia affects all ages, that there are different kinds of dementia, and when you have met one person with dementia, you have met one person with dementia. We are all different with our own personalities.

I am a member of the SUNshiners group, which is part of DEEP, and I am also one of the Dementia Envoy's for the KMPT.

I also enjoy being active despite having had a stroke in 2015 and a TIA in 2018. I mobilise with a stick but enjoy walking and swimming. More recently I have started to swim in the sea, which I find freeing.

I try to learn new skills every so often to keep the brain active. Skills like loom knitting and macrame. I also enjoy doing different courses on the computer, even if I might not remember them later. I enjoy reading, writing the odd poem, and gardening. I play word games twice a day.

When I was first diagnosed with dementia I self-published a poetry book. Writing poems at the time was cathartic and helped me with my diagnosis.

Concluding thoughts

We hope that these self-penned biographies support what we intended to achieve by way of diversity, and will give readers insight into the lives of these fifteen people before embarking upon them talking to us about life with dementia. In this way, you will get to know the person before you get to know the person with dementia. Given that the group is so diverse, we discussed at length how we should refer to the group collectively in the book. Interviewees or participants felt inadequate. In the end we decided to refer to them simply as the Fifteen.

4   Practicalities of the interview process

Keith Oliver

Reinhard and I were delighted that fifteen people living with dementia agreed to spend an hour individually with us talking about their lives both before and since being diagnosed with dementia. The structure of these conversations was based upon the Kitwood flower model, which features on page 92 in chapter 5 of *Dementia Reconsidered, Revisited*. As authors we have tried to retain a conversational style to the content of the book because we recognise that it may be widely read by – and needs to be accessible to – other people who are affected directly by dementia, either with a diagnosis or living and caring for someone who has dementia. One consequence of this I hope is that you, the reader, will feel as if you are sitting alongside Reinhard, myself and the contributor who is speaking with us – and, indeed, to you.

Our first task having recruited our participants was to consider an outline to what we were seeking to discuss with them. Using the Kitwood flower model and Kitwood's writing we generated the notes in Box 4.1, which later became the basis for our prompts and questions.

Box 4.1: Thoughts for questions to use in the book with people diagnosed with dementia

Identity

- Knowing who oneself is – in cognition and feelings
- Narrative – connection to one's past, one's story – life history, help with holding on to it
- Consistency from past to present situation
- Sometimes one's identity is confirmed by others
- Everyone is unique
- Empathy – I-thou
- Dementia world and condition can at times feel like taking one's identity away – institutionalised/expectations

Occupation

- Involved in the process of life in a way which is significant to the individual drawing upon person's abilities and powers

---

- Opposite –apathy, inertia, boredom, futility
- Sense of agency
- Involved with others or in solitude
- Often involves having a project – work/leisure
- If unoccupied, then one can decline and self-esteem falls
- Person with dementia wants to help, take part, support
- Important to know about person's past to support occupation in activities

Inclusion

- Needing to fit into different social groups
- Group identity? – family, friends – longstanding and recent, neighbours, colleagues (current/ex), others with dementia
- Clinging/insecurity – seems to us to reflect attachment rather than here, as Kitwood places it
- Being viewed as unable to be a part of a group due to the dementia (diagnosis?)
- Care homes – people isolated/grouped together, sheltered housing complexes – inclusion in a community
- Risk of person with dementia retreating into themselves – decline
- Having a place or role within a group

Attachment

- Connections and interdependence – social society
- Bonding – safety net to deal with uncertainty
- Using attachments to overcome uncertainty, unfamiliar situations and fears

Comfort

- Calming anxiety
- Warmth and strength to overcome challenges – avoid falling apart
- Towards self / towards others / from others to you
- Overcoming feeling of loss so common in dementia – failing of abilities / loss of self-esteem / jobs / loved ones, etc. / way of life
- Needing to feel comforted

Love

- Nothing as such in chapter 5 of *Dementia Reconsidered, Revisited* on this but is intrinsic within the chapter and book.

I then took these thoughts and, in no particular order, started to let my mind wander into deeper thinking about what we had written in this outline. I re-read Kitwood's book and the 2019 commentaries and with the support of Ellie, one of the students, I accessed some of Kitwood's articles and read them with interest. I wanted to explore and think through the plan in Figure 3.1 by amassing a greater understanding for myself of the key issues relating to the labels on the flower and gain some sense of what inspired Kitwood, which I hoped would in turn inspire me and then those with dementia we were talking with. Knowing Reinhard's great depth of knowledge, I wanted to do this before getting too deeply into the book with him so that I felt confident occupying a parallel space alongside my co-author in constructing the questions or conversation prompts we were going to base the Zoom and face-to-face dialogues upon.

Starting with a sense of the person we were engaged with, I wanted to find out what their sense of being a unique individual was, who in some ways had things in common with me and the other members of the Fifteen but who was also very different. There was no question in my mind that this would be done with respect and humility, and we would speak as equals, which made it easier for me since I share some similar experiences with each of the Fifteen. I was interested to hear if my experience of how relationships and connections have taken on a greater significance for me since I have lived with dementia was something the others had experienced and can relate to. Then to support this I was keen to give each person the time and space to open up further into these relationships and the part they play in their lives. If personhood is defined by social interactions, then dementia creates risks to this – namely, social exclusion, vulnerability, loneliness and isolation. Are people good in their own company? On a personal level, I am not unless immersed in an interesting and engaging activity but would this apply to everyone else?

I wanted to find out if each person felt that their personhood and sense of self had changed over time, by thinking in terms of 'Who was I? Who am I now and who am I becoming?' As well as, 'Where have I come from and where am I going in my life?' I was curious to know when each individual spoke about their future, what their hopes, dreams and ambitions were opposed to their fears, concerns and doubts, and then how their expectations and beliefs brought them to a balanced outlook on life. I then hoped to take this further by considering with each person what changes they saw in themselves by way of influences, taking into account what has been lost or gained since diagnosis. This is what Kitwood referred to as the 'core self' and I hoped through the conversations to be able to reach as many of the core selves of the individuals as possible and then to record them in this book. As we outlined earlier, this book is not a scientific study so at no point did Reinhard and I consider utilising measures to assess each individual's personhood; indeed, it could be argued that personhood cannot be easily measured as each individual is unique and different.

Knowing each of the Fifteen, I anticipated that the conversations would reveal and unveil each individual's abilities and potential interests, intellect, ability to relate to and communicate with others, relationships, and how they perceived being wanted and needed by others. Many of those we spoke with have been part of groups and projects that I myself have been involved with, so consequently, I expected that creative activities would form part of their conversation and would link in closely to the structure of Kitwood's flower. Some of these projects are funded and supported by DEEP, so I thought it interesting to see how engaged and empowered each individual felt by participating in those projects and events. Often people wish to feel busy and occupied and I often muse on whether being busy and occupied equals being engaged and empowered. Viewing this both before and since being diagnosed and if any changes had occurred was something I was keen to explore in the conversations.

This sense of self is something that has a bearing upon a person being self-motivated, able to communicate and self-aware (Warren 1973) and when selecting the Fifteen, I gave thought to these considerations in helping them to form a picture of themselves through the Kitwood flower model.

Reinhard and I spent long periods of our regular catch-up meetings talking, sometimes with the student supporters, about the concepts of 'i-thou' (i.e. around genuine human exchanges) and 'i-it' (i.e. where the person is objecti- fied). While I do not remember using these phrases in our conversations with the Fifteen, it was certainly in our minds as we always sought the 'i-thou' route into and throughout the conversation.

Looking beyond the person's inner feelings and thoughts, we wanted to examine relationships – with family members, friends, members of the com- munity and professionals – and their impact upon them as an individual. We wanted to look at boundaries and if they were helpful or a barrier to positive, meaningful relationships, again for them as an individual. We also wanted to look at the person's experiences of health and social care both relating to their dementia and/or any other health issues they live with. Reinhard writes in the next chapter about malignant social psychology (MSP) (Kitwood 1997), the aspects of which include: labelling – being defined by others or oneself; stigma; treachery – being lied to; outpacing – interactions that are too fast or too slow and also possibly patronising; infantilisation – being treated as a child rather than an adult; and condemnation – where the person may be dis- believed, blamed or accused of doing something they either did not do or had no genuine recall of having done it. For me these were the main aspects of MSP running through my mind when thinking ahead to the conversations. There is no question that the use of negative language does impact upon the individual and it was my expectation that this would feature when people were talking about all of the petals within the flower model. From this, I then wanted to ask what support – both professional and personal – each person received to combat malignant social psychology and dementia generally or, to put it positively, to enhance the flower.

Given the influence religious faith had on Kitwood's work, we were inter- ested to ask the Fifteen if it was also important in their lives, and if it was, how did it shape their personhood. Although when he died he was a humanist, not only did Kitwood base his thinking on his Christian theological background, he grounded it in the importance of where people live, and clearly this needed to feature in the conversations. Each of us has a sense of belonging, familiarity and security in where we live and function, and again I always had notes on this in front of me when speaking with the Fifteen.

While anticipating that the conversations would be essentially serious, I did hope that each contributor's sense of humour would get the chance to shine through in their responses, and that this would showcase their broader attitude to their life living with dementia. Ageing for many holds few laughs, especially if the person is living with any other serious health issue that affects their physical abilities, which in turn may impact on their mental wellbeing and quality of life. I would resist during the conversations use of the medical term 'co-morbidities'. Also, I was interested to hear how people had been treated as an older person with a dementia diagnosis by family members and friends, as well as professionals they had interacted with, beginning at the point of diagnosis and what support they may have subsequently received. Related to this, the balance between dependence and vulnerability with independence and confidence was likely to feature in a number of overlapping petals.

The conversations took place as the world was still coming to terms with the impact of the COVID-19 pandemic, on us all as individuals but also as a society, so it was inevitable that this would come up. I anticipated that some contributors' experiences would be similar to mine, in that while COVID-19 and lockdowns were predominantly negative experiences, maybe there were some positive aspects people took forward into the post-pandemic period. As we all became more reliant on technology and all of our preparation and communications were conducted using the computer, we felt it important to ask how the use of technology contributed to each individual's quality of life.

We then needed to settle on ways forward with the questions by:

1 Using the above thoughts and prompts to construct the questions and then direct the responses to the flower for writing in the book.
2 Using the flower to structure the interviews by placing the prompts under the flower headings before embarking on the interviews.
3 Placing the emphasis on the quality of being human in combating pressures around dementia causing the individual to feel a 'non-person', and then taking this forward as each unique person with dementia against person with dementia and the ME in dementia.

In addition, as always when seeking to construct a plan in preparing the prompts, I resorted to my tried-and-tested openers: How? What? Where? When? Why?

With these thoughts printed in front of me, I was then able with Reinhard to devote my energy to the next stages of the process.

This sense of active listening is something we tried ourselves to utilise when talking with and listening to the Fifteen. We had an outline (see Box 4.1 and Box 4.2) for use with each conversation, although we were very happy to be led in different directions by the contributor. All of the conversations took place during the summer of 2021 either on Zoom or face-to-face. The conversations were recorded with prior agreement and then one of the students typed up the transcripts for us. Each conversation lasted around an hour and were extremely interesting and as varied as the individuals we talked to. Though the outline may have been the same, the conversations clearly reflected the individual experiences and personalities of those we were talking with. We wanted each person to have control over what they wished to share with us and therefore to give them each a sense of agency.

Box 4.2: Semi-structured interview questions

Identity

You have now been living with a diagnosis of dementia for X number of years.

- How would you describe yourself now?
- Is that different from how you saw yourself before the diagnosis? And how?
- What is the same? Do you do anything to help you stay the same?
- How do you feel about any differences?

Occupation

- Has dementia changed your interests? Your activities? And how?
- What are the activities that help you to live well?
- What are the challenges in engaging in your interests and activities?

Inclusion

- Has anything changed in the way you feel close to, and connected with, people?
- Do you feel included in family, groups, society, the world? If so, in what ways / how?
- What do you do to remain connected and included, and what are the challenges?

Attachment

- Has dementia changed your relationships with family, with friends, with acquaintances, with wider society?
- How have any of your relationships changed?

Comfort

Dementia can be a stressful, frustrating experience.

- What provides you with comfort?
- What makes you feel better, gives you strength?

Love

We live in a society where 'love' can be difficult to talk about. How has dementia affected or changed how you:

- feel and express love for others?
- receive and perceive love from others?
- show love towards yourself?

Our semi-structured outline for the conversations was shared in advance with all of the Fifteen by email along with a follow-up reminder a day or two before we were due to talk together. Some chose to prepare detailed notes, others jotted down key points, while others chose to speak as thoughts occurred to them. This worked well for each person in turn, and for our book because it was centred around the individual talking with us. The only two common threads were that each person had been given a diagnosis of dementia, and that each gave us their thoughts on their lives past and present through the 'lens' of the Kitwood flower model – Identity, Occupation, Inclusion, Attachment, Comfort and Love.

All the participants who spoke with us on Zoom were comfortable using this means of communication, having developed experience of it during the pandemic. The face-to-face interviews took place either at Reinhard's house for participants who could easily travel there, or in one case at the person's own home with their wife also present. We were mindful of how tiring conversations of this type could be for people with dementia and the time we spent talking and listening seemed to fly by. Reinhard and I would use our pre-prepared questions as prompts and would not fall into the trap of speaking for the people who we were engaged with, even if at times the conversation seemed to meander and move away from the subject we were seeking to talk about. This did not matter at all because later in the process, with the students' support, we would edit the transcripts to provide us with the material for Part 2 of this book. It was always considered paramount that the person with dementia should feel comfortable and confident that what they were saying was valued and respected and all seemed very happy to share their thoughts with us. After completing the conversations, we contacted each of the Fifteen to secure their written consent for the use of their words within the book.

Summary and reflections

1 There is no doubt that the mutual knowledge and trust that existed between the Fifteen and myself helped the conversations to flow. While there are many things we have in common between us, there are just as many – if not more – ways we are different. I live with dementia, as all of the Fifteen do but we each live differently and it is only the individual who really knows what it is like for them. What I tried to do was to draw close to their singularity, and then to explore and highlight overlaps with myself and the other members of the Fifteen as seen through the 'lens' of the Kitwood flower model. Where there were gaps and differences I hoped that empathy and mutual respect would help fill some of this void to enable connection to be maintained.

2 I have many flaws, weaknesses and deficits, and most are highlighted by my dementia. Those we spoke with opened up honestly about this as it pertained to them, and we sought to use the Kitwood flower model to support each person find ways of navigating these vulnerabilities. I want to be treated as me, but more than this I want people to engage with me, be interested in me for who I am not what I have been, are or can be for them.

3 People with dementia need to have trust and confidence in the person they are talking to in order to be totally open and honest.

4 Active listening and engaging with the person illustrates how valued they are and how much respect one has for the point they are making.

5 'Deadly silences' are extremely uncomfortable for most people with dementia who are far more relaxed if the conversation flows.

6 Be prepared beforehand but also be prepared to be flexible and go where the conversation takes you.

5 Enduring themes from Kitwood

Reinhard Guss

Tom Kitwood wrote about dementia as an engaged professional, a learned academic, a sensitive observer and a passionate activist. He was an expert in many ways, though not by personal lived experience. This resonates with my own perspective in the field of psychological dementia care research and practice. Most of us who wrote commentaries on Tom Kitwood's original text in *Dementia Reconsidered, Revisited* came across passages that 20 years on seemed wholly anachronistic. For Keith and I, it was the assumption that people with dementia are unable to tell us anything about their experience of the condition, and the focus on the very late stages seemed to exclude the many years of experience of dementia most would have had well before a time when active verbal communication became very difficult. Hence, I am particularly pleased to remedy my outside-in perspective on living with dementia with the majority of this book containing the words of the fifteen experts we spoke with about their experience, but also Keith's perspective as first author and editor of the book series. In this chapter, I hope to complement his expertise with my perspective as a psychological practitioner, and share how Kitwood's concepts have influenced my practice and experience of working in the dementia field over the past 25 years.

My early life experience of dementia

My own experience of dementia lies way back in my early life, long before any notions of working in psychology or the field of dementia. As I age myself, the longer I practise in this area and the more I reflect on my motivations and interests in pursuing it, the clearer the importance of those early influences becomes. This especially applies to the concepts of relationship and attachment, both central in Kitwood's thinking.

My grandmother, Helene Völpel, called 'Nuna' by her own preference, lived with my family of origin from when she was 70 and I was 5 years old, until her death at the age of 96, when my siblings and I had long left home. While there was never a formal diagnosis, looking back today, it is likely that she lived with a form of Alzheimer's disease throughout this time. For her grandchildren, and perhaps particularly for myself, she was a warm-hearted, ever-present and open support, part of the overall household and thus easy to relate to. It is also easy to see that familiarity with her passions, her likes and dislikes as well as her life story and anecdotes alongside an emotional connection made it easy to relate and to communicate even in the very late stages of her illness, and years before Tom Kitwood wrote *Dementia Reconsidered*.

Nuna had a tough life. She lost her mother at the age of seven when her younger sister was born, and the loss of key attachments was a recurring theme of her life from then on. With her older sister and her much-loved younger brother, she was moved away from her home village to an environment where a mostly absent father soon remarried and the children were not welcome. Her uncle eventually paid for the children to return to the village and be cared for by a distant relative. Nuna was always conscious of being tolerated rather than belonging. Being sent to boarding school to receive a higher education was a highlight for her, opening opportunities for a career as a teacher. This separated her from her brother, who was subsequently killed in the early days of the First World War at the age of 17. She loved her career as a teacher, discovered anthroposophy and Rudolph Steiner, and met her future husband, whom she was not allowed to marry until after the death of her benefactor uncle. When the Nazis gained power, she had two young children and became the sole breadwinner as her husband was unemployable due to his opposition to the regime. The end of her career came soon after when the Nazi government stopped married women from working in the public sector, resulting in subsisting on a minimal income. Her husband seems to have become increasingly depressed, and died of cancer before he could see liberation and the end of the Second World War. She never remarried and it took many years for her to rebuild a life sub-letting rooms in her flat in Hamburg, rekindling relationships with relatives in her native village in the Harz mountains, with extensive correspondence with friends, and some much-enjoyed travel. She also lived with a sense of duty to transcribe and type up her late husband's enormous volume of anthroposophy-related writing, noted in his own shorthand that nobody else would be able to decipher.

Aged 70, Nuna walked across a road without looking for traffic and was knocked down by a car. It was thought that she could no longer manage on her own, and she moved to southern Germany to live with her daughter (and her young family including me aged 5) until the end of her life 26 years later. Nuna was known to pay little attention to mundane daily things, having her head in poetry and literature instead. It is possible that many of the early signs of dementia were put down to her usual personality of paying little attention to managing daily life. Many of her personal struggles with her failing cognitive abilities only emerged in the very late stages and after her death, when her many attempts to write notes or letters were found, which she had part-written, corrected, rewritten, crossed out and annotated in different colours, and eventually abandoned. While she has provided me with some precious examples of the possibility of communication, of emotional change and of coping in the later stages of dementia, the intensity of her lonely struggles in those many early and middle years of the condition are so sad to contemplate, and no doubt another motivation behind my clinical work.

My early clinical practice

My practice as a young clinical psychologist in the UK in the 1980s coincided with the last years of Nuna's life and the late stages of her dementia. I only met her for a very few but significant times on visits. Cared for by my parents, who were eventually supported by a community carer, she did not have to experience institutional care, and lived with people who had known her well for decades. In terms of clinical and professional development, these were the pre-Kitwood times. I was practising cognitive behaviour therapy (CBT), which was a relatively new approach then. There was a general view that because of the deterioration in cognitive abilities, psychologists would not have anything to offer that could be suited to people with dementia themselves, other than behavioural approaches to modify 'problem behaviours'. Carers and family members were seen as appropriate for CBT however, and if we could support carers, there would be indirect benefits for people with dementia as well. I developed an early CBT-based programme to assist carers with managing stress, involving the participants completing many complicated questionnaires, some translated from German, which demonstrated its effectiveness. A couple of participants appeared to be struggling with some memory problems of their own, and much of the material was reminiscent of family experiences of living with Nuna. It made me wonder whether there would be a way of making some of these approaches useful to people with dementia themselves alongside families and carers. However, until the emergence of Kitwood and his writings, I had found little appetite for this in the clinical psychology, no-framework, no-starting point in the academic world to develop psychological practice further with people with a dementia diagnosis.

Neuropsychology is another approach to dementia that has influenced my practice and continues to evoke discussion and attempts of integration into a holistic approach. While on placements to obtain UK recognition of my qualification, I was fortunate to work with Elizabeth Berry, a fellow German who was working at Salford's Hope Hospital as a specialist neuropsychologist. The caseload there included people seeking explanations for cognitive changes they had noticed, which repeatedly resulted in a diagnosis of a dementia. The ability of neuropsychological testing to establish changes in cognitive profiles that give rise to particular diagnoses, and strengths and weaknesses that might explain people's changed experiences and assist in living with the conditions, seemed a way in which psychologists could be helpful in the field of dementia care.

Utilising Kitwood in clinical practice

I got a post in Kent in the early 1990s to develop a psychology service for older people. At the time, I was busy establishing myself and dealing with the challenges of NHS mental health services. I attended a training course in Dementia

Care Mapping at Bradford University that was led by Tom Kitwood but the approach seemed too lengthy and cumbersome to fully put into practice. It was Tom Kitwood's book *Dementia Reconsidered: The Person Comes First* (1997) that introduced a range of concepts and ideas which were new to me, and which it seemed possible to apply. In the rest of this chapter, I will describe some aspects of Kitwood's writing that have had an enduring impact on my practice.

The formulae

I initially found Kitwood's use of formulae with their pseudo-mathematical appearance very odd. Only over time did I begin to appreciate the genius behind this approach: a simplistic way of engaging a more scientifically or academically minded audience in the consideration of concepts that were new and contentious at the time. Looking back, it is also clear that graphics and formulae have endured and gained wider appeal and use in a way that most of his more detailed writing has not.

Here is the formula that made the neuropsychologists listen up:

$$\Psi = b / (B^d, B_p)$$

This means that every psychological state, every individual experience (Ψ) is also a brain state (b), with the physiology and neurology of the brain inextricably linked to the psychological state, the experience. All of this happens on the background of a brain that has developed its structure and connectivity over a lifetime, and that continues to develop (B^d) even under the onslaught of a dementia, of brain pathology (B_p).

Kitwood did not live to see Linda Clare's work on learning in Alzheimer's disease (Clare et al. 2001) and the development of cognitive rehabilitation approaches for people with dementia (Clare et al. 2019), but the ingredients are there already, especially the idea that brains continue to develop even while brain pathology and deterioration are present. Therefore, it has to be possible to support people's ability to use as much as possible of their brain's capacity to grow and develop. This will necessarily be easier if we understand in what way 'brain pathology' affects an individual brain in particular ways, and work with that person to make best use of strengths to mediate difficulties. Neuropsychological assessment has to be a helpful piece in this mosaic, alongside an understanding of a person's interests, motivations and background.

Perhaps more enduring generally is the following formula:

$$D = P + B + H + NI + SP$$

This provides an alternative description (the enriched model) of the syndrome constituting dementia to the medical diagnostic categories (the standard paradigm). It aims to emphasise the wider influences on an individual dementia presentation (D) other than what is deteriorating and going wrong in the brain. NI, the Neurological Impairment here, is only one factor among many, which has profound implications for how assessments of dementia ought to be undertaken. Alongside the neuropsychological/cognitive assessment of the impairment, there needs to be an appreciation of the P (Personality), the B (Biography), the H (physical Health) and the SP (Social Psychology, social and relationship status) of the person, if we are to gain an understanding of how a diagnosis, and later on any change in cognitive ability/disability, will affect them.

The beauty of Kitwood's formula lies in its constant reminder of the interrelatedness of so many factors in how a dementia affects a person and how it is experienced. Mathematically, perhaps this would be better expressed as a multiplication rather than addition. Nevertheless, here we have a framework for looking at a whole person in their context, above and beyond the establishment of deficits that we may find in our neuropsychological tests. This has had a profound impact on the way I undertake and teach cognitive assessment for memory clinics. Even in current practice, there are detailed catalogues of questions that clinicians are meant to ask in order to establish all the relevant facts that allow for a meaningful interpretation of test results. By and large, these still seem to be focused on a deficit model, and all too often are solely used to establish or support a medical diagnosis, while neglecting the impact for the person and the possibility of rehabilitative approaches. If it is worth spending significant amounts of time on extensive and cumbersome tests, then surely there should be a way of maximising the positive benefits for the person participating?

P (Personality)

Working clinically in the NHS brings clinicians like myself into contact with people from all walks of life. Some of the Fifteen have talked about dementia as 'a great leveller'. It often affects people who had never previously been in contact with mental health services. In this way, I have had opportunities to see, observe and work with Kitwood's assertion that personality is one of the key factors in how people will experience and cope with dementia.

In CBT's vulnerability-stress model (Hawton et al. 1989), mental health problems can arise due to the accumulation of stressful life events in combination with daily hassles. In dementia, a diagnosis is certainly a major stressful life event, and the nature of the condition means people increasingly experience daily hassles such as lost keys or glasses, missed appointments, forgotten PINs or passwords. I am often amazed and in awe at the resilience that some people possess in navigating this without suffering constant frustration, anger or despair. Yet underlying vulnerabilities can also be activated. For example, I see that people with a more anxious personality may present with anxiety or panic, and people with a more negative personality may become depressed and despondent, often long before a dementia is actually diagnosed. They then have to overcome the additional difficulty that their cognitive disabilities are attributed to anxiety or depression by health professionals wary of a false positive diagnosis of dementia. This leads to delays, further stressful periods of uncertainty, and missed opportunities to address the underlying issue of a developing dementia while various anxiolytic or antidepressant medications are trialled and repeated testing is undertaken. It often appears to me that carefully listening to what people tell us of their difficulties, their coping styles, their lifelong tendencies and personalities would hasten us towards clarity and the possibility of positive support at a much earlier point.

In the assessment schedules of memory clinics, 'personality change' is a flag that is asked about and taken as a possible sign of dementia, yet at times it is what is seen as lifelong personality that masks the developing dementia. I wonder sometimes how long it might have taken for anyone to suggest that my grandmother's many mishaps and frequent disasters could be due to a dementia rather than what was assumed to be her scatty personality. Given how driven she was by guilt and duty to produce literary works of correspondence and transcribe inscrutable texts, how might she have been helped to make peace much earlier on in her dementia with what she could or could no longer achieve.

A final thought about personality in relation to the Fifteen: such remarkably different and individual people and from such different backgrounds, yet all have eventually arrived in dementia activism, in being open and vocal about their lives and struggles, in making new relationships with other people with dementia and engaging with a wider public. It makes me reflect on how much of this is due to their personalities, and whether there would be ways for professionals to understand for whom this may be a helpful avenue and for whom it would not.

B (Biography)

People's biographies are central to the therapeutic work of clinical psychology and are closely linked with identity and attachment. In later life, there is inevitably even more of a lived life to look back on, and who we are becomes increasingly experienced as what we have done and what we have experienced over a lifetime, rather than what our plans are and what we might want to do in the future. This is magnified by the arrival of dementia, where it becomes more difficult to plan ahead and more important to hold on to who we are, to the memories that define us. Here lies the power of life-story work (Kaiser and Eley 2017), which strengthens the connections with past experience, be that engaging in an activity of reviewing old photos, discussing historic events or shared cultural experiences, or used instead in a more psychotherapeutic way, revisiting difficult times or ruptures in the course of life, making sense of how these affected us and got us where we are today.

It was fascinating to read the short biographies that the Fifteen shared with us prior to our conversations. Few included much of their early lives, childhood and adolescence, the times that I often ask about in my clinical work in order to get an inkling of clients' attachment history and attachment style, and what the strengths and struggles might be in this area. The absence of early history in the biographies is perhaps not surprising given that people were asked in the context of a book of living with dementia.

Biography is also essential in understanding how the psychological needs of Kitwood's flower have been met throughout people's lives, where there might be deficits, and how to use past strengths and experiences to support continuity. Biography helps us to understand what has been of comfort for a person in difficult times, and how love has worked out for them, both in terms of love for themselves and love given to and received from others. So much of identity is linked with occupation and work histories during adult life, and many of the Fifteen use their past professional skills to best effect in activism, as well as acquiring new ones. Biography, perhaps alongside personality, tells us much about a person's tendency to join and muck in or to keep on the margins, observing. I am interested in knowing whether people are outgoing or more introverted and of need of one-to-one relationships in order to flourish. However, some of the Fifteen talked about how they have surprised themselves in their activism, when they had previously considered themselves to be more passive. This also serves as a reminder that biographical history with all the helpful hints it can give for best support and care in dementia is nevertheless not deterministic and new interests and ways of doing things can emerge or be learnt despite or because of dementia.

H (physical Health)

The importance of physical (and mental) health for cognitive functions is known to most of us. The experiences of pain, high temperatures, hunger, exhaustion, stress or fear will impact on our ability to function at our best. Taking account of physical health is well established on assessment processes in memory clinics. However, it still can be the case in many situations where the diagnosis of dementia overshadows further investigation of physical health problems. Changes in behaviour are seen as being due to the dementia rather than having a physical cause. The tendency to see behaviours or complaints by people with a dementia or by their relatives as an inevitable sign of a deterioration in their dementia that cannot be helped or treated is widespread in health and social care systems, despite many efforts to educate and raise awareness of the heightened need for good physical health care in people with dementia. As dementia progresses, it can become more difficult for people to notice what exactly is going awry with their physical heath, and to communicate this to health professionals in a way they can easily understand, making it all the more important that more attention is paid to the possibility of physical health issues.

NI (Neurological Impairment)

While there is much about brain function we can test, assess and measure, and while there are increasingly detailed scans showing us the physiological state of connections and key areas for specific brain functions, there is still much we cannot derive from them. My work as a neuropsychologist in diagnostic memory clinics has demonstrated many times how little of what can be seen on a scan correlates with the cognitive disabilities experienced by people. Neuropsychology is such a scarce and expensive resource and, given the vast number of people referred for assessment of possible dementia, it is only those for whom there are doubts or discrepancies between presentation and scan reports that are seen for more specialised tests. These are typically people who show obvious cognitive difficulties but do not show any visible signs on brain scans. People who are functioning well but who have clearly visible damage on a scan are usually not referred. I recently attended a specialist neuroradiology seminar run by one of the very few radiologists with a specialist interest in scans related to dementia diagnoses. There, I learnt what should have been obvious all along: that scans do not show us all that is relevant inside the brain. Even the most advanced technology does not manage to show changes that are smaller than what can be seen by the naked eye. Damage from a dementia-related process or from microscopically small strokes can be numerous and scattered widely, or happen to occur in places of vital significance for co-ordinating the different areas and functions of the brain, and have a very great impact, while larger, more visible changes may be in a place where the enormously complex brain can easily compensate or re-route signals.

While as a neuropsychologist I take account of what can be seen on scans and what neurology and radiology may conclude about the physiology of the state of a person's brain, my primary concern is how different aspects of the brain's functioning are working for and affecting that person. On the basis of the person's experience, observation in interaction and test results on abilities to concentrate, process information, carry out verbal, visual and motoric tasks, learn and recall different types of material, plan and organise actions or solve problems, conclusions can be drawn on the physiological state of the brain, and comparisons made with scans and medical histories. It is frustrating how often clear signs of a dementia in neuropsychological testing are ignored by medical colleagues when there is a lack of anything visible on a brain scan. This then leads to people being discharged, perhaps with a diagnosis of mild cognitive impairment (MCI), which precludes them from accessing the admittedly limited medications and, more importantly, any dementia support services at an early stage.

In Kitwood's formula, NI is only one of five factors, and arguably not even the most important one, but when having to live with a dementia it is often immensely helpful for people to understand how the physiological changes in the brain affect their experience and functioning. The availability of a profile of cognitive strengths and disabilities lies at the heart of cognitive rehabilitation and the possibilities this holds for managing daily life and remaining active and independent for significantly longer than anyone would have thought possible in Tom Kitwood's time. Speaking with the Fifteen, the importance of using strategies and understanding the challenges and limits imposed by the dementia became very apparent. Finally, it can also be immensely important for people to develop a sense that their struggles with supposedly simple tasks are not a personal failing but the result of a neurological impairment caused by a medical condition – an insight that is equally important for families and carers in order to avoid apportioning blame or constant self-criticism. Such understanding of neurological impairment might have saved my grandmother years of distress and despair over her failures to manage her correspondence, and given her and her family access to support and strategies that could have helped her maintain her long-distance relationships for much longer.

SP (Social Psychology)

Tom Kitwood's observations and descriptions of the influences of social psychology, particularly malignant social psychology, took place mainly within care facilities and in the later stages of dementia. However, the effects are also present in diagnostic clinics, in the early stages and even before a dementia develops. The issues described above of the ways discrepancies between scans and actual functioning are affecting diagnostic decisions, referral processes and ultimately the access people have to services and support is one example of the effects of social psychology, of the impact of beliefs held by powerful groups on the way that people with dementia are treated.

Social psychology is also at work in the way that people with dementia develop their views of what dementia is and means over a lifetime, and how they consequently perceive themselves when concerns surface that they may be developing dementia themselves and after a diagnosis. The beliefs about dementia widely held in society 50 or even 80 years ago are what people visiting memory assessment clinics and their partners and peers have grown up with and can be difficult to adjust. This is particularly difficult in a society that perpetuates negative stereotyping, unfortunate 'jokes' and memes, and a use of language that activists with dementia like the Fifteen have worked hard to challenge and improve.

Following a diagnosis of dementia, many people feel that they are no longer part of the mainstream of society and become something 'other', much in the way that Kitwood described. Meeting others who are living with dementia, especially if they can provide positive examples of managing and coping, is often the most helpful 'intervention'. My clinical experience is that I can talk to groups of people with a new diagnosis or meet with individual people to go through the many positive possibilities, doing my best to reassure that admission to a care home and total dependency are a very long way off yet, all with relatively little effect. However, when another person with dementia speaks about their experience and strategies for living with their dementia, the impact is far greater. Herein lies a reason why I passionately believe that more activists, more people like the Fifteen, more peer involvement and peer support are needed in our services, as well as greater efforts by professionals to facilitate and enable that to happen.

For the past 10 years, the DEEP network has increasingly provided an infrastructure for people with dementia to form their own 'in-group', not only in the growing number of local peer support groups, but also in wider national networks, through workshops, representation at professional conferences, through online materials and the regular newsletter, which is full of contributions from other people living with dementia. From speaking with the Fifteen and from observation in the field, it seems clear that this is beginning to accelerate a shift whereby a readily accessible group is available to people with dementia at the point of diagnosis, in a way that it had not been for Keith when we first met, and certainly not for my grandmother in her time.

Malignant social psychology

When Kitwood described MSP, it was based on his observations of people in the later stages of dementia and the ways they were treated in care settings and institutions. I have had little involvement with these settings for many years, but my most recent job includes working with a team of dedicated professionals advising care homes when there are difficulties with distressed behaviour in residents with dementia. After all these years since Kitwood's writing and given all the advances in understanding, training and support, it has been sobering to see how many aspects of MSP are still occurring in much the same way as 25 years ago. Kitwood stressed that MSP is not located in the individual member of care staff who is generally approaching their work with the best of intentions, but in our cultural heritage and wider social attitudes. Bearing this in mind is often helpful when faced with its ongoing impact in individual places, and in mustering the energy to work on the long, slow process of cultural change.

MSP can also be observed, however, in the early stages of dementia, in the way a diagnosis is reached and communicated, in the lack of post-diagnostic support and services, and in the experiences of the Fifteen and other activists. One aspect of MSP was apparent when I was working with Keith in the early days to represent views and experiences of a person receiving dementia services on NHS Trust boards and planning groups, in professional meetings and conferences, and on steering groups for policy development or research projects. Initially, there was much resistance and a view that one could not have people with dementia attend a professional meeting, as that would render it inefficient, ineffective and 'take over the agenda' in a way that was incompatible with professional working. Keith's lifelong ability to sense the mood in the room, to comment at the right moment, his diplomacy and skill at making key points in a way that others can relate to and hear, often led to surprised comments from professionals afterwards, and subsequently invitations to join more permanently. While such participation is today much more widely accepted – even expected – many of the Fifteen will have had similar experiences of having to prove their ability to function within such organisations where there is still a minimal willingness to make reasonable adjustments for people with cognitive disabilities.

Activists who engage with social media, speak at public events or publish blogs are repeatedly exposed to a particularly distressing effect of MSP when it is stated that they do not really have dementia at all. There are sections of the medical profession who subscribe to the view that dementia is not really present when people are still functioning relatively well, and that it is a condition that deteriorates rapidly, leading to the need for 24-hour care and death within around 5 years, as some textbooks still suggest. Consequently, a person who remains psychologically well and is able to live relatively independently 5 or even 10 years post-diagnosis must be misdiagnosed. Instead, it is assumed, they have a psychiatric disorder, or functional neurological disorder (FND), a form of what used to be called hysteria, and derive human contact, pleasure and meaning from their activism in dementia, which they would otherwise be lacking. On an individual level, this can be extremely distressing for people who have struggled to come to terms with their diagnosis and are experiencing the effects of deteriorating cognitive functioning on a daily basis. On a societal level, this is harmful in that it perpetuates the idea that dementia necessarily means dependency and an inability to meaningfully participate, thus taking away the voice that people with dementia and activists have only just begun to find.

Personhood and Martin Buber

When first encountering Tom Kitwood's writing, the concept that spoke to me most was that of 'personhood'. At a time when in my clinical posts I was rather focused on neuropsychological assessment of the nature, extent and patterns of deficits, or called onto hospital wards to 'deal with problem behaviour' of dementia patients, Kitwood emerged as a different way of thinking about and approaching referrals and the resulting encounters with people affected by a dementia. I also felt I recognised something here of my experience of Nuna in the later stages of her dementia: remembering her as the person I had grown up with and known for decades made it easy to relate to her and to find precious nuggets of deeply meaningful communication with her during my brief visits back home. It made me reflect on how, of course, Nuna was a person behind and alongside the dementia, and due to our shared history what I saw was the person first and the disabilities second, while in my work I had referrals that encouraged a dynamic of seeing deficits, disability, dementia and disruptive behaviour before anything else. I puzzled over the question whether and in what way it might be permissible in a clinical and professional context to take and apply something of a more personal and emotional experience in my own history, and how that might work and be safe for 'patients' as well as for myself. It was the starting point of many discussions with supervisors, colleagues and trainees over the years, more latterly with Keith and other people living with dementia.

I was interested in understanding more about Kitwood's ideas on 'personhood', and the undertone of existentialist philosophy or perhaps theology that seemed to permeate his writing and ideas. This led me to Martin Buber and his philosophy, in particular his book *I and Thou*, which for me was particularly meaningful as it linked to the other grandparent I had known: my grandfather, a minister in the German Protestant Church for many years and later a teacher of philosophy with a special interest in Martin Buber. I somewhat dimly recalled Buber being mentioned in the sessions my grandfather provided in support of young conscientious objectors when preparing for the all-important hearing in front of a military board to be recognised as a pacifist. In the times of the Cold War and the European peace movement, thoughts around relating to 'persons' instead of 'enemies' or 'communists' seemed much needed and helpful in arguing why we should be allowed to 'do our time' by looking after and caring for people rather than learning how to kill. For me, this closed a circle back to the older people in my own background, and to the people with disabilities that I had the privilege to meet and work with during my compulsory social service – all the key experiences without which I would not be working in these specialist areas today.

I got hold of a copy of Martin Buber's *Ich und Du* (1923) in the original German, another exercise of reconnecting with my linguistic roots while all my professional practice has been conducted in English. *I and Thou* appeared in English translation in 1937, 14 years after its first publication in post-war Germany. Understanding a little more about Martin Buber's thinking helped me to gain a better grasp of what Tom Kitwood meant when writing about 'persons' and 'personhood'. Martin Buber was a theological philosopher, steeped in the traditions of a western, Judaeo-Christian monotheistic tradition. On this background, he developed his ideas about two different ways of relating between humans (but also of humans towards other aspects of creation, nature or experiences). I-It, an instrumental way of relating, which follows a purpose, is a means to an end, or carried out while in a particular role. There are many examples of this in clinical interviews and therapeutic practices, or in neuropsychological assessment. Here we are in our professional roles, have a particular function to fulfil and tasks to carry out. We may become very good at our circumscribed tasks and produce great diagnostic letters or neuropsychological reports as a result, but gain a limited understanding of the person we have met in the course of these appointments beyond our tools and pre-set categories of understanding conditions or behaviours.

How are we to understand an I-Thou way of relating? I found the English translation helpful here, using the old-fashioned 'Thou' in its title, which is today mainly used in the context of hymns and old bible texts to address God. This conveys the religious, spiritual or faith background of the idea of relating in a different way: seeking the essence of the person, connecting in a way that is meaningful in and of itself, recognising and relating to what is unique in the person. In a more religious language it might be understood as relating to the soul, to the unique creation that is the other person, to the discovery of a spark of Creation in an interpersonal connection, to what is divine in the interaction and in the person.

Pondering Martin Buber's ideas also helped me think about Kitwood's concept of 'love' at the centre of the flower model of psychological human needs, and has helped my practice with people with dementia generally, but especially those in the later stages or having significant disabilities in communication. In precious and expensive NHS time, many tasks are to be performed, targets to be reached and goals to be achieved, all of which emphasises and encourages a thoroughly I-It way of relating. Introducing more of an I-Thou mode into meetings in this clinical context often leads to surprising results. As more analytic cognitive abilities fade, people with dementia use perhaps more archaic skills, relying more of what they sense in a non-verbal way, the tone of voice rather than the words, the overall feeling of an interaction rather than the content of what is said. These skills are often neglected across a lifetime but are honed and become more sensitive when other abilities are in decline. The example often used in training to describe this is finding oneself in a strange place where a foreign language is spoken that we do not understand. Here, too, we would rely on what we could glean from tone, mood and context of the situation to understand whether we are safe and whether an interaction is helpful. Sometimes, even an experienced psychologist won't be of much help in the difficult lives of persons with advanced dementia and, of course, much of the detail of any conversation is likely to be forgotten. It is especially at these times that it has been helpful for me to recall Kitwood and Buber, and the notion that the interaction, the meeting, the encounter in itself is important. I usually ask people at the end of an appointment how they have found it, meeting in this (often very bare) room, talking with me (someone they have never met before), and with very few exceptions people have got positive things to say that go beyond British politeness. I was especially proud of a reply from a recent client that made me think of and thank Buber and Kitwood – they said: 'Talking here today, it has made me feel human again'.

Psychological needs: Kitwood's flower

As a gardener, and one specialising in growing flowers, I have always been especially fond of the flower model. Graphically, it reminds me of the forget-me-not that has subsequently become associated with charities and groups working in the field of dementia. It provides an image that helps me to hold the overlapping psychological needs described by Kitwood in mind when meeting and talking with people living with dementia.

All too often, people referred to mental health services in the later stages of dementia are in desperate need in a whole range of areas, and the needs described by the model are, though intrinsically interwoven, are not the ones at the top of the agenda of statutory services. More basic needs in terms of Maslow's hierarchy (1943), such as physical safety, sufficient food and drink, a safe and warm living space, basic physical health care and safeguarding concerns usually trump concerns over emotional needs and wellbeing. In this context, the flower has been a helpful tool in reflective practice sessions, training and advising colleagues in the multidisciplinary team. 'Taking along the flower' to an initial assessment or subsequent appointments became an expression in one team to describe an alertness to Kitwood concepts while completing the myriad of forms that need to be completed in statutory services, helping members of staff to look for the aspects that are not covered in the paperwork.

Given my key interest in psychosocial interventions in the early stages of dementia and aiming to assist in coming to terms with a diagnosis, finding a positive attitude to living with dementia, maintaining skills and independence for as long as possible, and preventing deterioration into the distressing states that people often find themselves in when referred after all the above has failed, I have been pondering the uses of the flower at these earlier points in the dementia care pathway. In a BPS guidance paper on clinical psychology practice in the early stages of dementia (Guss 2014), a large section is dedicated to pre-diagnostic counselling. Practised more thoroughly and extensively in the early days of the development of memory clinics, it has since fallen victim to the need to streamline resource-starved services and what remains of it in reality is little more than a few tick-boxes on a form for a one-appointment assessment session. However, where it is still given over to a full session prior to undergoing tests and in preparation for a person-centred and sensitive way of sharing a diagnosis alongside personalised support offers, Kitwood's flower serves as excellent guidance for exploring the areas of life, relationships and functioning that are essential in achieving a good quality of life, maintaining hope and finding meaning.

Usually, such exploration of these key psychological needs is undertaken within different frameworks, alongside taking a personal history, compiling a family tree, looking at key life events, or talking about interests and strengths past and present. Working with Keith on the guiding questions for our conversations has also helped me think more carefully about how the flower and its petals can be included in our clinical conversations with clients, and I have since used it increasingly to structure my meetings with and thinking about people with dementia I meet in a clinical context. The model can be helpful in understanding how people cope with the unwelcome news, adjust to living with the diagnosis, and manage their fears about their future and the reactions of their families and wider social circle. In this context, too, it provides a helpful tool that allows clinicians to check on needs in each of the areas described by the flower petals, as well as help people with dementia to look at different aspects of their lives, make changes themselves or prioritise issues in therapy. It could be said that my practice has become more 'Kitwood-informed', and I am now including it in practice and exercises with junior staff and students, conducting 'Kitwood-type' appointments alongside or in advance of neuropsychological or therapy assessments.

These are some of the psychological needs that I have reflected on in my personal experience. For example, I sometimes wonder how helping Nuna, my grandmother, find a helpful type and balance of occupation might have worked to avoid the years of desperately trying to do what she could no longer manage. Perhaps she could have found the sort of peace earlier that she was able to enjoy in the last years of her life, when she had accepted that there were many things that she was no longer able to do. She could spend hours leafing through books, sometimes with the text upside down. She had a favourite book, her 'Angel book', a large coffee table format with many photographs of artwork and depicting angels over the centuries. My prevailing memory of Nuna is of her sitting in her favourite armchair, leafing through her angel book, focused and concentrating on what she could see, and when approached repeating one of the few phrases she was still occasionally able to use: 'Oh, how beautiful!'

For the Fifteen and for Keith, who writes about inclusion, it is about different aspects and areas of life to those described by Kitwood for people living in care homes and in the later stages of dementia. The fundamental themes of the need for belonging, for being part of a family and wider society are very similar for all of us, however. Some of the Fifteen describe the people they met in peer support and activism as their 'tribe', which seems an appropriate word for the form of inclusion it facilitates. At times it has felt an honour and privilege to be welcomed and included in the 'dementia tribe', and I have noticed how much I feel at home there. Relationships and friendships develop from there, such as the one with Keith. While reciprocity in who is including whom would be much in the spirit of collaboration and co-production as well as in Buber's I-Thou relating, as a professional and clinician, the question needs to be kept in mind to whose benefit these relationships are and whether there is a helpful and equitable balance.

Inclusion of people with dementia at any stage of the condition remains a very large work in progress. Having witnessed the developments over the past decades, it is heartening and exciting to see the changes that have happened over the past 10 years or so, much of it thanks to the Fifteen and their activist colleagues. At the same time, it is depressing to experience the slow pace of change of societal and institutional perceptions of, and attitudes towards, dementia. However, it is now possible to be part of a football club, to be a member of a golf club, to visit theatres and museums, as well as National Trust properties, some of which expressly welcome people with dementia as well as provide separate 'dementia-friendly' events.

When Kitwood talked about comfort, it was not so much in the sense of putting one's slippers on and one's feet up, but in the sense of being comforted, 'soothed of pain and sorrow', although both come together for me in the image of Nuna sitting in her favourite armchair with her book of angels. In the later stages of dementia, the task of a clinician or professional carer may well frequently be to provide a soothing and comforting presence. However, in most of my meetings with people in the early stages of dementia, this is only part of the story, and what I am professionally there to do is have difficult conversations about tricky and frightening subjects, and make those safe and bearable for the person despite the discomfort.

As mentioned previously, if the flower model has been used as part of an assessment, then we already know something about what a person will find comforting, how they recover from distress or are able to calm down after an upset. I often have conversations about ways of comforting oneself and bringing back the sense of warmth and safety Kitwood implied when working with people who have experienced trauma, which can often re-emerge to haunt them when a beginning dementia undermines their lifelong strategies for coping and keeping terror and distress at bay. Hearing from the Fifteen about the many and varied ways they are bringing about and experiencing a state of this comfort has been both reassuring and enlightening, and will also no doubt find its way back into my clinical work.

A final word on Love

In the Kitwood flower model, love is at the centre and holds the petals together, much in the same way as Keith's description of love for children or people in our care is what makes working in our professions worthwhile. 'Love' for 'patients' is not the terminology used in any NHS guidance, and it certainly was not part of my therapy training. In wondering how the type of love involved here might best be described or captured in a word, I at one point thought the ancient Greeks with their eight terms for different types of love might have the answer. 'Agape' might come closest, as a love of humanity as a whole, though the aspects of self-sacrifice seem less appropriate. When remembering my grandmother Nuna, thinking and talking about love among the experiences of dementia is simple and easy. It is not straightforward when considering a professional role in a statutory service, alongside the ethics and responsibilities of practice in psychotherapy, building respectful relationships with colleagues with dementia or maintaining friendships developed through shared times, interests and experiences. Perhaps it would be best for me to remain with Martin Buber and all that I-Thou relationships entail. After all, that was what formed the basis for the Fifteen sharing such deeply personal thoughts and insights with us in our conversations.

6 Reflections on Kitwood's flower

Keith Oliver

Since first being introduced to the work of Tom Kitwood, I have often thought deeply about his extraordinary ideas on dementia. It is my sincere wish that Kitwood hopefully is a constant thread throughout this book. That is not to say that I place him on a pedestal, but simply that 25 years after his death there are still enormous benefits from considering what he had to say.

Before embarking on exploring the thoughts and experiences of the Fifteen, I thought it might be helpful to outline and examine through my eyes my reflections on aspects of the flower model which resonate particularly strongly with me. In chapter 5 of *Dementia Reconsidered* (1997), Kitwood began, understandably, by stating that identity is to know who oneself is, and he underlined this in the context of one's feelings and cognitive abilities. The modern saying, 'When you have met one person with dementia, you have met one person with dementia' is true, and Kitwood articulated this by writing that the way in which each individual constructs their identity is unique. I interpret his point about creating consistency across different roles and contexts of present life, as the person trying to make sense of their own identity against the challenge of dementia seeming to take this away, giving rise to the many comments about the person not being the same as they once were, or others feeling a sense of losing the person.

Kitwood goes on to suggest that, to some extent, identity is conferred by others, as they convey to a person subtle messages about his or her performance (Kitwood 1997). The word 'subtle' is correct in some cases, but in others there is little or no subtlety displayed. A number of our conversations did include mention of this. It is not often I encounter people who are able to empathise with me in order to maintain or, indeed, boost my sense of self-identity, but when it does happen it is such an immense encouragement. I do try – and at times I am told I succeed in – empathising with others whether they have dementia or not. I try to do this by 'stepping into their shoes' in order to really get to know them as individuals and thus giving them the opportunity to enrich my life by sharing something of theirs with me in order to boost their sense of self. I am sure this is what Kitwood was highlighting in his writing.

When asked to deliver a talk or write a piece about myself, I am always keen for the audience to get a sense of the person first and foremost before addressing points around the dementia that I share my brain with. I tell them about my family, where I live. I wax lyrical about my hobbies and interests past and present, and then take others along a pathway of how my life's journey relates to my roots and has taken me from Nottingham to Kent via Sheffield and Cheshire. I explain that I used to be a primary school headteacher who was, at the time I retired, also working for the local authority as a schools adviser, alongside studying for a masters at a local university in education leadership. This then forms the bridge to explain about my early retirement from my career, an encouraged ending of the masters course and other life-changing issues that have impacted on my identity due to the confirmed diagnosis of Alzheimer's disease in December 2010.

Only after all this do I think it important to explain how dementia has and continues to impact on my sense of identity. Isn't it often the case that at social gatherings when we are meeting new people in our circle, the conversation usually revolves around family, career, places we've lived and visited, hobbies and interests? Seldom, I suggest, do we launch into telling people about a life-changing, incurable, largely untreatable disease that one is living with. The person must always come first.

When I retired from my school and education roles in April 2011, I did miss the children. So, to address this I arranged to spend one morning a week in another local primary school listening to children read, chatting to them about their week, enjoying the stories they had written and wanted to show me, and generally making a fuss of these 8- and 9-year-olds. On one occasion, soon after my story of living with dementia was published in a Kent NHS magazine under the title '*Dementia Doesn't Define Me* says Keith Oliver', Lewis – a 9-year-old I was helping – came to me with a broad grin on his face. Without prompting he said, 'I saw you in a magazine in my doctor's'. I need to add that I had not mentioned to the children that I had dementia and they always referred to me as Mr Oliver, a leftover from my previous boundaried comfort zone in a school environment. I expected then to be led into a conversation with this child about my life with dementia. I need not have worried, as he quickly added, 'yes, and I know your first name!' Clearly, dementia did not define or identify me in his eyes but he did identify with my name. If only adults would do the same as 9-year-old Lewis!

In the way I withheld my diagnosis from those children, it is unreasonable to assume that all fifteen people we spoke with revealed everything they felt about the six areas we spoke to them about. However, all did unveil their lives to us in a very open way, and they could easily have felt exposed by this. Both Reinhard and I, on a number of occasions, reminded whoever we were talking to that they should feel comfortable in what they were sharing with us, and that it was absolutely fine to withhold something of themselves.

I have told the story of Lewis a number of times since the event and I think it carries most potency with audiences of health professionals whose background and training sometimes leads some of them to see those of us with dementia as patients, service users, stakeholders or, worst of all, as sufferers. I often cringe at the way labels are attached to identify and pigeon-hole people, in ways to suit the person attaching the label rather than the person being labelled. I often saw this in schools where children were labelled in the staffroom or told directly they were 'naughty', 'a difficult or problem child', 'slow or even backward'. Was it any wonder that when the child was constantly made aware of these labels that they then lived up to them! Even very positive or flattering labels can make many people such as myself feel uncomfortable. I am quite at ease with the label 'person with dementia' because it puts the person first – years ago I think this would have been a 'demented or senile person' if I were lucky, as the labels used could be much worse.

People might struggle to form a new identity after a dementia diagnosis due to the negative labels that sometimes come with it. Moving into the post-diagnostic phase, I was curious to explore what the people we spoke with felt about reclaiming their identity, which may have been lost, damaged or negatively affected by the disease and diagnosis. Subsequently, some may have consciously or subconsciously created elements of a new identity while holding onto how they felt about themselves pre-diagnosis.

I am not totally sure that negative labels create fear but I am sure they add to fears that already exist in the minds of people. Dementia is scary. Often more so for those close to us or those who have little knowledge of the condition beyond what they see and read in the media. Sometimes I am scared, and this did very occasionally come out in the words of those fifteen people with dementia we spoke with.

When giving a talk, I try to structure what I am saying with a sense of narrative, sometimes using techniques such as Tree of Life and Journey of Life, which I have taken from Denborough (2014). Kitwood writes about the use of a narrative in telling a person's story and providing a sense of continuity and connection to one's past.

All of the petals plus Love are important to living as well as possible with dementia. However, I feel that identity is central to an individual's sense of personhood. It sits at the core of an individual's sense of themselves.

Inclusion is another petal of Kitwood's flower that resonates particularly strongly with me. To me, inclusion means I am not just allowed to be here or to be present, but I am valued, included, welcomed, encouraged and involved as I am. Inclusion has elements of influencing change or direction. This can be in terms of words or actions in myself or at times in others I care about. Other people can help create and facilitate these changes but I recognise it is also up to me to take opportunities when I see them presented to me or to others.

The COVID-19 pandemic had an effect on everyone to varying degrees, and for some this impact continues to this day. Perversely, not all of its impacts have been negative, and everyone with dementia involved in this book feels included as a member of a number of communities not just where we live but also virtually, out of necessity, both during and post-pandemic.

Social acceptance is part and parcel of positive interactions for people with dementia and many contributors confirmed that their volunteering activities gave them a genuine sense of fulfilment and inclusion, both of which contributed to their wellbeing. When we were planning our commentary for the *Dementia Reconsidered, Revisited* book (Kitwood and Brooker 2019), it struck me how little has changed even though the people Kitwood worked with who had dementia were a more narrow group of people with late-stage dementia than that of today. Kitwood spoke of it being hard to include people with 'mental impairments with ease'. I would be very surprised if he would write this today, but I do know what he meant. Perrin (1997), a contemporary of Kitwood, wrote about people with dementia seeking self-stimulation in a bubble, their own body space, somewhere they felt safe physically, emotionally and psychologically. I relate to this now that I am living with dementia, in that I no longer feel included or safe in certain situations. I feel confused by messages said or left unsaid and when this happens, I withdraw into myself or into a room (usually my office, which is my safe space). Relating this to care homes where residents often have little control of where they spend their time is very worrying. Kitwood touches on this and refers to 'the old style' – well, I would suggest that there are still examples of this 25 years later.

When Reinhard writes about malignant social psychology in Chapter 5 of this book, I am mindful of Kitwood's writing about this, and I am convinced that when people are not included in relationships, groups or activities, then so many aspects of MSP come to the fore, and with the person's needs not being met it is little surprise that they withdraw into their shell. Engaging with the person can address this and their social life need not dwindle away.

Kitwood wrote also about people that he witnessed in care homes with dementia seeming to cling or to hover. I identify with this in the sense that I get very concerned if I don't know where my wife is, even in the house when we are both together, and I also cling to friendships now far more than I think I did before living with dementia. Endings in friendships are very challenging and I often worry about upsetting or letting someone down to the extent it will have an impact upon our connection. Kitwood also described 'attention-seeking behaviour', which even today is still called 'challenging behaviour' by some care professionals. When someone feels vulnerable, isolated, bored or in pain, it ought not be surprising that they call for help or attention, and as their dementia progresses I have seen people who genuinely believe their needs have not been met by professionals. I saw a great deal of this in a geriatric ward in an acute hospital recently when my wife Rosemary was a patient for 8 days. The more understanding – and possibly better aware and trained – staff attended compassionately to the needs of the patients, most of whom had advanced dementia, but sadly I saw a lot of ignoring and dismissive behaviours on the part of some ward staff. There was little evidence that the needs of the patients as individuals were being met or that they or visiting family members were being included in their care.

Beyond this experience, I saw my mother, whose dementia was diagnosed in her mid-70s, display 'attention-seeking behaviour'. This was compounded by living with bipolar for the previous 30 years, though she never used this label, sticking instead to her late 1970s diagnostic label of 'manic depression'. In both the residential and then later the nursing home where she lived, she often presented with 'attention-seeking behaviour' as Kitwood described. This behaviour was only reconciled when her unmet needs were addressed. Sometimes it was solely the need for someone to talk with her, other times a drink or to be moved – for the last 4 years of her life, from the age of 77, she required a hoist to move from her favourite armchair.

In a similar context within the acute hospital geriatric ward where my wife Rosemary was treated, she observed one female patients who loudly demanded a lot of care and attention, and was the cause of some agitation and distress to other patients. On the fifth night of my wife's stay, the duty nurse sat with this woman patiently listening to her and Rosemary said the lady was the most lucid she had been all the time Rosemary had been in the ward. Sadly, this was the only time this happened and for that brief hour the person was respected, valued and included in a civil conversation, something we all take for granted.

Inclusion for me gives me a sense of connection and belonging. This can be to places but also most definitely to people, and both people and places current and in my past give me a safe and secure feeling of being grounded. While I would be the first to acknowledge that the COVID-19 pandemic had an immense impact on society at large, indeed on the whole world, drilling down to myself it changed my life in a number of ways, just as the diagnosis of dementia I received on New Year's Eve 2010 did. On 14 March 2020, Rosemary and I landed at Gatwick airport after a lovely 4-week trip to Adelaide. This was just 2 days before Qatar airport was closed to travellers. That was the last holiday we had. What dementia had failed to do in 2010 when the neurologist suggested we cancelled our ninth trip to Australia, COVID-19 succeeded in doing after our nineteenth. A mixture of our ageing, fears and uncertainty leading to diminished confidence in travelling unsupported and my dementia have all excluded Rosemary and I from joining the millions who take an annual holiday (or two as we, like many retirees, used to do). During March to July 2020, when COVID-19 first raged throughout the UK causing the initial lockdown, I like everyone else saw my diary decimated. I looked at it recently and saw, repeated throughout those months, 'cancelled' written through meetings and events I was so looking forward to.

My issues with spatial awareness now made the 2-metre safe distancing very difficult and I was constantly being told helpfully by Rosemary about this. I was someone who welcomed opportunities to hug friends and family to show how much I cared about them and how pleased I was to be with them. This stopped and 'elbow bumping' just didn't seem the same to me. I grew a beard for the first time in 25 years and kept it from April to July 2020, saying I would only shave it off to celebrate being able to connect again with people in what I termed the 'new normal'. I used extensively the phrase 'physically distanced but socially connected' as a response to the UK Government directing the public to stay socially distanced, though subsequently it was revealed the public kept more closely to this than some close to government. During this time I tried to keep busy in my own home and garden, appreciating that both were pleasant places to be. I immersed myself in painting the shed and fences, getting the Spring garden ready for Summer and tidying drawers indoors that had been neglected for some time.

These activities helped initially, but that was short-lived, and apart from sharing 24 hours a day with Rosemary, and clapping in our street for the NHS on Thursdays at 8 pm, we saw no one. No trips to the cinema or the coast.

No London trips for meetings or events and the social 'debriefing' afterwards, usually over a drink in a pub with friends who had been at the same meeting or event. No Forget-Me-Nots meetings where we attempt to put the dementia world to rights. No browsing in the local bookshop and enjoying a coffee in their cafe while chatting with Rosemary, people-watching or catching up with friends. The latter did not change for 3 months until, at the end of June 2020 Jess Shaw, a friend of mine supported me by walking into Canterbury with me so I could buy Rosemary a birthday card. Each day the television reports became worse and worse. Although we felt a need to be informed and wished to be included in the national response to this awful situation, this was tempered by fear, confusion and utter disbelief that this could be happening to us – actually, rather how living with dementia is like some days without the pandemic! We were lucky that although our youngest son was quite ill early on with COVID-19, he made a full recovery at his home, and we video called him every day from his isolated flat to keep his spirits up. Rosemary, myself and the rest of our family caught COVID-19 later in the pandemic once vaccines were able to curtail its worst effects.

Fortunately for me, I had learnt how to use Zoom for meetings with the 3 Nations Dementia Working Group a year or two before, so this was not totally alien to me. Once connections and meetings started up virtually I was better placed than many to be included. Then as 2020 moved towards late Summer and Autumn, my diary became fuller with six or seven zooms a day and me having to say 'no' to some as I found I could not function effectively in more than two lengthy zooms in one day. The professionals were very understanding, as one sensed they were experiencing the same issue.

A line I wrote and meant so sincerely for the poem 'Give Me ... I Will' (reproduced on page 204), 'Give me inclusion and I will belong', summarises for me what this chapter is all about. Since writing the poem, I have been moved by the impact it seems to have had on those who have read it or heard it being read, and I never tire of sharing it with both professionals and those affected by dementia. The second half of the poem was very much inspired by Kitwood's flower. Kitwood placed love at the centre of his flower model and that in my view is its rightful place. And I emphasise this in the poem 'Give Me ... I Will' (Oliver 2019).

I am not sure what the NHS line would be on encouraging or supporting staff to show love towards patients. I have spoken to numerous people working in the NHS and many share my view, which I believed when working with children for 33 years, that love is the fundamental principle of any life worth living, and is part and parcel of caring compassionately for – and about – another person. Others are uneasy with this viewpoint and seem embarrassed to talk about it both professionally and personally. Of course, everyone is different and I fully respect the wide range of views there are on this subject. I think the media and possibly society in general in this country have issues with what love really means in many contexts, but in this case love brings together the head and the heart of what it means to be human as it relates to caring for – and caring about – other people whose wellbeing will benefit from it.

Many examples emerged during the pandemic of staff in health and social care settings going the extra mile and putting themselves both at risk and great disadvantage for the benefit of patients or residents. This I feel served to remind us of the 'angels' who work at the front line caring for older, vulnerable people. This for me is love, and I hope we in turn can reciprocate and return this with gratitude.

Some would say it is a person's vulnerabilities rather than and alongside their strengths that cause us to love them more. The conversations with the Fifteen certainly drew out of each of them a sense of both where they felt strong and where they felt vulnerable. Often people with dementia like me, and I suggest many others, need affirmation and validation to be reassured that they matter and that their presence is important to someone. This is even more important when the person is close to them.

Part **2**

The Fifteen's Experience of Dementia through the Lens of Kitwood's Flower

Keith Oliver

In the chapters that make up this part of the book, we employ the same format to discuss each of the six aspects of Kitwood's flower as a means to examine and discuss the psychological needs of people with dementia.

It is fair to say that the experiences shared by the Fifteen resonated with me in that aspects of all of the conversations I believe apply equally to me. All fifteen spoke to us of this connection we have. I am convinced that this helped make their answers and statements much more open and revealing. The conversations contained elements of relaxed chat, talk about anything that came to mind in the moment, deep discussion, reflections on feelings and events, the consequences of situations, words and actions, and honest reflections. I was a bit surprised that no one moaned or whinged about their living with dementia. I share in my life many of the highs / lows, challenges / rewards, successes / failures, frustrations / achievements that all fifteen spoke so honestly about.

Each of Chapters 7–12 begins with a poem written by a person with dementia, followed by some reflections of our discussions with individual people in our semi-structured conversations. Each chapter will then give ample space to the thoughts and words of the people talking about their experience of living with their dementia. We will precede this by empathetically examining and summarising people's experiences in the light of Kitwood's writings. Our comments are intended to support and provide scaffolding to the Fifteen's words, although we have deliberately not overdone this so that you, dear reader, can reflect on and add to what the person with dementia has said. In order to structure their contributions, we have devised a series of sub-headings which we hope will prove helpful to you when navigating the conversations.

At the end of each chapter, we address dilemmas in dementia care and what learning we can take from the Fifteen from the perspective of both service user and service provider.

In what follows, the words of the Fifteen are italicised to help distinguish them from Keith's commentary.

7 Identity

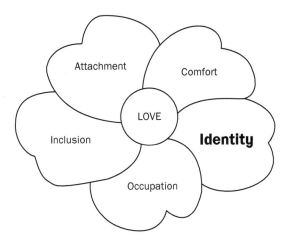

I am still me, why can't you see
The same face, the same smile
Dementia can't hide
Just see what's in my heart and inside
You will be pleasantly surprised, I am still me

– Chris Maddocks

The Fifteen on Identity – narrated by Keith Oliver

Each of the Fifteen was very different, and while united by the common bond of dementia along with often being friends with some shared experiences, beliefs, interests, fears, hopes and expectations, everyone spoke in a singular way about *their* identity and place in *their* world.

Agnes Houston

While sometimes I feel like the senior member of the 'club no one would want to join' (i.e. living with a diagnosis of dementia), Agnes has been a member for much longer than me, in fact longer than anyone else we spoke with. She has worked tirelessly in Scotland and beyond for better dementia care for everyone, including as a leading figure within the Scottish Dementia Working Group. Her opening comment to us spoke volumes in terms of the impact dementia has had on her identity.

Identity within the family

Having met Agnes' daughter Donna on a number of occasions, I know how much her family mean to her and how supportive they have been, and how she sees them as a central part of her identity, so it seemed fitting to begin the conversation with her talking about her family.

I've been living with dementia for 15 years now. I would say that before dementia, I wore many hats. I was a wife, a mother, you know, a daughter, a sister and all of those things. I don't wear as many hats now, so I don't have as many identities or roles to fulfil if you like, that makes life a wee bit easier for me because sadly my parents are dead so I'm no longer fulfilling that role ... [laughs] ... I've been, I'm going to use this word because I don't know if it's correct, but I've been 'downgraded' in the family if you like. They don't see me as 'Agnes' as the person that you would go to now, so I don't have that role in the family. I do feel that I've been relegated; I don't know where they've relegated me to, quite frankly, in the family. So, yes, my identity in my family has changed.

Attitude towards living with dementia

Dementia certainly changed that, because I no longer felt I was contributing by being employed and giving back to my community. So that was a big, big, big thing, you know, I felt worthless, and I felt shoved in the corner. I was looking and thinking, 'God, my life is over, there's no place for me here'. When I was diagnosed, it was all loss and doom and gloom. And I thought, you know, you're still the same person! being not a human do-er. You don't find time 'to be', if you get a sense it's like Agnes wearing these many hats in the community. Now, I'm trying to find time to be still and 'be', and appreciate what Tom Kitwood wrote using the petals in the flower. They do overlap, and don't they have a lovely scent?

I am now taking time to enjoy my life more – I don't know if you've got the sense of change there. It took me a long time to accept many of the identities and labels that I have been given. To be seen as disabled, you know, I totally wear my yellow and green sunflower lanyard. Why? Because it makes life much easier for me ... [laughs] ... You know what I mean? I realise that I want to have an easier, smoother journey, and wearing a lanyard means that someone in the train station will come up to me and say, 'Can I help you? Is there anything I can do for you?' Well, I'm accepting that now, but that didn't happen overnight. I think it would be easy to possibly have been one of the reluctant, stubborn people. It really took a while before I realised that 'this is to make you safe, life easier and smoother, this is where you are'. I am not ashamed of where I am at this moment. I'm using these words very carefully because I was ashamed to not be the 'Agnes' that I took years to portray, which was the nurse, the academic person, the go-to person. I liked that. I was quite comfortable with that thinking ... [laughs] ... thank you very much. But then on the other hand I'd been downgraded, you know. Nobody knew what they were gonna do with 'Agnes', so shove her in the corner. So, I created this new part of my identity and I'm now comfortable accepting that I need help which I am comfortable accepting with a smile and a thank you.

I am very aware of when anybody asks, and I'm very open, and I'll say to them, no, no, no. 'Have you had a stroke?' is one of the questions. I say, no, no, no, I have dementia. It's affecting my gait, and my balance. Consequently, my stability muscles have been put under pressure, and I'm having a lot of pain. And I need to retrain my gait. So, I think that's where it is, you know. So, the identity or just embrace who you are, and do not be ashamed of it.

Agnes covers a lot of points in this part of the conversation, including disproving the point that Alzheimer's is solely about memory loss. She describes her life with a poignancy alongside displaying the humour that I know gets her through some very dark moments. Although she does not use the word 'pride', I sense that Agnes is a proud person in the positive sense of the word alongside recognising that pride can become a barrier to living as well as possible with dementia, and that clinging to some elements of one's identity can be counter-productive.

Activist

So that's when I found that there's still something in there, that not everything had been taken away from me with a diagnosis of dementia. My activist identity didn't just happen overnight. It took a long time, because I was still getting nurses coming in saying that ... [laughs] ... you know you will get depressed, you will get this, and they weren't giving me any hope. I had to re-find this person called 'Agnes' who had limitations, but there was still a lot there, still a lot there. Later I discovered the campaigning and being an activist.

Yes, I think what it has done is it has taken me a long time to get a balance back. When I found activism, I threw myself into activism and it was all-encompassing, because it gave me a purpose. It gave me a reason and I was included and valued as a person. So, I was finding that I was creating a new identity if you like. I took control a wee bit by being an activist. But to live well, you need to have balance.

Often you get professionals and universities asking you for something. But if I say 'yes' to everything and then I stop and think, I know it gets very tiring to appear well in public.

Do you know what? It's like two different Agnes' in our setting. People, especially in the beginning of the activism movement where there weren't so many of us, you know what? I was like a bad penny. If there was anything needed to be said Agnes was there and I wasn't a quiet observer, I was the first up, the first to point out things. But, that is draining, you can only keep that up for so long.

That took a wee while because it was always ... [laughs] ... that I was looked upon as a leader and you take ... [laughs] ... them on board, and then you become comfortable doing it. It was very strange not to be in control and be a leader. But at the same time, it was quite comforting to know that if that went wrong, it weren't your job to fix it ... [laughs] ... unless there was a strange new step. So, there was a wee bit of adjustment, and I think in the activism, there should be more help to make that adjustment.

Whenever Agnes and I talk either face-to-face or on Zoom, we both feel a real sense of connection, and this is in part because of our efforts as dementia activists who both care passionately about making the world a better place for others. Some would say that wisdom comes with experience. This may be true to an extent but I know many who are very experienced at what they do but I would hesitate to describe them as wise. In Agnes' case, being wise is a very fitting word to capture some of her identity. I 100 per cent relate to her statement about the two Agnes' and the exact same could be said for myself. Putting on a brave positive face is often a good thing to do but has its drawbacks when it causes people to over-expect from us or treat us with disbelief.

Job

I don't think I'm as judgemental as I used to be when I had my nurse's hat on. I wasn't really a judgemental person, but now I think I am much more understanding. Sometimes I just smile, and I think, yeah, well, you know, your attitude changes with life circumstances and age. I feel much more mellow in that thought.

Hobbies

While Agnes did touch on her creativity and occasionally joining the DEEP virtual art group, she expressed this more in the sense of occupation and did not seem to convey to us that this was a part of her identity. The conversation instead turned to Agnes telling us about her love of walking.

I was always a great walker, which was well known to family and friends, you could hardly keep up with me. Now, I'm walking with a walker on occasions and even my neighbours are a bit surprised at the moment. The walker is for my gait and my balance. I may not have that walker forever, or maybe I will. I had to come to terms and make friends with my walker, and be comfortable with my walker, to go outside and be seen using it in public, which I thought was less than perfect. It takes time for people like me to accept and adapt, and be comfortable with it. I do it with a wee bit of humour and laughter. Well, I was walking last Sunday. It's a real struggle for me to keep my balance and gait. I was laughing with some of the children in the pushchairs. And I'm saying, this is my pushchair. I'll bring my doll the next time and you'll see it ... [laughs] ... I just laugh and I'll put it in the wee bit on the walker because there's a seat on it, so I can take the doll for a walk.

In a nutshell

When I am in that zone, and it just – it's all so beautiful that I can't express or explain where I'm at that moment. I'm just being me – an internal, real Agnes. It's an amazing feeling. You know, a truthful me.

Chris Maddocks

Job

At the time of her diagnosis, Chris was in the police force.

I was doing the law enforcement side of the business and I was writing policies and procedures and when I went back, they asked me to read some of them and they just didn't make sense to me. So that was it. I was only 52 when I retired from the police.

When I had my diagnosis, it felt like I was given a life sentence or maybe a death sentence from a police perspective. I felt useless, and I felt hopeless, and I lost all sense of purpose in my life.

Activist

While each of us who takes on an activist role recognises that we are only one voice among many, and that it is not usually possible to speak for other people, there are times when what we say rings true for others who can identify with our words.

I can remember one lady when I gave a talk, and she came up to me afterwards and she said, 'thank you so much for telling my story'. I said, 'I didn't tell your story, I told my story'.

Chris' activism has led her to be offered a number of roles, and she comfortably describes herself as '*an ambassador for the Alzheimer's Society and now the*

Lewy Body Society and NAPA' (National Activities Provider Association). Since writing her biography, which appears on page 18, she is the first person with dementia to serve as a trustee on the board of the Alzheimer's Society.

I think my best label is I'm a dementia activist because I really want to raise awareness of dementia.

Attitude towards living with dementia

Well, dementia is a huge part of my life, it is my life now.

I think this sentence from Chris summarises so much, both positive and negative about how each of us who is living with dementia see the impact it has upon us. In Chris' case, dementia has not just been a diagnosis restricted to her, but has influenced her identity through others in her family having dementia.

Yes, my, my dad had Alzheimer's disease and ... erm, so you know my brother, my sister, myself saw dad's journey with that and also my grandmother had Alzheimer's disease. So, when I had my diagnosis at the age of 60 and I had a leaflet about vascular dementia which I gave to my brother and my sister because it explained it better than I could explain it. They never told me that they read it, and they never discussed the dementia with me.

I'm a fighter. I've always seemed to have had to push to get to where I wanted to go ... And I've always been the one in the family and in a circle of friends. If there's a problem, speak to Chris. I was always the problem solver. I think my dementia has affected me in as much as I lost my sense of purpose in life. We all need a sense of purpose, it's coming back now. I did feel I lost my identity because I didn't know who I was when I had dementia.

What health professionals give to their patients to read can have a counter-productive outcome and an adverse impact on their sense of identity. Chris illustrated this point with this example from soon after her diagnosis.

I remember reading a leaflet that said with vascular dementia, the average lifespan is 5 years. So, that's where I felt I was given my death sentence, and that was 5 years ago. I'm still here. So I think that helped me lose some of my identity, because I thought, what's the point? I'm not going to be here in 5 years' time.

Chris' partner Heather was then brought into the conversation by Chris explaining:

Heather had pulled me up once when I first moved to Eastbourne, and people were saying, 'Why have you moved to Eastbourne?' I started by saying, 'Oh, well, because I've got dementia and Heather is caring for me'. Now I've built up resilience. I think that's a big thing, and very important.

Seeing herself and others as caring

I have often spoken and written about the way my thinking now works with dementia, in that previously, although I had a good emotional intelligence, my professional role necessitated my cognitive intelligence to be more to the fore. Now, since having dementia and dealing with its progression, I find that my emotions overwhelm at times my ability to think more objectively. If one viewed this as balance scales, the scales have most certainly tipped away from the cognitive to the emotional. Chris seems to experience something rather similar and explains it in her own way.

I think kindness is a big thing to me, that's me being kind to people, but them being kind to me as well. I don't like confrontational issues, although if I'm faced with one I will deal with it.

I've always been a very tactile, loving person. I was brought up in a mining community and lived with my grandparents when I was first born.

I think I get satisfaction and fulfilment from helping others. So maybe that's how I show love to myself. You know, what goes around comes around, comes around I suppose.

I really do care about people. I've always found myself in a situation if somebody has been rudely spoken to or, or anything, I would step in and say something.

Maybe some of this desire to help people comes from not only her childhood and upbringing but from her years in the police force; clearly it is deeply ingrained in Chris' sense of her own personhood and identity.

In a nutshell

I think people consider that you're a different person. I'm still Chris, and my emotions are still there, and my feelings are still there. I think that I want to shout and scream sometimes and say I'm still me.

Chris Norris

I have known Chris since he joined the Forget-Me-Nots in April 2014 alongside the life writing project in Canterbury which became the *Welcome to Our World* (Jennings 2014) book. We are good friends and he was the first person I knew would rise to the challenge of sharing the Dementia Envoy role with me in Kent. We often talk openly during breaks from meetings and events we both attend, or when he kindly picks me up in his car to travel to a dementia-related commitment which we both are attending.

Hobbies and dealing with his diagnosis

When referring to stopping playing music for 5 years as recommended by his consultant, Chris described the experience.

I really, really missed it because now I had lost that major thing in my life. It was almost like a bereavement, not being able to do it. Then in the end, when I got my diagnosis of dementia, on top of my heart problems, I thought, 'Well, blow it! If the heart doesn't get me, the brain will get me'. I'm so pleased and relieved to having gone back to doing it. Suddenly, I feel complete again, there was a big piece missing. That's not to detract from what my family provides. It's because playing music has been with me since the age of 11. I'm now 67, it's been such an important thing in my life.

I am unsure if it stems from the many years Chris has performed music in various brass bands, but sometimes one gets the sense that in certain groups he created a persona of the 'funny guy' in the mix and is often expected to crack a joke or express some witty comment on Zoom meetings. This is great when Chris feels up to it, but one senses it can place extra pressure on his own sense of identity. Being positive or funny all of the time is impossible, and having strategies that either one has developed oneself or suggested by others can certainly help to maintain one's sense of self-worth and identity despite what dementia and other life challenges come our way.

Certainly, since my diagnosis, I try and be upbeat, as much as I possibly can. That can be very challenging and tiring actually. I'm happy in my own skin. I am what I am, and I do what I can. Sometimes I'm frustrated because I wish I could do more, and sometimes I look at other people and think gosh, you know, on the grand scale of things, they do so much more than I can achieve. But it's another avenue that I try not to go down – that's why I never go fishing because sitting on a fishing bank for hours on end, you've got time to dwell on what is good or not in your world. All the time you're busy you know, you haven't got time to sit down and smell those flowers. Although it's good to do it sometimes, I try not to do it too much because you then start thinking about your negatives rather than your positives and I like to focus on positives.

So now by being involved in all these various things, that still gives me that identity, the music, the playing in the bands, the requests to play on the bandstand through all the various bands during the summer, that gives me an identity. That's Chris Norris who plays the horn. Then being involved in the various dementia groups gives me an identity because that's Chris who has dementia, but he's also involved in other things and so that's filled up the void.

Activist

Chris reflected deeply when talking about his high-profile dementia roles both locally in Kent and nationally. I was particularly interested by his Clark Kent/Superman analogy as I do not remember hearing him articulate his thoughts in this way before. But I do know exactly what he means because outsiders do only see one side of the activist identity and not the deeper person which Chris clearly describes here.

Involvement in things is good for my self-esteem. It makes you feel that you still have significance in life. That sounds very self-orientated, really, but it isn't. In life, you've got to feel that you have a purpose, and you have a place to be, and so that's why I'm so involved in other aspects around dementia.

But I kind of look at it – I've said this many times before, but it's always the Superman bit. The person that people see, initially of me, and for quite a while is Superman, you know, with all powerful, all wonderful, and I don't allow people so much to see the Clark Kent than I really am. Because, you know, Superman is very extrovert, isn't he? But Clark Kent is the true, quiet person that he is, and I am. I'm a quiet person. But gradually as I get to know people, then I allow them to know the other side of me.

Job

The careers which Chris has spoken to me about over the time that I have known him began with him being a soldier, then a police officer, followed by being a driving instructor and examiner.

I was always regarded as a bit of a rebel or possibly the black sheep. My five brothers and sisters all went off to university. I didn't. I left school at 15 and went into the army, which is the University of Life. Back when I was a teenager about to leave school, you saw the careers master and they suggested a career that you'd probably go into. Most people then went into that career and stayed in that career for 40/50 years and came out the other end retired. Whereas I've always bucked the trend because I've had seven careers in my working life. So, I've always been a bit of a – that's the other thing I like - I'd like people to think, 'Chris is a bit of a rebel'.

You carry a label with you of whatever job or career you are part of, particularly when you're working, because working at a job, that's kind of a label for you to hang your stuff on. And then if you have to cease work, which I had to because I couldn't continue doing the job that I was doing, then you lose a tremendously large part of yourself identity-wise. You then think 'well, what am I?' We should never define our own identity with the job that we're doing.

I'm now retired but I'm very involved in music-making. I love supporting bands. I think that would define me. I mean I might mention also the dementia, I suppose, but I don't want that to be the main label, I don't want people to go, 'That's Chris Norris, he has dementia'. I want people to think 'that's Chris Norris, he's these other various people'.

In a nutshell

So, identity is very important I think. Because you've got to feel that you have a place in this world rather than just another one on the treadmill of life.

Chris Roberts

I have known Chris for almost 9 years, during which time he and his wife Jayne have become good friends of my wife Rosemary and myself and prior to the COVID-19 pandemic we would share many platforms followed by a convivial debrief afterwards usually in a nearby hostelry. Jayne sat in the background on this Zoom call with Chris.

Attitude towards living with dementia

I'm less of the man anymore and I was always the man of the house in the relationship, wasn't I? I spoiled her but I was in charge, and that's totally turned with totally reversed roles you know. We were also very close … erm, emotionally you know. We're still close, we're very, very good friends and always probably will be. I can't imagine going out with anyone else for a pint, I can guarantee that. We have a great time, but dementia does stop you emotionally and it stopped me emotionally anyway. Sometimes I can't stand being near someone. So I've pushed Jayne away a lot.

Activist

We asked Chris what were the main attractions for him of being an activist.

Meeting peers and people like yourself you know, I mean both of you. When I got involved I thought I was becoming a bit of an expert now in my own dementia so what can I do with that because that's the only thing that I knew about because I couldn't do anything else properly anymore. I thought well that's got to be a positive. I was looking around for something to do with using the knowledge I had about my own dementia which I have researched. I first went on the Dementia Friends session and did the awareness raising. I thought that's something that Jayne can assist me with but I can do a lot on my own. And because we can still answer the phone and she can run the business from her phone. We were lucky to be in a good place, or rather in a bad place as it were. So that allowed us to do things. And the first time I ever did a session, assisted by Jayne obviously, but it really built my confidence up as I knew all of a sudden I could do something again and I could do it well.

One early venture for Chris and Jayne was to be involved in the Dementia Friends initiative, which drew them into the Alzheimer's Society.

The Dementia Friends filled a massive void in my life I think … erm, being able to get out talking about something that I knew from experience plus what I researched helped me a lot. Erm, because how can you cope with a life-changing illness if you don't understand it? So I had a lot of knowledge about it because I had nothing else to do but read you know and google. So that's really changed my life and how I see myself. It filled the void and from there led to ... erm, going to peer support groups which I never, never agreed to before because who wants to sit with a load of people with dementia? You know? Erm, yes that filled a big void in my life I think, and that's when things started to change you know and I felt a person again.

Seldom, if ever does anyone sit down with those of us who take on an activist role and talk with us about an exit strategy at a time when the role is starting to have a negative rather than a positive impact. Also, Chris talks here about how his childhood position in his family has helped forge his sense of identity today.

I used to think, especially the younger you are, you cannot go through life without having a role, a role and a purpose. Well, I did anyway. I found that I guess, which saved me. But now I've reached the stage where I don't need a role. I don't need a role at all. I've realised this and it has helped me. You know, the isolation and being on my own has prepared the way for me, and that's helped a lot in me coming to terms with no longer needing a role. I always thought I did. I always had to have a purpose. I was the eldest of six children. I used to look after them when I was very little. You know, I was cooking for them all. And so I've always had this role. And you're the psychologist, Reinhard. But now, for the first time in my life, I don't need a role.

Well, I'm not retiring. I've just changed roles. I'm just a gardener now. I'm a motor home enthusiast. I'm just a happy traveller now!

Time will tell whether as Chris moves into the 'new normal' as I term it, will he wish to rekindle the flame of passion which burnt for his activism prior to COVID-19. Who knows, but what is certain is that this decision will rest squarely with Chris and his wife Jayne.

In a nutshell

I was quite surprised by the way Chris brought this part of the conversation to a close. I got the impression that the pandemic had influenced his thoughts and that while still keen to maintain his activist role within the European Working Group, which he co-chairs with enthusiasm, he was stepping back from some groups he had previously been closely identified with.

But that's all I'm less of that person. Now. I really can't be bothered being bolshie and forceful. You know, I just, I've just gone so lethargic. I really can't be bothered to do things sometimes and I felt very disappointed with the Alzheimer charities I have supported.

Dianne Campbell

I have known Dianne for over 10 years, having first met her at a UNISON conference in London when with the support of Nada Savitch, I was asked to speak about the needs of people with dementia. Following this our friendship and collaboration was encouraged by our joint membership of the IDEAL study advisory group and the ALWAYS group linked to this project. Later, in 2018, we both travelled to Chicago supported by the Alzheimer's Society to address the Alzheimer's Disease International conference.

Attitude towards living with dementia

We asked Dianne how she saw herself now, and if she felt that dementia had changed her as a person.

I think I have a bad memory, and it's changing me because I think different, I look at people different. I think I'm a good-hearted person. I would think so. I always put people in front of me. I'm very considerate with other people. I think that's me. What do you think? I just like to help. I'm always a fighter ... [laughs] ... I think that's one of the things that my mom always taught me. My mum always tell me I'm a fighter and I know what to do. So, I should just get on with it.

While I have always been like that, as I said things have changed for me, I try to understand people from my perspective and where I'm coming from. With me this young, having all these issues with dementia, I just think to myself, 'Okay, what is it that I know?'

Religious faith as part of identity

You know, my mom was a Christian and I was born as a Christian girl, and so that's my faith as a believer.

In a nutshell

It was interesting to note that despite the changes Dianne felt in her identity that are stated here, fundamentally her roots and faith are her bedrock, and these have not changed despite her dementia.

I am a typical Jamaican. I was born in Jamaica and I'm gonna die a Jamaican because that's me!

Frances Isaacs

One very sad consequence of the COVID-19 pandemic is that at the time of writing, while I know Frances very well, it is a totally virtual friendship formed during 2020 when we collaborated on the 'Time and Place' poetry project and which we built further in 2021 when I joined a DEEP Zoom art group led by Frances.

Job

You know, once upon a time, I was quite an astute businesswoman, and now ... [laughs] ... I'm just a complete fool.

That was how Frances self-deprecatingly saw herself. While it is certainly not my remit to challenge any of the comments made by Frances or the others we spoke with, I do honestly feel that Frances is certainly not a fool. Reinhard, who did not know her at all, then pressed her to tell us more about her working life.

I was a fundraising consultant. I had the kind of brain that could work out why people's charities were not doing as well. Charities from all over the country would come to seek my help.

Attitude towards living with dementia

Having lived in London for many years, Frances and her husband Barrow moved to a rural life in the Brecon area, and having seen herself as a Londoner we wondered if she now felt she would identify herself by her rural Welsh home. Also, Frances is never averse to some friendly banter with George and myself during our virtual art sessions, and clearly she has a sharp sense of humour, which I was keen to ask her about in relation to her living with dementia. My experience tells me that those who come over as funny usually have a very serious inner self that the humour sometimes masks. Again, this was something which, as with Chris Norris, I was interested to hear Frances talk about.

I've always been a bit of an outdoorsy girl. We just got trapped by school, jobs, life, you know, as you do. This is a better life for us both. I had no interest in bringing London here. In fact, I was quite happy that all our London friends thought we were stupid old hippies and had finally gone off the rails. Hooray. Leave me here, please.

In chatting with my friend about the hospital experience of my diagnosis, she said you've always been a bit of a fruitcake ... [laughs] ... I was always trouble. Yes, it's because I've lost my inhibitions to some extent and with that goes even worse jokes.

How do I see myself now? Well, just probably a miserable old sod, actually, you know. A lot of people who are quite funny, like me are miserable old sods. I don't like being miserable because it is not good for you. Well, not much of a change as I was always dreadful. What I am now is worse, because I just can't stop laughing.

In a nutshell

Although she was too modest to say this, Frances is one of the most creative, intelligent people with dementia I know, and has on many occasions expressed some frustration that she feels she is not as capable of the quality of art work she did previously. However, because of her creativity and intellect, she has changed course in the style of art she undertakes which is, to those of us lucky to see and admire it, worthy of the plaudits it rightly attracts. Indeed, Frances did the artwork for the *Time and Place* book (Jennings et al. 2021) and the front cover of *Reconsidering Neighbourhoods and Living with Dementia: Spaces, places, and people* (Keady 2023). Frances sums this up in this way:

Look, you know, I may have dementia, but I'm not an idiot. I never was. Yeah, I mean, at the hospital, he said to me, the fact that you come in at a high intellect will always help you.

Gail Sharon Gregory

Hobbies

Gail began her conversation with us by highlighting the importance to her identity of hobbies and interests and how they can enhance selfhood but also how others can damage this.

I think people need to realise as well that the things that we are learning now, some of us was told at school that, that we were useless. Now, we're actually producing poetry. I was one of the bottom in the English class and they said I'd never ever succeed in English. Well, despite being told at school that we're useless, obviously we're proving our teachers wrong.

Attitude towards living with dementia

I wasn't a very, sort of, huggy person before but I am now, especially with my close friends and family. I don't like big groups ... I used to be the life and soul of the party. I was always the silly one ... I don't like the noises, I don't like all the background chattering. My head feels like an explosion of different noises. I get quite agitated.

Having heard Gail tell us how she had changed in a social setting, I was interested to hear her further thoughts around her views of herself.

I think I am quite bubbly, but then again I can be quiet. Erm, confident in some areas ... erm, I always try to be happy and positive, even though sometimes we do have the down days, I think we all have those, but most times I try to be positive. I have a more positive outlook on things, and that is a big change in me. I think for me it was, I didn't want to be sat here doing nothing, and let it be, let it take over. I wanted to fight it the best way that I could, if that's the right way of putting it. I just wanted to, to live. I didn't want someone or something telling me what to do in a way. I've never liked to be told what to do. My mum said as a child, I never wanted to be told what to do, and I suppose with the dementia, I'm not letting it tell me what to do.

Recognising the influence others close to the person can have, I then asked what impact Gail's husband had on her identity.

He just likes to get on with it. I'm the driving force and always have been, and I've been like that in the family as well. It's always been me that's sort of held everybody together. I've been a single parent and I think it's the struggles that you go through that make you a strong person, and I think that's why I can cope better now because of some of the things I have gone through in my past.

Sensing Gail's strength of character, I felt able to ask her how comfortable she was with that label of 'person with dementia', and then to explain her reasons for how she felt. Her reply was instant and without any sense of hesitation.

I don't. I don't like it, because I'm Gail. I know I have dementia but I'm Gail, I'm still the same person. I was an only child, so I had to learn to do things for myself, and bringing two children up on your own, you learn to adapt to your own self. Then as a person you become stronger and learn to love things because you have to. You have no other option. There's nobody else there.

I hate asking for help, I think that comes from being an only child. I have always found a way to do things on my own and yes, so I think I will struggle having to ask somebody to help me, in fact I know I will because it has to be done my way.

I don't like awards and things like that, I just don't think there's any need for it whatsoever … I don't know why, I just don't get it, because there's always somebody that's meant to feel bad because of that award and I just don't think they should.

In a nutshell

Not once when talking about her identity did Gail touch on her activist activities connected to DEEP or any former jobs that she had had before her diagnosis. For Gail, her family background and arts and social activities were the keys to understanding her sense of identity.

George Rook

George was one of the Fifteen who had prepared notes based upon the outline sheet (see page 36) I had emailed to them before our Zoom conversation. My experience suggests he is a very deep thinker and this was evident from the start of our conversation through his opening comment.

I see occupation and identity as quite, quite closely similar.

Activist

I increasingly turned to blogging because I enjoy writing. I started to blog about living with dementia and, and of course at the same time I was introduced through Chris Mason to the DEEP network and people, and that's where I found what I had begun now as my activism, which is very much to do with raising awareness, trying to improve support and care alongside supporting Dementia UK to get more Admiral Nurses. It is so important meeting different people and with completely different views but all tending to have the same thoughts about dementia is an incredibly validating and valuable thing to have in your life.

Within the family

We asked George if he felt his identity had changed within the relationships in his family, maybe starting with his wife.

She's worked from home instead of away, and whenever she's away with people who are, quote 'normal' … um, she comes back and expects me to be quote 'normal'. Whereas if we're together all the time, she doesn't have that sort of different perception, and she's more understanding and accepting of it and that is the big change.

I think people see me, and this will probably include my family, people see me as now being quite quiet and possibly withdrawn, because a lot more goes on inside my head now and a lot less goes on outside my head. So I will be thinking a lot but I don't feel the need to actually talk to people, and I don't necessarily want to. I'm quite happy to sit there and just listen. Now I'm not, I hope, I'm not stereotyping or having dementia … [laughs] … I might do one day, but, but equally I am convinced that people who are that stereotype, maybe further on, a lot further on than me, I'm convinced that they actually still have a lot going on in there, it's just you never see it or hear it. And they may look as if they're sitting there doing nothing.

I think we tend to judge even without knowing we're judging.

Creative hobbies

Whether or not George sees himself as this, but others certainly regard George as a creative person, both in thought and deed. A personal connection for this is that we both joined the DEEP art group led by Frances Isaacs at about the same time. Each of us had no background or experience of painting watercolours or any kind of painting on paper but we have both surprised ourselves and probably others by what we have achieved over the past 2 years. Whether or not we would identify ourselves as artists is open to question but artwork by us both features on the covers of books in this series. I applaud George's opening statement in this section.

I am what I do. I am what I write, I am what I create … um, that's who I am.

George then stopped to think and, with a little encouragement, he then took this further.

Perhaps going back to anxiety and self, lack of confidence … um, I am very insecure on my own, and when I have the affirmation we've talked about,

I can write or speak whatever, knowing that this is really, this is really me, but then I have the confidence to be me. Um, for my identity is what I do and if I didn't do it, I suppose the logic of it is I would not really have any real sense of identity. You know I mean the fact that I, and this fills me with enormous pride – the right sort of pride folks – I think, that I can carve and paint a bit, and always that stuff with gardening and growing flowers you know, I just, I just feel 'well, I can do that'. Yeah it just comes. So that's who I am.

In a nutshell

When asked to bring this part of the conversation to a close with a sentence to summarise his sense of self, George said this:

How do I see myself, well I've always been a bit of a … bit of a loner. I also have this very strong affinity with the natural world, and that has always been incredibly important to me. I can remember as a child, being in a pretty unhappy family. I remember wishing that I was a bird, not just to fly away, I mean it just happens that I'm a rook but there we are [Keith and Reinhard laugh]. Yeah I know … um, I would have been a sparrow though. And … um, I just wished I could be a bird to fly, to fly above and look down rather than be in it, because I hated it so much. So, where why did I say that? Er, ah, yes in my identity.

Jennifer Bute

I have known Jennifer longer than most of the other people we spoke with. Our paths originally crossed in 2013 when we were working together on a project with the Alzheimer's Society to give a clearer voice to those of us living with dementia, and I suspect our different, yet people-focused professional backgrounds – she as a GP and me as headteacher – helped forge some common ground and mutual respect between us. Once a caring GP and educator, always …

Job

I've always cared about people and always tried to help everyone make the most out of their situation. I've always tried to educate and explain things, and we do retain some skills from the past, and I do think that is one skill that I still have. I think I'm more confident in a strange kind of way. I feel that I'm an expert in dementia, which I certainly wasn't before and I'm still learning. My job as a GP ended when I had to take early retirement because of dementia.

I have an obstinate spirit, and I would educate them because often it's fear around not understanding, you have to allow people to change and by allowing them to take time they're not going to switch suddenly. I believe I can always learn. I'm aware of other people's feelings and their embarrassments and how easy it is to get it wrong. Well it's sometimes difficult to know how much we have to just accept and how much we can alter.

Jennifer told us about a recent incident in which she was witness to a man who had a fall. Without thinking, Jennifer switched into the role of doctor as this is how both she saw herself in that moment and how others nearby saw her, knowing this was her previous career.

I snapped into medical mode – I knew exactly what to do and I only relaxed when the ambulance had come and taken him off to hospital. Afterwards, looking at all these people looking at me and I thought where am I? Who am I? What am I doing? They said, 'Jennifer, you're going home now'. My reply was, 'Home, where's home, I don't know'.

Clearly deep within her psyche Jennifer had moved back into her former doctor role where she saw herself at that moment, before then reverting back to the Jennifer of the present time.

Religious faith as a part of identity

I think my faith is important because I honestly believe that I'm accepted and loved by God no matter what. I don't need a role as a person, and I believe that for other people it's not what they used to be, or what their role used to be, it's that they have worth and value now and I think since I've lost my professional role that has become more important.

Hobbies

I love going for walks but I don't always know where I live; however, people can bring me back so I daren't go out of this place by myself to go for walks.

Jim McNee

Reinhard and I met with Jim in his garden and he was accompanied by Kathy, his wife.

Hobbies

Jim was keen to begin the conversation talking in his comfort zone about football, and I asked him which team he supported.

Celtic. I don't see much of them, and Arsenal as my grandson is a fan. The Celtic connection is since childhood. I was a very keen footballer. That was all you could do where I came from. Yes, a wee small boy from a working-class family in Glasgow.

Keith: 'You're still that small boy?'

To a certain extent yeah, I was hoping that instead of a 5-foot 7, I was 6 foot and then I could have played for Celtic, life never worked out that way so that was my ambition.

I read a lot, I remember little and don't remember much about the story later. I also do crossword puzzles. I enjoy going on long walks and I do the same route for a while and then try and make changes to the route. This helps me try to keep physically fit.

Attitude towards living with dementia

At this stage, I don't feel any worse or better than I was, from when I was at the end of my teaching career. But I was diagnosed with dementia, so I have to deal with it. You know there are times when I think they made a mistake and other times I think, no they didn't.

Obviously I have to rely on Kathy a lot more than I did in the past but relationships with friends are much the same and with family who treat me the same as they did before.

If they're worried about me they would tell me.

I've got two daughters who worry about me all the time. That's something that keeps your brain tumbling, is worrying about your kids, whilst they worry about you.

I can continue to behave normally, I might need Kathy's backup at times but normally I'm okay.

Mainly forgetfulness has become a point. I do forget things, for example, what was the shopping list that we have to take? But I'm not convinced as a younger man that I was much better!

Kathy said little during this time but her body language said a lot as she nodded when Jim spoke of his flawed memory and smiled at this last comment.

Activist

Having spoken to Jim about his family and life in general with dementia, I was interested to ask his views on the East Kent Forget-Me-Nots group we both attend each month. This is a business-type group who alongside organising creative projects, set out to do things to make the dementia world a better place for us all. Jim attends regularly and is usually one of the thoughtful, quiet ones in the group, happy to share his wisdom when prompted.

To be honest, I just go along as part of the company and try and enjoy myself and build relationships. It's about having conversations with like-minded people, realising they have the same problems as I have, and that they deal with things in different ways, and that their diagnosis is slightly different from mine but that we are all the same. Trying and getting by as best we can.

I think it was partly Kathy who felt I should go. I have this problem and I'm not going to do anything about it from sitting in the house. Even if all you're doing is talking to people with the same problem, it does make a difference because you realise that you're not the only one.

I'm quite happy, I suppose. Through the years looking back I was quite happy to be on my own. I had a few friends but I wouldn't say true friends.

In a nutshell

Jim was absolutely clear in his response to how he identified himself:

I would identify myself as an ex-teacher. If someone identified me as a dementia sufferer I would say I'd be surprised. I don't feel that I'm a dementia sufferer.

Reinhard then closed by asking 'and within your family?'

Yes, things have changed to a certain extent, Kathy is now head of the family [amid laughter from us all, Kathy's response was: 'I thought I was always head of the family!'].

Julie Hayden

Attitude towards living with dementia

It's sometimes difficult to kind of keep the accurate perspective of yourself and because I don't have anyone to bounce ideas off, and I don't have anyone giving their opinion. It's not like having a partner with me that I can kind of do a reality check of how things are.

Activist

For most of our time together on Zoom, Julie was happy to steer the conversation into areas of her activism and how she saw this as a key part of her identity. This did not surprise me because I have got to know Julie well sharing roles within the 3 Nations Dementia Working Group in which we are both active on the Steering Group.

I think that essentially I'm the same person. I have the same values that I always had, but what's changed about me is I am becoming perhaps more intolerant of other people who come out with grand words and phrases and promises. It's more about action if you're not gonna do rather than what you say. I get very impatient with that kind of thing, and I have to kind of try and keep myself in check because when it comes to myself and my own rights and the things I need help with, there's only me to fight for me. I know to a lot of other people I sometimes will come across as perhaps as being unreasonable or a bit irritable.

I wrote a blog about this for Dementia Alliance International (DAI) for World Alzheimer's month, writing 'if I don't fight for me, then who will?' I have to say the words because there's nobody there at the side of me backing me up or saying, 'Julie does need this, she isn't being unreasonable, this is why she needs this'. That can jar with the difficulties that I perhaps have because of my dementia. Juggling those difficulties with how I sometimes put myself across.

Today I still hold the same values that my parents brought me up with. I still feel as keenly as I always have about the rights of people. If I feel that someone's not been treated well, I will speak out a lot of the time when maybe it might be wisest just to shut up. That's the way I look at things in the world. Generally, I've become much less party political than I used to be. Though I am still interested in what's going on in the world and I have my political views but when politics comes into everything, it becomes very difficult when people say you can't talk about politics or you can't talk about religion, but these are issues which become interwoven in so many areas of life. Every single aspect of life has a political angle to it, so it's about pulling away from the party politics and just keeping it to the little people politics. I do feel passionate about seeing myself as an advocate for demanding the rights of people with acquired disabilities.

Religious faith as a part of identity

When Reinhard asked Julie about her religious faith, this was her response:

That's a strange one because I used to be very religious. I was brought up in the Church of England, but as a teenager I actually moved away and got into the charismatic movement of the church. It was a Billy Graham type of thing and I used to go to church instead of just once a week, several times a week. Now I would not exactly call myself religious, that has dimmed over the years but I do still talk to God even though I don't have that formal religion.

In a nutshell

Living with dementia is tough but it would be so much worse if I was just turning my face to the wall and feeling sorry for myself all the time. Whereas if you can balance it up with, 'yeah it's tough for you, but it's tougher for other people', then you can use that as a balance to keep your identity.

Keith Day (Cam)

Attitude towards living with dementia

Cam outlined in the conversation how his attitude towards having dementia changed from at first being in denial, moving then to acknowledging and finally to comfortable acceptance. To support this he spoke not only about his own inner thoughts but how he identified himself at work and with his wife and family.

We went to the GP, then he referred me back to the mental health for older people and they found out that I had frontotemporal dementia. At that particular time, I was in denial of it and I wouldn't accept that was me. After about a good 3 months, I started to read about dementia and I noticed there were changes in myself. This led me to go to a group. As soon as I got to the group, I could relate to everything they were saying because this was me – I was doing what they were talking about and it was from then that I realised what was happening.

At first I didn't want anyone to know, but then I started to accept myself. I now have no qualms at all in telling people I have dementia, it's simple because I think I've accepted this way of life and my wife and daughter have accepted it as well.

I went back to work and I was talking to my supervisor, and she was talking about how I caught up with that and the thing is because when I had the stroke I wasn't able to speak. I also wasn't able to write or read or anything, so I knew what it was like to not have a voice and that is how I felt at work. Unfortunately, all the children I worked with come from abusive pasts and they were taught you can't talk about this and I knew in a way I had an insight into what they were going through. I felt I couldn't talk about having dementia.

When asked if Cam felt that dementia had changed his view of himself or the views others such as his wife had of him, his answer was very direct and to the point.

Yeah, your character changes doesn't it? Yeah, it does. What she said to the doctor was, 'This is not the man that I married'.

He then illustrated how he felt he had changed by sharing a story of a recent incident with us.

I realised it was silly little things I was doing that I'd never ever done before which can offend people. A little while ago I spoke to a woman. She was quite a big lady right, she'd keep saying about how her knees were hurting. Normally, I wouldn't say to her have you tried this to help? I got to the stage where I was saying, 'well actually, if you lost weight you wouldn't feel so bad'. She said it was quite rude but to me but I felt it wasn't. The lady looked at me, and I told her I had dementia. She said, 'if you hadn't said that, I wouldn't have thought you'd have dementia'. I felt like saying it's like, 'well I don't have a uniform!'

I have only known Cam since just before the COVID-19 pandemic, partly through our involvement with the 3 Nations Dementia Working Group but we also both live in Kent and are Kent and Medway NHS Dementia Envoys. Cam had seen a film I had made in 2012 on YouTube [www.youtube.com/watch?v=CPulwcrkcxA&ab_channel=DementiaTraining] and had identified with much of what I was describing there as my lived experience with dementia. Cam has told me a number of times that watching the film was really helpful to him. Consequently, it came as little surprise when he said,

I have dementia and you and I have a lot in common.

Thinking about this statement from Cam, it reinforced in my mind that while all of us with dementia are unique individuals, it is quite possible to see elements of oneself in others, and to take some strength from the notion that we are not alone travelling this pathway. For many, this sense of shared identity is really empowering. Conversely, Cam then went on to describe a more negative line of thought.

I think the only thing I would say I find difficult is when you when some people get to know you have dementia and they automatically write you off. I say what others also say, you know we've all said before, the thing is we are still human, we're the same person. We might be a little bit slow in doing it, and that's the downside of it you know. Sometimes as well I think if you can explain to them the fact you have dementia, they can then prepare themselves and accept a lot better. Before, when I was first told I had dementia, I wouldn't tell anybody, it was as though it was like a stigma.

I didn't at first like it but I can say now I'm quite happy to talk about dementia.

Religious faith as a part of identity

Cam had on a number of occasions in our conversation touched upon the importance of his Christian faith. I wanted to give him the opportunity to tell us how he saw this as a part of his identity, and if dementia had affected this, whether positively or not.

I would definitely identify myself with my religious faith. We'd class ourselves as born again Christians. It's something important to us, as we've been with the church 26 years now and I would never, ever walk away from it. I mean the thing is, I have my faith right and I'm not gonna knock other people because they have a different faith to me, that's up to them. But to me I don't think I'd be able to go through all that's happened like a heart attack as well as dementia unless the people from the church were there.

As so often was the case, Reinhard recognised that the threads of the conversation based upon the petals of Kitwood's flower overlapped at this point. Reinhard explained that Cam had mentioned his faith as being really quite important in attachment and in what Cam did in many aspects of his life, but also in inclusion through Cam's participation in community life. Reinhard then emphasised the importance of recognising Cam's faith as a central part of his identity, to which Cam said:

Yes to me the church is a big part of me and gives a lot of comfort as well to me and to my wife. I really think sometimes it's our faith that's taken us all through all the things that's happened to us and we believe it's there for a reason.

In a nutshell

My favourite thing for me now is I have dementia, but dementia hasn't got me. In a way, we are so quiet and normal. I think about having a bad memory, it's just changing me because I think different, I look at people differently.

Masood Ahmed Qureshi (Maq)

Impact of dementia on his identity

In the days, weeks, even months after receiving a diagnosis of dementia, there can be an enormous impact upon a person's sense of identity. For some, it provides answers to challenging questions which have stirred in the mind, and in the minds of those closest to them; for others, it can have a devastating effect upon their lives and sense of selfhood. Each person needs support at this time in order to come through it. In my own case, I told those who needed to know within my family and at my place of work from the outset, but withheld telling others for several months. Maq chose to deal with it as follows:

To start off with I didn't tell a lot of people about my dementia because again there is a stigma. When you say dementia, first of all there's no word in my native language, so it's difficult to explain and secondly, the minute you mention dementia, I believe that it is number one associated with memory and number two with old age.

It is still difficult to talk about this, and it's difficult to talk to strangers about this. I can safely say that friends like Keith who've I've known for quite some time now and that has brought all this out of me, so I'm in a sense of coming out. I'm able to talk and go into depth as I feel a lot more confident about it.

5 or 6 years ago, I wouldn't have actually gone out there in a strange sort of situation not knowing people and being able to say I am living with a diagnosis of dementia whereas now I can and I'm prepared to stick a badge on me saying I have dementia.

Hobbies and interests

Maq was very proud to tell us of his prowess as a calligrapher, and this clearly helped him to feel positive about himself. It is a skill learnt before his diagnosis but through continued practice, is something he retains and enjoys.

I'm a calligrapher as well by the way … in English as well as Urdu Arabic and you know I've written the letters handwritten and spent time on them, and you know the phone calls I've had and the thanks I've had from them, it's unbelievable. I don't think that dementia has made any less of me than I was and I'm okay with that.

Job

I'm a lot more caring – I was ruthless when I was an accountant.

For some of us, our professional background has better enabled us to maintain a mask to screen from others the dementia, and better maintain an identity that is more in keeping with our former professional self. Maq commented on this.

Because now I understand it fully and because I know what areas it affects, and because of my professional sort of background I can hide it to a certain extent.

There are some people that do see colour obviously, you know and it does exist. When I moved into this street I was the only Asian, and because I had a good job with a company car it wasn't liked very much. Whereas at work I became one of the lads, I earned my respect that way.

Activist

I first got to know Maq through our shared responsibility on the Steering Group for the 3 Nations Dementia Working Group. His involvement with the 3 Nations has allowed Maq to retain a sense of belonging to and respect within a group, which has contributed to him maintaining his identity. Being involved with the 3 Nations helps Maq identify himself nationally but he was also keen to tell us about his more local activism in the area where he lives.

I belong to 11 different organisations and do Zoom sessions, on average 15 zooms a week. I have got contacts everywhere and if I'm not on one of the meetings, I get a phone call asking, 'Where are you? We are missing you, we want you'. In a sense, people with dementia have made a star out of me you know.

In a nutshell

Maq senses the responsibility he feels as a public voice for the Asian community, many of whom he often states struggle to come forward to talk about their dementia, and this in part is a big motivation for him to encourage others to join organisations.

'You meet one person with dementia, you've met one person with dementia' – we all say that professionals say that, but people living with dementia live by that and practise it whereas professionals don't, they treat everybody the same. We're all individuals and I think it's made a better person out of me.

Nigel Hullah

I was very interested but not at all surprised by the way Nigel began his biography on page 29 describing where he lives allied to his political affiliation. Although all of the Fifteen mentioned where they lived, Nigel began our conversation and his biography by stating his allegiance to his hometown. One often hears people state that they are a Cockney, a Brummie, a Geordie, a Scouser, a Glaswegian, Welsh or, in the case of my two eldest children who were born in Nantwich, Cheshire, a 'Dabber'. Or maybe it is others who identify people in this way due in part to their accent.

Nigel was the only person to do this. He is a big man in so many ways and occupies a big space in the world of dementia activism through a number of his roles and allegiances. It indeed seems appropriate to begin our conversation with him by exploring how he saw himself in the activist role.

Activist

Well, I mean, you get thrust into the limelight, that's the way it goes. Sometimes you have to say, 'No, I'm not the person for that'. I did say yes to everything in the beginning, I took every opportunity to have my voice heard, but it suddenly dawned on me that I wasn't the best person to talk about that. For instance, somebody asked me to talk about the Tree of Life. Well, I said to them, 'I don't know anything about it. All I know is it's a narrative therapy, and it's very useful for some people'. So, I said, 'I am not the one for this'. On the other hand, if asked to talk about human rights, I could talk … I could talk a sheep to sleep, but that bores people and I've moved away from that now, and I've set my own agenda. My own agenda is what I follow very, very closely because I've developed a new mantra in life: you can't change my dementia, and you can't change the world in which I live. I think that's what I live by now, in making these little tweaks to life or encouraging organisations to suggest maybe just little tweaks to life, which will in part, now or in the future, make my life a lot easier.

Taking on an activist role does take some courage; putting yourself in the public domain opens one up to all sorts of comments and pressures. And beyond that Nigel has for the past 4 years been the chair of the 3 Nations Dementia Working Group which, like all leadership roles, requires a certain kind of personality. I asked Nigel about if he saw himself as a leader. His response might have surprised some, but good leaders think about, support, encourage and celebrate the efforts of those they are leading, and knowing Nigel as I do, I know how sincere he is making the following statements:

I think one of the great things about activism is that over the last couple of years our voices have become heard in different places. It's absolutely remarkable. I mean, a lot of people who stand up in front of large audiences and whilst they're squirming inside, they do it anyway. It's ultimate bravery.

*The 3 Nations Dementia Working Group is a clear example of when people like us get together. The changes that **we can make**, and that's the kind of person I am now. I've got to be honest. I like being a captain of a team, but I'm also quite happy to play in the team. I'm a better follower than I'm a leader, and so I'm happy to follow.*

I think now, I'm more open to other people's opinions. I look towards getting people's voices heard, I look towards preparing a platform for people and helping them achieve from where they are. You know, I mean, this is so important that we are genuine and not just say it because some people say it, but genuinely support people in achieving, that is what a peer support group does. I've got personal goals around having confidence to join whatever I'm doing, and that people have confidence in me.

Attitude towards living with dementia

Nigel began this element of the conversation focusing upon himself as an activist, and while I wanted to encourage him to do so, I was also keen to hear about his thoughts on himself outside of this role. In probing how he saw himself, he was clear about which label he was most comfortable with:

Just Nigel. I think most of us are like that, aren't we?

Well, from a personal point of view, I'm a much different person now. Even on my former sunniest days, people would say I was not very pleasant to be around prior to dementia because I had this coil spring approach, you know, and I had a very structured mind which still comes out now and again, sometimes when we do the 3 Nations stuff. I see boundaries. This is where we should be, and this is what we should be doing, and not everybody sees eye-to-eye, not everybody agrees to that. But since dementia, I look for different things in people who are around me.

More often than not, people say, 'well, dementia hasn't really changed me'. Well, I don't believe that for one minute. I think it's bound to change everybody who's ever had a diagnosis simply because, you know, it invades every part of your life.

Being creative

I never would have believed that Nigel would have been told that I would have a poem published one day. I thought you are insane, and I think it's because I'm ham-fisted. Next I'm going to take part in a kite-making workshop ... where we make our own kites on the beach and we fly it and I will try make a dragon kite. Has to be that with me being Welsh! I've never been a sort of creative person in those terms. I was once. I've always been a sort of get my hands dirty, get stuck in bloke with a full agenda. I don't see life from a personal point of view, I mean, getting a diagnosis of dementia has given me a period of self-reflection because in the past my days were so full, and now, I need that space. I need that space, and without it, I don't function. I'm more self-aware and I'm calmer now, believe it or not.

Seeing oneself in a technical world

In our conversation, I also wanted to ask Nigel about his attitudes towards feeling included, comfortable and identified by the use of technology and social media. I did this because I know Nigel sits on many virtual platforms in his various roles in the UK and in Europe and uses some aspects of social media to support this.

Yes, I do use social media but it can be a horrible place, and you have to take it for what it is. If you have a sensitive nature and you get offended or upset by it, don't go there. Yeah, it's not the end all and be all. It's a great tool for engagement. It's a great tool for swapping ideas. It's a great tool for looking at what's happening elsewhere. But you get the odd one or two things that come up there which are best left alone. I use WhatsApp quite a bit, that's a great communication method if you just want to do one or two things. Having said all of that, I like to talk to people. I've got a Zoom account of my own, which I use quite a bit. I think communication is probably the biggest tool in my personal armoury. I think I'm a good communicator.

I'm immensely proud to be chair of the 3 Nations and I won't stop telling people that. I'm immensely proud of the work we do with the Welsh Government, but I'm only there because of the work I've done with other people who've got me there. You know, who have helped me see a broader view. If you're not careful, dementia narrows your view of the world.

Job

Before I was quite non-descript. I was considered a bit of a bully, although I never bullied anybody in my life. I just had a set of values and ideas which were unshakeable. I was very difficult to deal with … yeah, which meant I worked alone. I didn't play well with others.

People I worked with don't live in the past because that's where they made all the mistakes. They live in the moment and people with dementia are similar. You know, we live in the moment, don't we, to a certain extent and, I mean, there was experiences like that which kind of changed me, and then I had to negotiate everything I had to do, it drove me mad because I had to learn all these skills of getting people to agree with me. Here comes Nigel, he must be right. You know, once in a couple of previous lives, when I was working, I had to get people to agree with me. But some of these skills, I re-discovered these negotiating skills, particularly from when I worked with IBM, were so vital because if you revolve without socialising and you had a product hiccup, then you had to get down to it and you have to get people to agree with you so that things could be done. You couldn't force your way on, and even before my diagnosis of dementia my perspective had always been you can say something which is good for you, or you can say something which is good for everybody. So, you might as well say something that's good for everybody.

What Nigel outlines here shows that he still relates to his former identity within his past profession and recognises some continuity but also acknowledges some changes to his identity, many of which he regards as for the better. He also clearly describes how he has built strategies based upon those developed when he was working. We certainly understood how hard it is to do this but he is showing it can be done. Often the expectation is that living with dementia solely causes a decline in one's sense of self-identity – clearly Nigel disproves this theory.

Tracey Shorthouse

Hobbies and interests

Reinhard and I were consistently told of hobbies and interests that the Fifteen had, many from before they were diagnosed with dementia, but others they had developed subsequently and were proud to express as part of their current identity, different from their former selves. Tracey actually began speaking about her identity in this way.

I have always loved gardening, I just love seeing things grow. My garden is full of wildlife, so it's got bees and butterflies and foxes. That's the positive side, the strongest plants in the garden survive. So that is how dementia is, it's a strong piece of us that survives over the diagnosis. We are strong as we are with our minds, as we can be, to fight against the dementia, and I think that's how I think of my garden sometimes as well.

While I personally do not see a fight against dementia, where Tracey and I adopt the same stance is when she uses powerful metaphors to help explain how she sees herself living with dementia.

Tracey self-published *I Am Still Me* (2017), an anthology of poems written by herself, and she also contributed to *Time and Place*, a collection of poems edited by Jennings et al. (2021). One of her more recent poems appears in this book (see page 96). When I asked Tracey if she considered herself a poet, this was her response:

I don't really think of myself as a poet, I never think – it doesn't come naturally with me, no – other people think it might do, it might have done in the beginning after my first diagnosis. But I don't really think it's there now.

Dementia in its various forms does so often impact negatively on one's self-confidence, and to counter this we do need other people to give us a boost from time to time. While I respect and understand Tracey's comment about her current ability to write poetry, clearly her recent poetic piece shows that with encouragement she can still create poetry of great worth.

Job

I did mention earlier about how we are often identified by ourselves, or by others, by the job we do or did before retiring. An example of this is how Tracey used to see herself and how this has continued, remained or changed since she was diagnosed with dementia in her 40s.

I was the catheter queen of nursing – it's those sort of things that will never leave me because it's part and parcel of being me. I still think of myself as being a nurse. I remember one of the union reps from the Royal College of Nursing told me I would never stop being a nurse. I might be retired, but I'm always going to be a nurse because the knowledge is in my brain. It never goes.

Activist

All fifteen people we spoke to could legitimately be described as activists to varying degrees in the realm of dementia service user involvement, although some decried this and did not see themselves as such. This is how Tracey described it:

I see myself as a speaker as well, because even before lockdown, I used to do lots of activist work, trying to change people's ways of thinking. I might do that through my blog or through Twitter, because it's important for people to understand.

Being an activist, in Tracey's case an NHS Dementia Envoy in Kent, does not only entail speaking at events and meetings – she is also a very keen blogger:

I can be myself in my Blog. I can be as open as I want to be. I really just think of myself as a nurse and speaker. I've still got my independence, I'm still quite active, but just in a different way.

Attitude towards living with dementia

So why can't we all be more kind and caring – it's quite scary being a patient, since I've been a patient, it's quite scary when you want people to be understanding. It's hard being a patient, it's hard being a nurse but you try and get that happy balance.

I did ask Tracey, by way of her personality now, whether she thinks her personality has changed?

My friends have all told me that. Even my mom has said to me, she's really pleased that even though I've got dementia, it hasn't changed the way that I am. She sees my personality as the same, I still come across as caring for others. I might lose my temper at home on my own, because I get frustrated. But I don't lose my temper with other people. My friends will say that I am probably a better person since having dementia because when I was nursing, I was quite stressed all the time, whereas I'm much calmer now.

I see myself as a team player in more aspects, and also on my own as well.

In a nutshell

The word 'dementia' changes you, changes the way people perceive you, and it shouldn't do because our identity hasn't changed. We're still the same people.

As soon as people hear the word dementia or even more than any other label there is out there, we still get treated slightly differently. Some of my friends tend to overcompensate, so they try and help me more, when I don't really need help.

I have got dementia but I'm more than the dementia. I want people to see me over the dementia. I feel people should just accept me for who I am rather than anything else. We are all unique individuals because of the way that we are.

So what learning can we take from the Fifteen?

These interviews provided a rich and varied account of how dementia impacts on a person's identity. We reflect here on what we can generalise for others living with dementia and those who support them.

From the point of view of someone living with dementia:

- We each need to be treated as a unique individual with strengths, challenges, wishes, needs, hopes and expectations based upon our past, present and future.
- When looking in the mirror, try and see your real self, what lies behind your eyes; dwell upon that identity of your self and then consider how others might see you.

There are also implications for those who provide professional support and care for persons living with dementia. For them, the main takeaway messages are:

- The main task of dementia care is to maintain personhood.
- If one main need is met, this will have an effect on the other needs too. As the whole cluster of needs is met, it is likely that there will be an enhancement of the global sense of self-worth, of being valuable and valued.
- Labels and ways of identifying oneself or others are a part of life, and all of the fifteen people we spoke to could be identified, to varying degrees, as activists. If asked, I think they each would respond in one of three ways: some are born to activism, some achieve activism, while others have activism thrust upon them. If wishing to engage with a person with dementia or seeking an activist collaborator, please determine which one of these three you are likely to collaborate with before embarking on the co-created piece of work.
- To help maintain the identity of a person with dementia, professionals need to be alert to their needs for swift and clear communication that engages and empowers rather than alienates and confuses.

8 Occupation

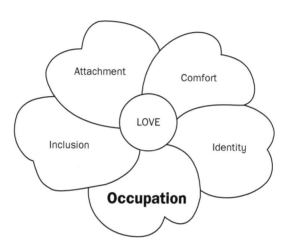

Life's quality means feeling useful
Give me a reason to carry on
Show that I'm still needed
A purposeful life rather than an
    existence
My own valued song
One which allows others to hear the
    message in my music
And see the person that remains
I am not dementia I am Julie, value
    me

– Julie Hayden

What is Occupation in the true
    sense of the word?
What does it mean? For me
A structure, A purpose, A way to fit
    in, to be part of the herd
I am a retired nurse, which helps to
    be a key
In opening doors of a different
    sense of the word, Occupation

– Tracey Shorthouse

The Fifteen on Occupation – narrated by Reinhard Guss

The importance of meaningful occupation, things to do that show an effect that endures over time, was apparent in my earliest venture into co-production and joint planning with people with dementia and their families. Over 20 years ago, I remember facilitating a workshop on what to do with a small pot of 'left-over' grant money from the Alzheimer's Society. Around a dozen people with dementia took part and what they told us very clearly was that they wanted somewhere to meet others, but not just to sit and chat. There should be something to do. A vote was held on a list of suggestions from art and craft to exercise, and much to my gardener's heart's delight, gardening was chosen, and the YOD (Young Onset Dementia) Horticultural Project was set up. It ran for 8 years, supported by a half day of clinician time and numerous volunteers and in several locations over that time. It provided occupation on a level suitable for each participant, similar to groups nowadays provided in some locations by Thrive, the horticultural therapy organisation [www.thrive.org.uk/get-gardening/gardening-and-dementia]. Of course, the social contact was important, but it was the satisfaction from the activity itself that energised people most, aided by taking home bunches of flowers or vegetables, and photos of the dug plot or the tidied border before and after.

Most of the Fifteen received a diagnosis of dementia when under the age of 65. This meant that most were engaged in an occupation in the sense of a job or career that they tended to talk about first, before mentioning what could be classed as hobbies, other interests and their work in dementia activism. Clearly, the loss of the structure of work or employment and its large contribution to identity during a working life is a particularly difficult challenge for younger people with dementia. It may not be that activism provides a particularly attractive form of occupation for someone who had to give up work they had expected to be continuing for some time to come. A regular blog, an advice and sharing site on social media, preparation of talks, membership of committees, all require much dedication, time and effort, and many activists have seen the demands on their time increase exponentially. Speaking with the Fifteen, it struck me how many had found this overwhelming or exhausting at times and needed to find ways of keeping a balance with other interests and down time to retain wellbeing. This echoed some of the early concerns and work with Keith on evaluating usefulness and enjoyability of different types of involved activities.

Some of the Fifteen talked about times prior to discovering activism and other dementia inclusive activities, feeling despondent, watching daytime television and doing very little. Many people I meet seem to need a period of time after the diagnosis where they do very little other than perhaps let the new situation sink in and settle before they are able to venture out again. The insight from gerontology about retaining skills and fitness in later life is that 'if you don't use it, you lose it' and applies all the more so to living with dementia. Remaining inactive, avoiding challenges, and staying away from situations and activities that may expose cognitive disabilities is a more or less conscious coping mechanism many people employ who are experiencing a developing dementia, and often by the time a diagnosis is reached, this process has been going on for several years. As a result, the radius and range of activity has shrunken, and to rekindle it may feel too challenging emotionally or too difficult given cognitive disabilities.

I often talk with families or carers who would very much like their relative with dementia to be more active, to engage in sudoku, brain training or crosswords, to go for walks, read a magazine, help with the garden, the cooking, the shopping, do something, anything! At times, it is a case of adjusting expectations, finding what the person is actually interested in and providing the reasonable adjustments and support that makes the occupation possible. At other times, it may need recognising that following a strict morning, mealtime and evening routine and spending all the time in between in front of the television or playing the same game on a tablet or phone may be the only form of activity that the person is able to tolerate.

In what follows, the words of the Fifteen are italicised to help distinguish them from Reinhard's commentary.

Agnes Houston

I first read about Agnes in a newspaper article about the Scottish Dementia Working Group around 2010, where she appeared as one of a group of people with dementia who visited the Scottish parliament's ministry for health to advocate for rights and services of people with dementia – an unheard-of concept at the time, and great encouragement for my more or less extracurricular activities in the health service and psychology. Meeting her in person at conferences and DEEP meetings were opportunities to experience her energy, kindness and humour at close hand. In 2014, Agnes agreed to help with the launch of the British Psychological Society's documents on Psychology in the Early Stage Dementia Care Pathway and we jointly presented on these at the subsequent UK Dementia Congress and at Alzheimer Europe conferences.

While, of course, some things have changed for Agnes in the intervening years, and much has become more difficult, she remains one of the trailblazing examples of people with dementia advocating for themselves, utilising a wide range of options to remain active and involved, trialling innovations, and in the process remaining much more well than textbooks suggest or professionals would have thought possible. I am often grateful for her prolific online presence, her book on sensory issues, which I use a great deal in staff training, her many presentations and, of course, her MBE – one of the examples of positive role models of hope to suggest to people following a new diagnosis.

Job

Occupation, was my paid job. So, dementia certainly changed that, because I no longer felt I was contributing by being employed and giving back to my community. So that was a big, big, big thing, you know, I felt worthless, and I felt shoved in the corner. I was looking and thinking, 'God, my life is over, there's no place for me here. Dementia has just, taken a rubber and scrubbed me out'.

Activism

When I found activism, I threw myself into activism and it was all-encompassing, it was out of balance. That was all I had. I spent a lot of years giving a lot of hours and a lot of me to campaigning in activism. I've no regrets but it took finding the creative 'Agnes' to get it a wee bit more in a balance.

Finding a balance

It's taken me a long time to get a balance back. Yeah, it took me a while to realise that I was saying 'yes' to everything. Almost the same way as I did before dementia. And now what I'm realising is that with the diagnosis of dementia, with my information and sensory overload side of dementia, I can't always say 'yes' to everything. If I do say 'yes', I'm now getting the strength to be able to say, 'Yes, I can do it, but here are some things that I need for me to be well while I'm doing it'.

Finding new interests

Do you know I'm dabbling? I haven't found my niche if you like, in the creative side. I thought it might have been sketching. But I'm dabbling. I'm being playful with all. So that is where I'm at the moment and I haven't found one that is all-encompassing. My creativeness, you know, it's almost putting the world into a perspective and being able to see it through a creative lens if you like. And just to enjoy, be still and enjoy. So that's when I am in my creativity. I'm doing mindfulness and meditation and yoga. They're my mainstay, you know, and I just, you know, I just be in that zone.

Attending one of Frannie's classes, the colours and the enjoyment – it's just a whole new world that I never stepped into, or the door was never opened for me. It is just an amazement, it's like a child in a toy shop. There's so much to choose from, you don't know what to do and you lift one, put it down, go back to one. It's just an overwhelming feeling of joy.

In a nutshell

To think, well, at my age and stage, where in the dementia world, people who follow the medical model feel and think that your world has diminished. And everybody feels sorry. And I'm thinking, 'Why? Why?' I've got more and see more, and then more coloured in detail than the ordinary eye – that I wouldn't have got I don't think if I hadn't had dementia. But by God, it's got its downsides too!

Agnes describes the devastating impact of losing her job that so many younger people experience following a dementia diagnosis. Discovering dementia activism can fill the gap in a way that other 'retirement hobbies' perhaps cannot, contributing to the largely younger demographic of this generation of dementia activists. Over the years, we had a number of conversations about the expectations on dementia activists, that lack of thought and consideration for their needs often displayed by organisations asking for their input, and how to address this. It was therefore particularly uplifting to hear more about Agnes' discovery of creative activities, and her descriptions of how she uses meditation and yoga in a regime of self-care are sure to find their way into many discussions with clients looking to adapt to different life parameters following a new diagnosis of dementia.

Chris Maddocks

Chris was one of a group of people living with dementia I first heard speak at the National Dementia Action Alliance and at a UK Dementia Congress. I particularly admired her work in raising awareness of the needs of people with dementia in the LGBTQ+ community and her eloquent descriptions of the benefits of peer support. I contacted Heather during my time working in Hastings and was so grateful for her support in setting up a peer support and involvement group there. With her partner, Heather, Chris travelled repeatedly from Eastbourne along the coast to Hastings, to give the Brightsiders group a good start.

Loss of job

I found that when I was going to log in into my work account and my emails, I couldn't remember how to do it. And I'd asked for help and be shown and 15 minutes later again I couldn't remember how to get into my email accounts etcetera.

I had my dementia diagnosis and within 3 months I lost my job. So that wasn't my decision at all.

Discovering involvement

One day I thought I've got a choice, I can either sit at home and watch daytime television or I can try and do something with the skills that I still have.

I did a course they were running called 'Living Well with Dementia'. That was my life-saver. I realised that it wasn't just me that was going through certain things, other people were going through the same things. When I started getting involved in doing things like that I had some sense of purpose back, and I started to feel hopeful instead of hopeless.

When I moved here, my details were passed onto the local Alzheimer's Society, and very soon they got me involved in doing talks with them to members of staff.

Letting go and finding new activities

I used to do a lot of walking. But because I've got Parkinson's disease and Lewy body dementia now, I was struggling quite a bit with my walking. So, I do some exercise now with the Parkinson's group. And I've got a friend who's a personal trainer, so I'm starting to do exercising with her now.

And Heather and I like to go and visit friends, we go for walks and meals out.

What else do I do? I used to love doing cross stitch, but I have actually had to give it up. I like playing games on Facebook, which drives Heather nuts. And in the pandemic, initially I started doing the singing lessons via Zoom.

'And I enjoy your photographs of the sunrises in Hastings' [Reinhard talking about Chris' photography posts on Facebook]. *Yeah, well I had to leave early yesterday for my walk on the beach, because I was doing a free spirit talk straight afterwards. Then I had some lunch, and I was supposed to be doing another Zoom at 2:00, and another one at 3:00. It was for the 'Time for Dementia' programme with Brighton University. I think we're helping to educate medical health professionals of the future.*

One of the best things has been 'Wellness in Nature' I think it's called, where I've done the course in the woods. It is for people, you know, with early-onset dementia. We've had a craftsman, a woodsman and a cook and we made things! We cooked things on an open fire. We were allowed to light flat fires and we would be given knives to whittle with. And that has been one of the best things I have ever done to help for me, because I am one of these people, people say I do things always for other people and I don't do much for myself.

Chris described the difficult lead-up to a diagnosis of young-onset dementia, and the abrupt end to her working life adding to the message of despair in the diagnostic process. She describes one of the early courses on living well with dementia as a 'lifesaver'. Some of the encouragement and support she received there has been vital in facilitating her developing into a nationally recognised expert by experience who has made significant contributions to the development and quality of services for people with dementia in the NHS and in the voluntary sector. I sometimes wonder what Chris would be doing today if this initial support had not been available?

There is an echo of some of Agnes' points in Chris' conversation about activism, where she considers doing more for other people than she does for herself. It contrasts with the thrill and excitement of the wellbeing in nature programme designed with younger people with dementia in mind. Here people were 'allowed' to light a fire, to whittle with knives! It was so good to see Chris' enthusiasm for and enjoyment of the activities shining through here. At the same time, I reflected that these are the activities generally deemed too risky and not suitable for people with dementia to engage in, with an underlying message that they are, like the job, like a working life, no longer allowed.

Chris Norris

As one of the founding members of the East Kent Forget-Me-Nots DEEP group, I have known Chris for almost as long and we have worked together in a range of projects over the years, becoming good friends in the process. Chris' attention to detail and his ability to use frameworks of rules and processes to manage his difficulties has helped him over the years as a reviewer of memory services for MSNAP from the point of view of a person living with a diagnosis. This programme is a work in progress to ensure reasonable adjustments can be made to the reviewer role to ensure that more people with dementia, rather than carers, can contribute. It is a great loss to the programme that Chris felt he had to give this up recently.

With another member of the group, we took our conversations about living with frontotemporal dementia to the UK Dementia Congress to raise awareness and to share some of my clinical learning more widely, which Chris and his colleague had enabled for me: that even this particularly devastating form of dementia – according to textbooks – does not necessarily follow the course or adhere to the catalogue of symptoms generally assumed by clinicians, that profound insight into the changes caused by the condition is possible and can be facilitated, and that a good quality of life is possible for very much longer than generally assumed.

Given the absence of medication-based approaches to frontotemporal dementia, Chris has been particularly interested in psychosocial interventions, and has been a wonderful advocate for their advancement and use, especially in the development and dissemination of the 2014 first edition of the BPS *Guide to Psychosocial Interventions in Early Stages of Dementia* (updated 2022). More recently, I have been particularly taken with his videos and contribution to the new online materials of the *Living with Dementia Toolkit* (IDEAL 2022) and cognitive rehabilitation resources.

Music

I have a basic interest, which, of course, is music. Music is my first love, which doesn't make my wife very happy, because … she was. I tried to explain that to her, you know. Music has carried on through. When you start off, it's a curve, isn't it, you start off and then you get better and better and better. Then in recent times, my ability to carry on doing my music has become more challenging. In as much as when you read music, you read it in lumps and passages, you don't actually read each individual note, but now I've had to go back to reading each individual note. So that's become more challenging, but it's certainly a ride that's carried on through, keeping me going really. I mean, that's my main hobby, I mean, in the past, I was very involved in scouting, but now music is my only hobby. Music is the only thing that takes me out and away from the house. I don't do an awful lot of music playing at home.

Music to me – it's almost my whole being. It's so very central, and so important in my life. And there was a period of time where I stopped playing for 5 years because I was told to by the heart consultant to stop playing.

Changes due to dementia, strategies and support

Yes, music playing can cause frustrations as well, because I'm very aware that I'm no longer as good at doing it as I was before, and that can cause frustrations. I try not to let that happen; I just have to accept the fact that the dementia is there. And that is what's causing the problem, not me as a person; my musical ability is still there, but the sort of dementia is chopping away around the corners.

I do find these days that I'm actually counting the length of each note now, I'm very much immersed in it. Whereas before, I didn't need to count the length. I could just feel the length and feel where it is. But now, if I've got a dotted crotchet, then I have to kind of count the length in my head.

I mustn't think of anything else when playing music. I find that it's easy for my mind to drift off, like the other day where we were practising with the police band, and we're out on the field. I became aware of the gate and people coming in through the gate and there's a particular way you must come in through the gate. You know, you've got to stop, let the gate open, then when you go through, you've got to stop again to make sure the gate is shut behind you. I was playing, and suddenly I was aware of what was going on, my mind went over to the gate. It wasn't any longer concentrating on what it should have been concentrated on. I really have to make sure I don't get distracted because it's so easy now to get distracted.

Even more now I do focus on the sheet music and on what the conductor is doing. Not that I ignored the conductor before, but now I'm really watching his beats to make sure that I'm doing the right thing in the right place. And reading the marks on the music as well, so that I don't come in really loud when it's a quiet bit. Sometimes I miss those marks now as well; sometimes I give it more than I should, and everyone can hear it.

I'm already really aware of how things have changed and possibly deteriorated or become more difficult. In the band there are people in their 80s, they're able to look at it from an age point of view. I have to look at it from a dementia point of view. I am aware that could be a challenge, but I'm prepared to just carry on as long as I can. And I'm very well supported by the people around me.

The people that play alongside me on the horn section, they're very supportive, and they're very aware. And gradually, I've educated the conductors and other members of the band, just letting them know. So that if I do something that's a bit odd, or not quite right, or if I've forgotten what we've already been told the way that we should be doing something, they can take it on board.

Social aspect of music

The difficulty over the last 18 months is that people haven't been able to come together because of the pandemic. It's all well and good playing, having a practice on your own. But it's nothing like coming together with other people to make music. That's what it's all about really. It is like building this isn't it. You look at building this thing. 'Why? Why do they do that?' I think there's a social element of bell ringing as well. It's being able to clang the bell at the right time, and also, that feeling of being a part of something and being an integral part of it and suddenly I feel complete again.

Driving

Yes, driving is very, very important to me. I really enjoy driving. I enjoyed the drive over here to meet with you both, it was only half an hour, but I enjoyed that. Driving keeps you very active as well, doesn't it, because you're looking around, you're needing to concentrate.

Although I can no longer be a driving instructor or an examiner, I still want to keep the driving going. I like the challenge, I like the cut and thrust. You speak to a lot of people, and they say, 'Oh I hate driving in London', but I used to love driving in London, and I used to love the ducking and diving and weaving around and the challenges that presented because that just somehow kept you alive and your mind active.

I now have to renew my license every year, but at the moment the professionals are still happy with the way things are.

In a nutshell

I try very much to continue doing the things that I've always done, and not just the hobbies and that sort of thing. But I try very hard to maintain those things, I have this feeling inside me that if I let it slip, I step back a bit, then I'm not going to be able to get that skill back. And that I'm not starting down that slippery 'Helter Skelter' – because it's very hard to climb back up a 'Helter Skelter'. Easy to slide down, but to climb back up is really hard. So, I'm constantly – sometimes it is the word 'worry'. Yeah, I suppose the word is 'worry' really. I worry that if I give an inch, then, you know, dementia will take a mile from me. And I'm constantly fighting that.

Having given up playing the horn following his cardiologist's advice, Chris took this essential part of his interests back up following his dementia diagnosis, on the basis that a demise from a heart condition might be preferable to deteriorating with frontotemporal dementia. Now over 10 years later, the importance of playing in a band has in maintaining his mental health and emotional wellbeing shines through in our conversation.

Chris' awareness, observation and analysis of his difficulties in relation to his music playing has long been an example to me of how the principles of cognitive rehabilitation can be used to good effect when coupled with insight into the difficulties and a motivation to persevere with strategies on the one hand and raising awareness in the social environment on the other.

Chris is also one of the people whose diagnosis and profile on cognitive tests might suggest that driving would be out of the question, and in the past would have led clinicians to declare that he has to stop driving. Thankfully, there is now an independent route to establishing driving competence through an annual driving assessment with the DVLA, and there is no doubt his professional life experience as an advanced driver in the police force, a driving instructor and examiner helps to maintain his skills.

I was struck by the image of the Helter Skelter, the constant fight against sliding and how exhausting it must be. Activism and activities seem for Chris to be very much part of the fight against dementia itself and its effects as well as providing moments of feeling alive and complete.

Chris Roberts

Before meeting Chris around a decade ago, I had heard him speak at Dementia Action Alliance and heard about the BBC Panorama television documentary filming his and his wife Jayne's lives using discretely placed CCTV cameras. I had been asked to chair a conference in the 'Dementia 2020' series, a title which was at the time suggesting something in the distant future, and was looking for a co-chair with lived experience. Chris kindly agreed at the time but before the date of the conference, he had a stroke and thought about 'retiring' from his more public activities. The airing of the programme fell only a few days before the conference and I spoke with Jayne about my concerns of what it might be like for him to take part in this very public event so soon after having some of his difficulties shown on television to a wide audience. She suggested we meet up to talk on the day before the conference so that Chris and I could discuss in person, and this resulted not only in the fabulous experience of sharing the event, but also a lasting friendship within and outside of dementia-related activities.

Given my interest in all things European, and dementia politics and policies in particular, it has been especially fascinating to see Chris' activism in the European Dementia Working Group and his addresses to the European Parliament, but I am also very grateful to Chris and Jayne for their support at the launch of the BPS Dementia Guidance papers in Wales, and continue to follow Chris' Facebook page on dementia information and support as one of the longest running peer support initiatives.

Loss of driving licence and motorbikes

Dementia interfered with my driving, it interfered with my biggest interest, which was motorcycles. You know, if you can't ride a motorcycle, what is the point of having one? I haven't got one now, it's a massive hole in my life when you've had one forever! Also, then you don't see all your motorcycle buddies or your friends anymore.

Jayne: 'That really brought it home how he was feeling about the loss of the licence, that rite of passage into, you know, masculine adulthood'.

That really was my biggest interest. I had a motorcycle publication shop. I built motorcycles! And now I couldn't even have a drive on private land or on a campsite, not having a licence anymore, because I knew that if I drove even once again or rode a motorcycle again I would do it again and again.

Losing DIY skills

I started to slowly lose my do-it-yourself skills, my maintenance skills. The more I lost that, it was so frustrating, because I had to employ tradesmen to do what I could've done myself for a fraction of the price. That was so frustrating and so annoying, especially when I don't like spending money anyway. And they never did it the way I wanted it done, because it's hard, they don't have the same investment, and they don't know what's in my head or how I wanted things to look. Then the knock-on effect of that was ... depression, I suppose, and what I was doing to the bank of mum and dad. I wasn't contributing anymore financially.

We've got a property rental portfolio. Jayne runs the financial side and paperwork of the business and I used to do all the maintenance. So, when you're maintaining 19 properties and then you're not so good anymore, it's a huge, huge bill that wasn't there before and the finances aren't so good anyway if you start to slow down and not work anymore. I've been self-employed my whole life. So, I was very adverse to any benefits or anything like that because I've never been on them before, I didn't know what to apply for. You don't know what you don't know. So those two things had a massive effect on my life.

So progressively it's had a massive effect. I think it was because the isolation, the not doing so much, I would spend days not even going on my iPad where I was permanently on it before. I would just go in the garden and just use my chainsaw and my axes, and the lawn would get mowed several times a day. But I was nearly turning around and talking to people with machinery in my hands and for a while I just stopped doing gardening at all. Because it was so dangerous, I just thought the best thing to do was stop.

I just stopped everything, that's all I've done. I just absolutely isolated myself. I left everything I was involved in, completely.

Filling the void

Meeting peers really helped, and people like yourself, you know. Yourselves, both of you. When I got involved I thought I was becoming a bit of an expert now in my own dimension, so what can I do with that, because I couldn't do anything else properly anymore. So I thought, well, that's got to be a positive. I was looking around for something to do with using the knowledge I had about my own dementia, which I had researched. I had knowledge!

Advocacy

That filled a massive void in my life, being able to get out and talk about something that I knew from experience plus what I researched. How can you cope with a life-changing illness if you don't understand it? I had a lot of knowledge about it because I had nothing else to do but read and google. That's really changed my life and filled the void and from there then led to going to peer support groups which I never, never agreed to before because who wants to sit with a load of people with dementia?'

The camper van

Not working, the camper van filled a massive void. It also got us out of the house. Now being out of this surrounding that I'm sat in, where I can't find my tools properly and I'm sat looking at all the obstacles. When we go away in the van, I don't have to mow the grass, I don't have to do any maintenance or don't feel like doing any maintenance anyway.

I do want to have time in my motorhome, I thoroughly enjoy going away. I don't want to be in the house anymore. I actually sleep in the van a lot on the drive … because I find it's so comfortable and relaxing. It's so dementia-friendly, I can immediately sit in my chair which looks at the whole van, this little one room and I can see anything I need. You know and it's great.

There's no obstacles or hurdles. I can see everything, where everything is, right from where I am sitting. You can't lose anything. There's nothing to worry about, apart from someone bringing me food, obviously.

New tools

And now I've discovered cordless, fantastic. I didn't have to mess about and try and work out extension leads and how many it would take me, you know, and because the battery runs out after 30 minutes or whatever, you have to stop and have a rest, which was good because I also have lung disease so that was good for that as well. And if I don't get so tired, because of my emphysema, then it doesn't affect my dementia so much either.

In a nutshell

Jayne: 'I believe he recovered as well as he did from the stroke because of all the advocacy work he was doing. Because he had to go out and he had to do the walking. He had to do the talking. And you know, if it had gone wrong, we would just get a taxi home. So I think the advocacy work definitely helped'.

Yeah, I just want to do it, I've always had this feeling that I'm not going to be able to do it forever, and anyway, who wants to talk about dementia forever? I've always said, I'm not going to do it forever, and I want to spend time in our motorhome …

While I had heard Chris speak about the difficulties of living with dementia before, it was usually in the context of his thoughts about projects, peer support and policy, his ideas on how things could be better, the experience of living with dementia improved. Here he described in some depth and detail the struggles of adjusting and the impact of losing skills, occupations, activities and their associated social life and contribution to identity.

What helped in that process besides Jayne's special approach to the 'carer' role? Chris hints at his determination to gain knowledge and understanding of his diagnosis, which predated the discovery of activism and peer support, and was essentially self-organised and self-taught, giving him the tools for the Facebook support group, activism and policy work.

Dianne Campbell

I first met Dianne around 10 years ago, when she gave a presentation on her role as a peers support worker at an early event on examples of working with experts by experience in dementia services. Subsequently, our paths crossed repeatedly at the Dementia Action Alliance, the IDEAL project advisory group, and we spent some particularly memorable times together at the Alzheimer's International Congress in Budapest.

Activism

I think the first dementia project that set up in London, it was just me. That is up and running for a couple of years now. The second attachment for me was a project with my church. Then we tried to set up quite a few more in Brent. Yeah, so the first one was when I set it up in London. I don't think people know where to go to really, to get out of their house to talk, explain themselves, what is really going on in their brain or how to express themselves. So, we set up the groups. I think the second one was with Rachel. Short Rachel. Philly was there as well. [Rachel and Philly are members of the DEEP team supporting people with dementia in setting up new groups.] I don't remember the other young lady.

Because I do volunteer work, sometimes I just want to go home and rest. While as you finish, you just want to go home, but sometime my head is so tired. I don't want to hear any noise at all. I just want to go home and chill. It's not because I don't live with anybody but because I'm tired and I just want some quietness around me.

I used to say 'yes' to everything, but now as I get older, I just say 'nope'. 'No'. I also do a lot of voluntary work for the British Heart Foundation. I realised that's okay, every month or every 2 months they want me to do something – and I just said, 'no'. 'No, no, no'. I think they were kind of a bit shocked when I said 'no', because people maybe who know me and that I go to so many places out-of-London, they say 'Diane, I saw your picture!' I thought okay, I just wasn't up to do it.

Travelling

Apart from me doing my voluntary work at the moment, I like to travel. I like to travel but for a couple of years the pandemic shut me down. So, I thought getting up back on my feet to travel, I love it!

I think because I travel with friends, that kind of makes it easier. What I normally do, I try and put things in place. If I travel by myself, I make sure that things are in place. I know some people don't want to travel by themselves because they're scared and whatever, but travelling is so enjoyable.

In a nutshell

I would still love to go and do something. But what I did, I threw myself into voluntary. Because I think there is so much there for me to do and I give it my all. We did a food aid project. I still run the dementia group, though, with the closing down in the pandemic, we are trying to get things up and running for the dementia club again at the moment. With that, with the food aid that I get involved with at my church, it gave me a buzz because I like it. I like it, but as I said, things changed for me and I started to say no.

Having heard so often from people who find travelling with dementia particularly demanding, stressful and disorientating, and their coping by maintaining routines and a stable environment, it was good to be reminded of a very different perspective and Diane's continued enjoyment of travelling.

Like others of the Fifteen in our conversations, Diane describes the buzz and excitement of volunteering and activism activities, but also how demanding and tiring this can turn out to be in the long term. She links her increased ability and confidence in saying no to requests to having grown older, and indeed reaching the age at which people who do not live with dementia expect to retire.

Frances Isaacs

Frances is one of the Fifteen I had not met before. I had, however, spoken with people with dementia who took part in one of her online painting courses during and after the pandemic, and I admired her talent of awakening an enthusiasm for a creative activity some people had never previously considered.

Teaching art

I had always decided that in retirement, I would follow the hobbies that I had, until I got bored. I've always been keen on painting, but the pleasure for me is in handing on the skills. And the joy, the total joy of seeing other people who never thought they could do it, get the same pleasure and discover that the new way of seeing things, and perceiving the perception that you get, that you never thought you would have. This for me is the total joy of it.

Practising and adjusting art

I have changed, I have changed my style quite a lot. My eyesight has gone really horrible. And I just had new glasses so I can see a hell of a lot better, but for a long time I really haven't been able to see properly and consequently my art has become much more about colour and feeling and expression than actual detail. Actually, I've found huge pleasure from that. I no longer stress over it if some days it doesn't look like a daisy – so long as it kind of feels like a daisy, it'll do.

Frances describes the adjustments she needed to make to her approach to her own painting in order to be able to continue to find pleasure and enjoyment in this activity. It mirrored conversations I have had with other artists who needed to adjust to living with dementia, who had found that moving from a realist approach to an impressionist, expressionist or abstract framework opened new possibilities and avenues for their art.

Her enthusiasm for and enjoyment of teaching art, and especially her focus on artistic perception, give a glimpse of the reasons behind her ability to inspire and enthuse others.

Gail Gregory

I had heard Gail speak about young-onset dementia in an online event and had seen some of her YouTube videos of her craft activities which I thought would be really helpful in encouraging and inspiring others. I was looking forward to hearing more from her on the subject of meaningful occupation.

Negative messages at diagnosis

Embroidering teddy bears, so crafting and things like that has always been a big part of my life. When I was diagnosed, I was sort of told that I wouldn't be able to carry on doing the things that I was doing now, to take things easy.

Discovering new occupations

When I got my diagnosis, I found out that I could write poetry, but I could only write poetry if there was something bothering me. If I'd had a bad experience, I found that writing things down, it was like a release; so poetry become like a release for me. The 'Time and Place' poetry project obviously helped a lot of people because we found out about all the different types of poetry. That was absolutely wonderful because it was something that I wanted to look deeper into and it just gave me that experience, it was brilliant.

Adjusting loved occupations

I suppose you go into a sort of depression, because you believe that you can't do things anymore, well I did anyway. And so for me, I stopped doing the crafting, and I stopped doing the things which I loved because I believed that I wouldn't be able to do them, that I'd forget how to do them.

But then I started thinking, well surely there's a way that I can carry on doing things by looking for little sorts of things to help me. So in my card-making, for instance, I used to make a card and make notes as I was making the card …

The challenge in doing things is that you can do it one day, and the next day it just doesn't happen. You've forgotten little pieces of what you should be doing and I think this is where I find the strategies of writing things down, recording things, making notes to help me because I know that tomorrow I might go in to make a card that I could make today, but tomorrow I wouldn't have a clue, it'll just be a blank piece of paper.

I didn't used to keep calm. It used to really annoy me and I used to get quite angry, but now I suppose I've learnt to live with the fact that this is how it is, and it's no good getting angry, and it's no good getting all frustrated. This is why I made the notes because it was easier and it kept me calmer to be able to do things.

Me with my crafts, I started making fairy houses because the weather was glorious, so I started making fairy houses. People were asking me how I'd made them, so I did little recordings on YouTube, which was quite frustrating at the time because I had never used YouTube before. Again it's something new that I've learnt to do. It took time, but I got there, and I think that's what it's all about. It's trying new things, doing things slowly.

In a nutshell

I'm not as quick as I used to be, but I can still do it, and that's the important thing, is to keep doing things. We're not going to pick things up straight away, but we can still learn new things, and it's all about learning.

Watching one of Gail's YouTube videos it is hard to imagine her giving up all her crafting activities following a disheartening diagnosis process, but not surprising that this loss would lead to depression. It seems more due to her irrepressible spirit than help from services that she was able to move on to discovering new occupations and rediscover old ones while incorporating strategies and providing heartening ambassadorial pieces for the uses of cognitive rehabilitation in dementia.

George Rook

Since I lack Keith's meticulous records, I am not sure when and where I first met George. I had read some of his blog posts, heard him speak at dementia-related conferences and DEEP events, and had some brief conversations over break-time coffees. He struck me as a natural political operator with an eloquence well suited to making the voices of people with dementia heard in the world of health and social care policy.

Preface

I always preface this sort of comment or discussion with, because, mine is, like yours, young-onset dementia rather than being diagnosed in my 80s, therefore we are in a sense in a different place in our lives anyway, so we are probably more open to doing things that are new to us, and probably physically more able to do them as well.

On the other hand, having dementia and all panoply of acquaintances, and knowledge of dementia that's come my way now, all that I've found, have opened my mind to possibilities that I never thought of before.

Post-diagnosis

I like gardening, I have got a big garden and I like the natural world, and photography. I suppose I just pottered around for some time.

I increasingly turned to blogging because I enjoy writing. So I started to blog about living with dementia.

Discovering activism

At the same time, I was introduced through Chris Mason at the University of Bradford to the DEEP network and its people, and that's where I found what I had begun now as my occupation. It is very much to do with raising awareness, trying to improve support and care, supporting Dementia UK, to get more Admiral Nurses.

DEEP stuff really is incredibly important. I'm really happy working with it, doing jobs and things.

Discovering creativity

During the pandemic, it was just whittling at the time, just sort of making whistles and things, and I gradually got into that. I taught myself to carve and use various tools, and did that last year. I'm still doing it, but less so now because I've now started to learn to paint, like Keith with Frannie [Frances' online course, see above]. I tell you what, some days I think, shall I craft, carve, or shall I paint and it takes hours to think, 'oh, which one shall I do', and then I think about the painting all bloody night, because I can't get it out of my head!

So that, the artistic bit, that is the bit I would have never imagined, because, you know, I had always been written off and written myself off as not having any sort of artistic creativity.

Effects of dementia

I can have a day when I just can't, just don't want to do anything. I could still paint or carve on those days, but I certainly can't do the garden. I don't do anything with any great determination on those days, I suppose you might say. I think that's the handicap. I do have a number of physical illnesses that mean I get tired very quickly, but the ... the brain disease is on top of that and when it kicks in for one reason or another, who knows why, you just can't or don't want to do anything.

Adjusting activism

Um, I have chosen to exclude myself from some of the stuff I used to do because, oh maybe, just maybe that is a little bit due to dementia, but it's mainly due to COVID-19, which helped make my mind up, in a sense, you know. Lots of us are umming and ahhing about whether it's worth going to this committee or that committee.

In a nutshell

So, I'm not sitting here thinking, day after day, I wish I could do this, I wish I could do that, because actually anything I wish I could do, I'm doing.

Reading George's comments on his discovery of painting doesn't seem to convey the sheer excitement and joy I remember him expressing in our conversation about this new found occupation. Frances' online painting course and George's response to it is an example of people with dementia using the pandemic-related restrictions as an opportunity. In addition, George describes the break from usual activism as helpful in reappraising which meeting or committee is really worth attending, and when to engage in other occupations.

Jennifer Bute

Having read some of her online materials and parts of her book, I had never met Jennifer before our online conversation. Knowing about her deeply held Christian faith, I had recommended and used some of her writing in the South East Spirituality and Dementia Group, now many years ago. Having met Dr Daphne Wallace and spoken with her about her approach to living with dementia on the background of her professional experience, I was also curious about Jennifer's ways of thinking about or using her professional experience.

Continuity post-diagnosis

Certainly, dementia has focused attachments for me. I've always cared about people and tried to help everyone make the most out of their particular situation, everyone is different. That hasn't changed; I've always tried to educate and explain things and we do retain some skills from the past, so I do think that is one skill that I still have.

I used to educate, of course, and I used to write educational literature leaflets and things like that, so when I first got the diagnosis, I would write, because there was nothing in those days, nothing!

Previous experience of dementia

Yes, but you see, we learn! When my father had dementia, that was many years ago. He was very intelligent, so I thought I could get things going with him again logically, and of course it was a complete waste of time, because logic does not work, does it! Nowadays, I would've used memories and photos and explored his interests. He was interested in books and stamps and people but I didn't understand that. I did make a book of people over his life time, all in chronological order, and each morning he would read this book from cover to cover, because that enabled to remind him who he was.

The dementia blog posts

I started writing leaflets and that was how I got involved with education, because the Alzheimer's Society picked that up and that's how it all began. It was most odd wanting me to go and talk about it! Well, I wasn't just going to talk about leaflets, was I, so that's how it all began. But the blogs have only happened since I was making educational videos. My son is brilliant, he makes the films and he runs my website and he's helped me. He says you need to do it regularly and a few more educational leaflets every year. Oh, and videos which are free and used all around the country, even in medical schools apparently. That led to people asking me questions all the time and I became a bit overwhelmed with it all, so the easiest thing was to say, 'well, read my blog!' So in a sense it all started to contain the avalanche of questions.

Living in a care setting

I have the privilege of living in a dementia inclusive village, where I have the opportunity to learn to walk the path with many others. I've been here for 10 years and I know what works and what doesn't work. There are almost 200 of us here, I guess at different stages, and everyone is different. I mean we are all here until we die. Well, we are all going to die one day, but it's wonderful, it is absolutely wonderful! You see, I can see what makes a difference, so I do more of that, and if it doesn't work, then I need to alter it to find something different or better. I am learning, learning, learning all the time.

Using Alexa

Alexa helps me with taking my medication because I live by myself and because now I'm getting worse about that, it checks on me: did you actually take it? It reminds me to have a meal, and it reads books to me, because I can't read easily anymore unless I know what it says. It is wonderful. I couldn't live without it anymore.

Running groups

I run my memory groups here. I was speaking to a conference at the Excel Centre and heard Professor Karishima speaking and I thought, crumbs, if what he says is true, why aren't we doing it and I've had the privilege of learning over these 10 years what works and what doesn't work so the group has grown and grown. I keep it on my computer, it's my backup brain. I keep statistics and I think over the years over a hundred people have been and gone. Now I've got 40 people still on my list who want to come. It was costing me a fortune, but the management here pay for it all now, because they have seen the differences made to the community.

Yes, I have help now, they do it for me. I don't have to get out my CDs and search for things, it's wonderful! I also help other people to understand that. We used to have musicians, coming in to help us and I'd see people wake up and light up. If I want to help someone talk again who stopped talking, you know, I'll go after the music sessions – I used to go to them, because that was a good time to do it, but of course, that's all finished at the moment with COVID-19.

Reining in activism

I like to put myself out for other people, I mean with all the talks and lectures I was doing, there were so many at one stage that my family put a limit on the number I was allowed to do. Before COVID-19, I was being asked up and down the country. You know how it is, Keith, don't you. We've been to many together and been on many others, lecturing and talking. But with COVID-19 that has got worse, because with Zoom I had two on one day once. It's not good, and that has been more difficult. Of course, my family aren't aware of that, are they, so I have to be careful, and I did turn two down recently.

In a nutshell

I keep a record of what helps me, and each week I do the blog. Not about me, enough people are doing that, but about what I've learnt, with a story to help others understand. And people are amazed, and they're so grateful ... so that helps me, doesn't it, you know it's not just me helping other people, it helps me as well.

Building on previous experience with dementia in the family and on professional experience in education and awareness-raising has helped and informed Jennifer's activities in this area. She gives us some positive examples of a care setting that provides person-centred support, and her use of technology in maintaining independence. She is not the first to mention the overload that can be caused by demand for input from activists, and the need to balance this to maintain wellbeing.

Julie Hayden

Before meeting Julie online, I had not met her in person, but had seen some of her online posts and comments, admiring her outspoken advocacy and her responses to the poor use of language.

From working to diagnosis and activism

I have had two previous professions. Way back I used to be a nurse, that was a long time ago, and my last profession was as a social worker.

It took about 5 years for me to be diagnosed, so with the diagnosis, at last I found out what's going on. I finally, you know, identified the enemy – and then you can deal with it.

One thing that diagnosis gave me was then a focus for how to carry on and get involved in the activism. I felt really written off by society, so activism opened up so many avenues, so many options in life. Now I feel that I have purpose, because this is work that I can get involved in and so many different ranges from peer support to research, to being involved in education.

The benefits of activism

With the dementia, sometimes it is going to a complete dip and being fully critical of myself, and then another day I can think: you know what, you just gotta deal with it and you've just gotta accept it. And it helps, the work helps, because especially living on my own, I need the outside focus. That helps you keep a balance in life, it helps you keep more of a reality check if you've also got to concentrate on other people.

Balancing activism

I said to Keith, getting involved in the poetry and painting projects was really just about that activism work, because with living alone and not having family living nearby, my life just became about that work since lockdown. I have actually become a bit lost for a while, so getting involved in the creative side, art and poetry, which I had never drawn or painted before, never composed poetry before, it's kind of given me a bit of time to invest in me as well.

In a nutshell

The benefits to me of the creative projects are, I think, if you are just out there concentrating on the work, and it's brilliant to just be involved in as much as you can on the activism side, but by … but hopefully by investing in creativity now starts to make me more sustainable with the activism side. As we are sat together and out and about more, that creates more of a work/life balance than I actually had before.

With ready access to activism opportunities post-diagnosis, this worked well for Julie in finding purpose. The pandemic and participation in creative arts projects provided a break from the very busy routine, and new ways of balancing activism with self-care activities.

Keith Day (Cam)

I had met Cam at several local Dementia Action Alliance events where he spoke both movingly and inspirationally about the impact of dementia and his efforts to adjust and make the best of his strengths.

Hobbies

I like to keep myself occupied, I like to do cross stitch and also I do needle felt, just things to pass the time, you know?

Activism

It was the best thing I did when I started to get interested in things this year, I joined 3 Nations and I do a lot of work now with the NHS and with the Pathfinders Group, Dementia Diaries, Dementia Voices, you know, so I help all of them.

What we are hoping to do with the Pathfinders, now the new term has started, we are hoping to get into schools and old people's homes, not to the residents but certainly to the staff, and let's get them aware of the things that can happen with dementia.

Impact and church activity

I'm not able to do a lot of things I could do.

And obviously, we go to church. We are very into the church itself. In the middle of the week we do a house group that myself and my wife run. I don't preach now, but I still went over to Uganda to work with the children and everything, it didn't matter.

Like others, Cam described the discovery and particular importance of activism in a portfolio of meaningful occupation alongside more traditional hobbies. While faith communities can struggle to adapt appropriately when active members are living with dementia, it was good to hear Cam describe a successful change in activities and continuing with those he is able to pursue.

Masood Ahmed Qureshi (Maq)

I had not met Maq before our Zoom meeting, but seen him from afar at a conference and was aware of his work in the Asian community, especially at a time when there was very little of this happening in the UK. I was also aware of his diagnosis of frontotemporal dementia and looking forward to meeting another person who is challenging the perceived trajectory of this particular form of dementia.

Ending work

After the diagnosis, I gave up my job as an accountant because I thought that I cannot give it 100 per cent. I don't know whether it's the condition or the thought of knowing that you've got a condition of that nature. I am still not sure to be honest, but I thought that I couldn't be fair to my clients, hence I gave up the job.

Community work pre- and post-diagnosis

I belonged to quite a lot of organisations within the Asian community dealing with some of the issues that Asian people have, language being the biggest issue. Of course, I assisted the police and the courts and the National Health Service, even hospitals. That was basically what kept me busy. You know, dementia has taken a lot away from me. It has taken the ability to translate away from me – to a certain extent, but not fully.

I still do community work, and that was the second thing that actually kept me busy, because there was a lot of need for it in them days. That was in a sense a full-time job, you know, although on a voluntary basis. It kept me busy and you know you get a boost from something like that. The satisfaction you get and the comments that people make: 'we couldn't have done that without you' and 'glad you were here' and 'you made life easier for us' and all that stuff – you can't put any money on it!

Adjusting community work

It was of such a nature that I didn't have 'no' in my dictionary. Whenever anybody wanted something, I was there and did it. It came to a stage after the diagnosis where I felt that I needed some me time as well, and instead of going out to per-form all those community duties that are there, I did it from home. I would rather have them coming here and I would sit in front of them and write or translate.

Moving online

I have found that they listen to me, and if I do advise something, you know, they actually take that on board and appreciate it! I mean, I've spoken to about 3,000 people since the lockdown. I belong to 11 different organisations and do Zoom sessions. I do an average of 15 zooms a week. I've got contacts every-where and if I'm not on one of the meetings I get a phone call saying, 'where are you, we're missing you, we want you'! So I believe that in a sense demen-tia, people with dementia have made a star out of me!

Previous community work in the Asian community has merged quite seamlessly into dementia awareness-raising and activism for Maq and has continued to pro-vide meaning, purpose and satisfaction. His is also an example of successfully moving online and embracing the changes brought about by the pandemic.

Nigel Hullah

I have seen Nigel in action with the 3 Nations Dementia Working Group and have lasting memories of a fascinating hour spent sitting in the sunshine with him outside the venue of a Birmingham Young Onset Dementia Conference, discussing human rights and dementia policy.

Pre-diagnosis

I've always had demanding roles, whether it's been in the private, charity or statutory sector. I fed off pressure. I loved it and, to a certain extent, I inject that into my life now. I like to feel I'm in a job. You know, not just another number, but I'm actually having an impact. When I worked for IBM, for instance as a business auditor, that was a huge impact. That meant long hours, and it meant attention to detail. I have still got attention to detail. It's like OCD actually. And I've always had it in my life. I've always had to be the best at whatever I do, which put huge demands on myself and I wasn't always the best ...

Post-diagnosis

I think when you are first diagnosed, it's the loss of confidence and many, many things you have to relearn. My first 6 months post-diagnosis were awful. I mean, I just locked myself away. I didn't engage with anybody. And then these very annoying ladies knocked on my door from the occupational therapy department and kind of forced me on a track. There is a tendency to second-guess everything you're doing. I call it the doorstep challenge. You know, my next-door neighbour goes mad with me because whenever we go out together, she has to wait 5 minutes while I check all the doors in the house, that I've locked them. Even though I've got an app to tell me I haven't, I still do it physically.

Managing activism

I'm quite lucky because I can pick and choose, you know, and it's where I'm accepted for who I am.

Oh, now, well, I mean, you get thrust in the limelight, you know the way it goes, Keith. I mean, sometimes you wouldn't be able to, blimey, ask me to talk just a little bit. Sometimes you have to say, 'no, I'm not, I'm not the person for that'.

Remaining well

If you have any psychological weaknesses, and we all we've all got them, they get set off. They do take different kinds of handling. You have to sleep well; you have to eat well. You have to have something to look forward to all the time. So, it's very important that you make sure that your days are full, and as full as you want them to be, because you can do too much as well and be no use to anybody. But, I mean, I'm a firm believer in sitting down, shutting everything off. Like I did yesterday, I shut everything off for a time.

For an hour of each day, minimum, I do something I really enjoy. Otherwise, you tend to lose focus or perspective. Or, I sit down and either keep a journal, keep a diary, read a book, listen to a play off the television, or listen to a play on the radio. I take a great deal of pleasure from radio plays on BBC Radio Four.

Recovery from the impact of a young-onset dementia diagnosis in the middle of a high-powered professional career was facilitated by *'the annoying ladies from the OT department'*, and I was relieved to hear of an example of services playing an active part in the process.

We heard again of the benefits and the strains of activism, and the importance of developing other enjoyable and satisfying occupations to balance the demands.

Tracey Shorthouse

As another Kent resident, I first met Tracey when she joined the SUNshiners DEEP group in Folkestone, and subsequently at many events by local and National Dementia Action Alliance, as well as enjoying her blog and Facebook posts, and often recommending her poetry publication to students.

Loss of job / vocation

The nurse role never leaves me, ever, ever ... What I miss about nursing more, I think, is chatting to different people, and finding out about their lives.

Recovery and diagnosis

I used to do a lot of writing, used to do it a lot. I wrote a poetry book, only because I wrote poems in a way to express myself. I couldn't really talk about it. I didn't really have anyone to talk to after my diagnosis and I had all these things in my head, all the time, because my dementia was quite bad when I was first diagnosed, it really was, and then the tablets kicked in and then I've got not too bad.

New activities

But I do a lot more different things now. I do jigsaw puzzles, I've learnt new skills, I've learnt how to macrame. I've learnt how to loom it, I go swimming in the sea now.

Gardening in the summer and the rest are usually done in winter when I can't get into the garden, so I'll do a jigsaw, I'll have a break, and all the arty, crafty stuff is all done in the winter. Summer is definitely swimming. As well as sometimes walking and gardening, those three things.

Blog and activism

I usually transfer things over on my blog, or sometimes I'll print off photos somehow and then put them in a photograph album, and then put down dates and where I was.

I thought, I could write a blog, because I like writing things down just for me. I just utilised it every day. But then I can't always, my brain doesn't always work every day, so it's about once a week now, and I write about what I've been up to, how I felt, if it's been stressful. I like using public transport, that's stressful, lots of people around me is stressful. And then with that, I help other people who follow me along with health officials who follow me. My parents and my family read it and then they might just send me a text saying, 'Oh, are you alright?', because I don't really talk to them about how I really feel and all that.

In a nutshell

I do lots of things, different things now. It's like having dementia has opened my horizons because of what I can do, rather than what I can't do.

The loss of her vocation as a nurse often shines through Tracey's talks, and yet her enthusiasm for all the occupations and activities she has discovered since this loss is so heartening as an example of the possibilities for living well with a dementia diagnosis. As a closing sentence for a chapter on occupation and dementia, I feel something Tracey said is a particularly suitable one:

It's like having dementia has opened my horizons because of what I can do, rather than what I can't do.

So what learning can we take from the Fifteen?

These interviews provided a rich and varied account of how dementia impacts on a person's occupation and activities. We reflect here on what we can generalise for others living with dementia and those who support them.

From the point of view of someone living with dementia:

- Negative messages during the diagnosis process and experiences of mistakes or difficulties can lead to people with dementia giving up on hobbies and favoured activities, which can add to a vicious cycle of less enjoyment and increased depression after a dementia diagnosis.
- Having to give up working and losing their driving license are major issues for younger people with dementia, but there are many examples of managing these transitions and finding worthwhile and practical alternatives.
- People with dementia develop strategies, at times with support from services or with the help of peer support, that allow them to continue with favourite activities.
- Many people with dementia discover new activities and meaningful occupations, often in areas that they had never considered before. The experience of enjoyment and learning of new skills can lead to a positive feedback loop of successes, growing confidence and better wellbeing.

- Activism in dementia awareness-raising and service improvement can become an occupation that has many helpful side effects, such as meeting others with dementia, positive feedback on making an important contribution, and a sense of taking charge of one's condition. It can also become stressful and overwhelming, and activists need to find a balance with time for relaxation and rest to maintain wellbeing.

There are also implications for those who provide professional support and care for persons living with dementia. For them, the main take-away messages are:

- As occupational therapists know, meaningful occupation is essential for good mental health, and equally important for a good quality of life with a dementia.
- Services and professionals need to pay attention to the activities and occupations of people assessed in memory clinics, and provide encouragement and assistance with building strategies to continue with valued activities.
- People with dementia can and do take up new interests and activities, and services and professionals need to encourage this with a positive attitude and person-centred programmes of support.
- Supporting people with dementia into roles of awareness-raising in activism can be a good use of resources, but care needs to be taken to adequately support people with dementia in these roles.

9 Inclusion

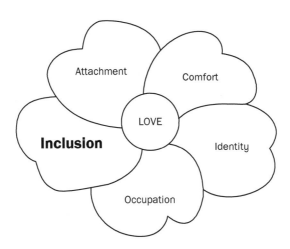

You come to see me
But you don't see me
We have a conversation
But you don't hear me
And I've been thinking if you don't hear me
How you gonna know what I'm thinking

Your eyes fixed on me
Sometimes you smile
I always smile
And I wonder if you know why

But if you don't hear me when I'm speaking
How you gonna know what I'm thinking
And if you can't hear me when I'm calling
How you gonna know that I'm falling

And though I no longer dance beneath quiet skies
Nor run across open fields
I wonder if you'd believe
The mountains I still climb

– Ronald Ferguson

The Fifteen on Inclusion – narrated by Keith Oliver

Having previously written at some length in Chapter 6 about my views on inclusion in the context of my experience of living with dementia and what Kitwood said about the subject, I would like now to turn to the conversations and how inclusion was expressed by the Fifteen. Each conversation understandably began with pleasantries about how the person was feeling, and this was genuine and sincere. For me, sometimes when I don't feel so good I am mindful of not wanting to moan, as this might draw to a close or bring a change of direction in an exchange. I will smile, thank the person for enquiring and then move on to talk about something else.

Kitwood identified how people with dementia often see their social life drift away. In discussions with the Fifteen, this generated a wide range of responses. Indeed, each individual suggested that although they each enjoyed a healthy social life, there were times when clearly aspects of malignant social psychology reared their ugly head to damage the quality of the inclusive experience. At times like this they told us, they felt excluded rather than included in a relationship, a group or an activity. While Reinhard and I acknowledged and noted these negative experiences, some of which feature in this chapter, our main focus was on how people felt included and what were the benefits and challenges each person associated with this, helping us to see any overlaps with others.

In what follows, the words of the Fifteen are italicised to help distinguish them from Keith's commentary.

Agnes Houston

Included in the community

Agnes illustrates the transition here from being strongly involved and included solely within a real, local community to being connected virtually, and is the one person who mentioned dementia-friendly communities.

I have always done things for the community. I ran a wee club for men that have retired – dances and things like that, when I was a member of the community group. I was involved in the community and was a more active person like that.

Yeah, well, what happened was I was interviewed about something. It was about dementia-friendly communities. They were talking about your local community. I said 'no, my community is virtual, you know'. I have a strong attachment to a virtual community. Some people I've never met, other than to the virtual screen, and, you know, you can chat to someone any time of night. So, depending on where they are in the world, you're never alone. I think it's a much more inclusive community.

Included in the family

It is within the family that people with dementia most wish and need to be included, although for many this is not always the case. The challenges that dementia often present with are often most apparent within a family setting, which can put pressure on relationships.

I do have a problem with information overload, sensory overload. So I could not go to family gatherings because of noise pollution and because of sensitive overload and too many loud family gatherings – you know, crosstalk and things like that. Now through knowledge, and through getting that out, I am more aware of 'Agnes'. I know what my triggers are. My family are now more accepting of 'Agnes'; so that 'Agnes' can come to a celebration, a christening, a party or whatever. But it will be on Agnes's terms, and thankfully they don't take it to heart. So, there's been a maturity in a relationship now, but it's taken a lot of years to get there.

Included with others living with dementia

Almost all of the Fifteen spoke at length positively about feeling well included within the DEEP network – before, during and since the pandemic. If anything, COVID-19 has strengthened these bonds by uniting people virtually more frequently than would otherwise have been the case what with meetings involving travel and expense. I knew Agnes before COVID-19 and our friendship has been maintained virtually, although she says her conversations extend beyond those that are dementia-focused.

I was so glad to see you Keith plus Chris and Jayne coming out of the woodwork, and I thought, 'Thank God! Pass the baton on, it's now time for my creative juices to flow'.

Well, yes, we've got the DEEP groups, right? Then you've got other communities that are out there that you can engage with, you know. It's not all about dementia, like you can engage with them, chatting about maybe art, maybe other things, you know.

Included by professionals

There are few, if any, people as well placed as Agnes to comment upon the changes which have taken place over the past 15 years to enable people with dementia to be better included in dementia care. I'm in complete agreement with Agnes here in describing how people should be included, and I relate very much to the positive but also negative perspectives she outlines.

Whoever's doing the conference – maybe it's run by people with dementia. I think we're going to have 'what is the etiquette here?' and have a conversation with people with dementia saying, 'How do you feel about this? What do you feel as you? Where do you stand on this?' Yeah, I think that's changing. I really think that's slowly changing now. At the beginning, when I started out it was … they take you there, they don't care how you get there, they don't care anything about you. Now, there's more care and more thought behind it. That comes from, if you don't show what your needs are, how can they be met? You know, it's like a married couple. If something annoys you, and you don't tell them, and then suddenly there's a big fight, and they say, 'But you never said that … [laughs] … before'. So, I think activism now – and I think it's coming through the DEEP movement. Collectively, in a kind way, they're saying, 'Yes, delighted to come to this event. If you provide these things, it's certain that Keith or Agnes will attend'. Now, Keith's needs would be different from Agnes' needs, so we put our needs down, and that is that. If they don't provide that, then they're being disrespectful; we send an email telling them why we won't be back. I think it needs to be like a healthy marriage, there needs to be open communication and respect, and the respect goes both ways. It's not, 'I've got dementia, and I expect you to be respectful of me'. But I have to be respectful of the university that I'm working with and the boundaries that they have to work under, the rules they have to work under. I do think we're getting to a healthier relationship. It's not, 'I've got dementia so you must do these things for me.' It's 'Let's have a dialogue. Let's have a respectful, healthy relationship. And then if you can't provide that, you know, let's have a discussion'. So that's where I am. That's where Agnes is now.

Frustrations around being included

Agnes' opening sentence in the paragraph below resonated very well with me, as she said something I have felt for some time. Being included is a two-way thing. With some people, I often feel it is me who has to initiate a conversation that goes beyond the professional, whether that be by text, email or WhatsApp message. Those that are initiated by others tend to be requests of my time or knowledge. I do crave at times that people I see as friends could take a moment to begin a dialogue, whether in person, virtually or simply through an exchange of messages. Facebook is a double-edged sword. I have had no nasty experiences with Facebook but at times I have found that for myself and others with dementia, it is difficult to feel included in the world when others are doing so much more with their lives.

Well, I think the big difficulty for me is always having to make the effort when others don't. There is a sadness, a tremendous sadness comes over me when I think why have I always to make and go the extra mile to attend something. To be included. It would be lovely if someone would do it for me … [laughs] … you know, and say, 'Well, Agnes, we understand and what we've done, is this, this, this, and that, isn't that good?' But no, they get you there. and then you've got to, you know, do it.

Yes, it's very, very rare that someone would ask me to go for a coffee. It's very, very rare. I may do it to them, and say, you know, for no other reason, 'How about meeting for coffee?' You know, but very rare it's reciprocated.

In a nutshell

I do really appreciate you both having this conversation with me, because it's very rare that I get a chance to have this sort of broad conversation, normally it's one topic and you can't stick to that one topic.

There's always somewhere and someone you can reach out to. I never feel alone now because of the virtual window to the world, as I call my iPad.

Chris Maddocks

Included when working

When younger people of working age are diagnosed with dementia, they are often presented with additional difficulties around whether to retire early or to carry on working. If the latter is the preferred or necessary option of the person, then the employer I feel has a duty to make reasonable adjustments to support this. I know from personal experience and from speaking to others such as Chris that this is seldom the reality and the person, rather than being included is often excluded from the workforce.

I really didn't feel that work was on my side, and I was devastated to be quite honest with you, because I had my diagnosis and lost my job all within a 3-month period.

Included by charities

Thankfully for Chris and for many others living with dementia, our energy and remaining skills have been identified and utilised by some of the main dementia charities in the UK, namely the Alzheimer's Society, Innovations in Dementia who host DEEP, Dementia UK and Alzheimer's Research UK. I have often said that the best thing about these charities is primarily the amazing people who work way beyond their job descriptions and who include us in their work so conscientiously.

At the end of a course I attended not too long after coming to terms with my diagnosis, staff from the Alzheimer's Society approached me and said, 'Chris, you speak very well, would you be happy to give some talks for us?' That's how it all started. When I started getting involved in doing things like this, I had some sense of purpose back. I felt included and I started to feel hopeful instead of hopeless.

Included with friends

It is sometimes the case that the friends of a person living with dementia find it difficult for the dementia per se to be a part of any conversation, especially as Chris says when they themselves have experienced at first hand the dementia of a loved one. We asked Chris if there had been times when she felt she was not included in a conversation with friends.

I have yes, and especially from my group of friends who have known me since before dementia. They don't want me to talk about dementia. Sometimes I think, you know that's a big part, well it's a huge part of my life, it is my life now, and sometimes I'd like to talk about it. But I've seen some of the friends have lost parents and things from dementia, so they don't want to hear it. I've found that hard.

I really can see both sides of this and I have often had to bite my tongue and either change the subject or allow someone else to do so in order to maintain harmony.

Included by professionals

Chris shared with us earlier a positive account of being included with a charity. Here she speaks eloquently and passionately about a much less positive experience she had with professionals. Again, this story is similar to many others we were told during our conversations.

When I applied to do voluntary work for the local hospice in Eastbourne, I told them I had dementia and Parkinson's and I thought that's it, they won't take me on, but they did, and I loved it. I used to work on the inpatient unit and take their meals around and chat to them and do other things to help.

I want to be included but I'm finding lots of difficulties as a result of dementia. I've been disappointed with the hospice as I haven't done any voluntary work with them for a while because ... erm, I kept saying, 'I'll do this shift, I'll do that shift' and I was getting, 'oh, we've got it covered'. I had surgery on my foot, so I was out of action for a little while. I rang the HR team and said, 'look, I'm ready to come back', and they said, 'oh, well, we don't think we can have you back in that role because you were forgetting things'. Now I had an agreement with them if there was an issue, they would talk to me there and then about it. I think it was the manager of the department didn't like the fact that I was there and had dementia. They then turned it round and tried to make it all about COVID-19 but I think my dementia was what caused the problem there along with something that they accused me of that hadn't happened. So that was an issue for me.

I had a real problem with my GP in Eastbourne because I didn't feel that she understood my dementia at all. She described me as a difficult case one time and I said, 'well I'm very sorry I've got all these conditions, I haven't asked for them' and she just didn't understand dementia and she kept ... speaking across me ... we then had a long talk about dementia. Her attitude changed totally when she realised that I could actually have a conversation with her. People with dementia really need somebody to give us counselling who's got an understanding of dementia. Because she didn't know what some of the problems that were linked to dementia and what weren't?

I've also been in hospital settings where the doctors have started to speak to Heather about me and not spoken to me. I said, 'you know, I can understand, and you know, you're talking about me, so please talk to me'. I have also had times when professionals have not included me in some things because they feel that maybe I'm not able to do it. Well ask me and let me say 'no', don't make assumptions for me.

In a nutshell

I do miss actually going to talks and meetings. I miss the social interaction. The other thing that we've done is set up a peer support group in Eastbourne which Heather and myself facilitate.

Chris Norris

I do know from our friendship how much Chris benefits from being included in the bands he plays in, and having heard one of them perform – they are excellent! I think Chris articulates extremely well what many of us wish for and fear.

Included with friends

Generally, I still feel accepted within the band, for the person I actually am. And I hope I will still be included when I start being a little bit sort of leery, or what I think is making comical remarks, which possibly … [laughs] … are distracting for other people.

In a nutshell

Well, involvement in things and being included for me is a part of self-esteem, isn't it? Of making you feel that you still have significance. That sounds very self-orientated, really, but it isn't. In life, you've got to feel that you have a purpose, and you have a place to be. That's why I'm so involved in aspects around dementia.

It gets me to meet other people when we are allowed to get out and to travel about.

Chris Roberts

Included in the family

I'd let Jane make thousands of decisions which I would say 'yes' to but now I don't have any involvement in the decision-making. I don't have any involvement in finances, I don't have a phone and I'm not to be trusted with money.

Impact of COVID-19 on one's own feelings of inclusion

Most of this part of the conversation with Chris centred on the impact the COVID-19 pandemic and lockdowns had on him and on his dementia. Chris was then – and still is – the same person I have known as a good friend for the past 9 years but there was a different edge to him and to his answers about being included. Before the pandemic, we both shared many platforms, meetings and bar tables but one sensed this was not going to happen again anytime soon.

During COVID-19, life changed drastically for me. First, I was thrilled not to be doing things so much, because we were so active, and we'd have more time for ourselves. Then I realised we couldn't have time for ourselves because we weren't allowed out anymore. So what turned into a good thing after a couple of months I found it very, very isolating – a very, very lonely place. I don't do well online with lots of others in a social aspect. I'm much better in person. So that the social side of being virtual did not really work for me. I quickly disappeared from that side as well.

The conversation with Chris was one of the last Reinhard and I conducted and took place in September 2021 after some of the worst days of the COVID-19 pandemic had passed, but it clearly was still having a significant impact upon Chris.

As I said, I found it very pleasing in the beginning, but I found it difficult in a short amount of time. It really had an effect on me, a massive effect. I isolated myself I suppose. I'm not very good in social situations anymore. I found it very difficult leaving our house because people weren't obeying the rules. They were coming too close to me. I was getting angry with them, that they just seemed to be bloody annoying people more than they ever did before COVID-19. You know, I didn't suffer fools gladly before, but now everyone seemed stupid, that's how I feel.

Still. I just started to isolate myself more and more and more, apart from going out with Jayne in the van and even then I was happy sat in a van on the road and not mixing with people like we used to. We stopped going out to pubs. We stopped socialising. My eyesight has deteriorated a lot. I don't know why. My thought processes have got worse. My dementia has become such a challenge now. It's really a big barrier now. Before I could live with it. Yes, I struggled to live with my dementia but now it's a really big struggle. I'm being retired from my activist role without me making the choice of retiring. I'm going to find it very difficult to join in again because I'm quite happy on my own now. I went through a phase of missing my friends. And now both of you don't take it personally but I don't miss anybody. Yeah. Then, if I do think I don't miss anyone, I then feel bad about it, which has its own effect, because really I'm a nice person.

I'm just I'm a stay-at-home hermit now.

In a nutshell

Although I cannot remember if Chris and I have met up in person since this conversation took place, we have shared a virtual space a number of times especially since the middle of 2022, so I am unsure whether, if we spoke with

Chris today, would he say the same things. I know he does less with the 3 Nations Dementia Working Group, which he co-founded with Hilary Doxford, but I feel sure he had begun this withdrawal before COVID-19. He is still at the time of writing the co-chair of the European Dementia Working Group and is very active in that role with Jayne's amazing support.

I've always had this feeling that I'm not going to be able to do it forever and who wants to talk about dementia forever? I've always said, I'm not going to do it forever and I do want to have time in my motorhome because I thoroughly enjoy going away.

Dianne Campbell

Included by professionals

Many of us who take on an activist role are initially concerned that, if we say 'no', then whoever has asked us will go away never to return. I used to think this, but experience tells me that while occasionally it does happen, more often than not the invitation will acknowledge the fact that we may be too busy, unwell or simply not attracted to the task. In such cases, when we exclude ourselves, the person who extended the invitation will likely retain our details to approach us again another time with another opportunity. This is especially the case when good relationships are built between the professional and the service user.

I used to say 'yes' to everything, but now as I get older, I just say 'nope'. I also do a lot of work for the British Heart Foundation. I realised that okay, every month or every 2 months they want me to do something – and I just said, 'no'. 'No, no, no'. I think they were kind of a bit shocked when I said 'no'.

Included in the community

There was a lot of laughter during our conversation with Dianne, as there always is, but among the laughter she always is able to get across some serious, thoughtful points such as the following:

People maybe who know me even in places outside of London say, 'Diane, I saw your picture'.
*   I can easily de-stress myself because my phone is always ringing … [laughs] … Yeah, so when people ring me, we always have a laugh.*
*   I love being with people but not all the time … [laughs].*

Frances Isaacs

Included in the community

Within the Federation of my Women's Institute, I was number two, next in line to be number one. I turned that one down thinking, you know, this is not a good idea, because if anything goes pear-shaped, we're all officially trustees and with that comes responsibilities, and to have one that's already been diagnosed with dementia is not a good idea, so, I stepped down from the Board of Trustees immediately, and just remained a member.

Well, sometimes I do feel that I don't fit in. You know, I will sit back sometimes. We're very 1980s here. We still go to dinner parties. Yes, terribly 1980s, we still eat avocados … [all laugh] … how about that?

In many ways, the above and below extracts from our conversation with Frances sit squarely alongside each other, the above showing her maintained connections to be included as part of her life before diagnosis. Then we read below how she has embraced the friendships and warmth that her involvement in DEEP with others who also have dementia has brought her since being diagnosed.

Included with others living with dementia

I kind of felt slightly, I don't know, out a bit. Just a little bit. But with my real friends, and particularly with my DEEP friends, I feel totally at home. I mean, I'm close friends with Dory, as you know, and we do speak a lot. She has a friend who occasionally brings her down this way. I mean, I saw her a few weeks ago, and you know, it's just a pleasure. Yeah, we are good friends, and we will be for life, and we're from very different backgrounds.

Well I found DEEP, because eventually, my husband, he likes Thursdays off and he goes to the Sailing Club at the bottom of our lane. He was finding that leaving me at home was a bit random, especially if I decided to cook … [laughs] … and set something on fire. DEEP was the best thing for me personally, signposting me to all the help I needed from the support services which were available, and how you can live with this. Rachel Niblock from DEEP was most helpful. She made me do a dementia diary. I had already heard a dementia diary, namely Wendy Mitchell's, and from Wendy Mitchell I discovered that you can live with this thing. All the things she'd been through, I was going through too, so I didn't feel quite so weird. I didn't feel quite so odd.

Then I started a group locally, because there were people like me that didn't really want to go to the centre because it was a bit too, you know, 'let's rattle tambourines'. I said to them, 'anybody ties a bell on my leg, I'm actually going to kill them' … [all laugh] … because that for me was the most humiliating thing. So, I started a group called 'Like-Minded' in Brecon, in the local bookshop cafe, it had a wonderful atmosphere. I invited Wendy and Dory to come down and we had a book launch in the cafe. It was just brilliant. People came from all around to the book launch and to the launch of the 'Like-Minded' group, boosted of course by having Wendy there. The bookshop had brought in a load of her books so that people could get them. We had people from the medical centre here in Brecon and people from all sorts of careers. It really was a big eye opener for people to see that. Here was the famous Wendy. She was so articulate. And there was Dory and I, and we were all laughing, because we knew each other fairly well ... we're all laughing and joking. People found it, I think, quite heart-warming that, you know, we weren't this sort of typical image of dementia, people sitting there with twiddle muffs ... [laughs].

In a nutshell

This line of thought led to these final words from Frances on inclusion:

Sorry, but if anybody hands me a twiddle muff ... [all laugh] ... *I'm gonna know my number's up.*

Gail Gregory

Included with others living with dementia

Although for me painting as a creative activity came after COVID-19 subsided, I was first introduced to Gail during the first lockdown when we both took part in the 'Time and Place' poetry project. I quickly recognised how creative a person Gail is and how she is able to use her creativity to connect to other people.

I think for me the lockdown was an absolute saviour because in a way, I met some wonderful people who were struggling, they didn't know what to do with themselves ... um, and boredom was kicking in. Me with my crafts, I started making fairy houses because the weather was glorious, so I started making fairy houses, and people were asking me how I'd made them, so ... um, I did little recordings on YouTube.

I think ... erm, everybody sort of ... erm, it's I can't think of the word ... we, we feed from one another. And I think if one person's doing one thing, it's like an inspiration for another person to try and have a go at whatever it is. It might be art, it might be poetry, I think we drive one another forward, we really do.

Included in the family

Although Gail's statement below begins by relating to her family, she extends this to anyone who she wishes to be included by and with. She is absolutely right to stress the point about choice, and it is widely understood that having dementia reduces the range of choices for the person with the diagnosis and their close family caregivers.

Sometimes I do feel as though I'm not included, yeah, a little bit. I used to look after the grandchildren quite a lot and sometimes ... I know it is harder for me now. I think sometimes they don't ask. They assume that I don't want to do it, and I keep saying, 'if you need me to help out, please ask me, because if I can't do it, I will say so, but give me the choice'. I need to make that choice. I don't want people to make it for me.

Included in the community

There is no doubt in the minds of all of us living with dementia that others knowing we have one form of dementia or another can be a barrier to being included in conversations or cordial relationships. Having said that, experience also tells us that once this is overcome those friendships can actually be enhanced with mutual understanding and warmth. Again, I agree with what Gail says about not pushing the inclusion and that being patient worked in this case – probably not just for Gail but also for her neighbour.

I live in a little town called Cleveleys, which is near to Blackpool, in Lancashire. I live very close to the sea, so I go off walking every day, but always on my own. I prefer my own company now, that's another thing, to being with other people. The neighbours, yeah, the neighbour next door was absolutely brilliant. He just carried on like nothing had ever happened, which I wish most people would do sometimes. The lady across the road used to make me laugh when I went into the front garden to do a bit of weeding, and she'd be there and she'd just turn around and, it was like she was nearly running down the drive back into her house. But now I suppose, I mean it's ... it's 2 and a half years on, she'd, she just comes out and waves and you know so, I never push anybody to speak, they'll do it in their own time. Obviously for her, she's watching me and thinking, 'oh well, she still looks the same as she did a couple of years ago, so I'll wave to her'.

In a nutshell

Like Gail, when I too was diagnosed in my mid-50s there was nothing age-appropriate available and I did try a few groups which did me no good at all in trying to feel included. While locally young-onset groups were quite rare, there was the virtual community, often supported by DEEP but also now driven to an extent by those of us with dementia who care about each other, and want to be included in each other's lives.

I was invited to join a group for people with dementia, which, when I got there, was horrendous because they were all older than me. That frightened me to death actually. It was like my life had just gone years and years in advance.

George Rook

Included or excluded

George began this part of the conversation by referring to his pre-prepared notes and was the only person to choose to explain to us how he saw the question of being included by first focusing on the reverse.

I don't really feel excluded, and I am included in whatever I choose to be included in. So, I'm not sitting here thinking, day after day, I wish I could do this, I wish I could do that, because actually anything I wish I could do, within reason, I'm doing. I mean, I'd love to go and spend a day beside the sea, but it hasn't happened for obvious reasons, and it doesn't seem to be going to happen in the near future because I need my wife to go as well and she's still working. We will one day. Um, I mean that's a small thing.

Included with others living with dementia

In terms of being included in my social group, well I haven't got much of a social group. Maybe that's it then, I haven't got a social group. My social group is on Zoom.

I recognised what I needed from people in DEEP who I'd met, I needed the reassurance of hearing that they were thinking similar things to me, and that I wasn't just some idiot in the middle of north Shropshire screaming blue murder about how awful the state of support is here. In terms of inclusion, I feel that I moved into a wonderful social group, which, apart from being friends share some feelings and experiences.

I've done it again, I've gone right off-piste. Um, so meeting different people with completely different views but all tending to have the same ... same thoughts about dementia is an incredibly validating and valuable thing to have in your life.

Yeah, absolutely. Absolutely it did, it was the first time I have felt that I really, genuinely had something to say that was absolutely right. I mean it sounds a bit arrogant but you know right, because it's being thought by other people as well. Um, and there I felt I have something behind me, a group behind me that actually backs me up. It helps address my anxiety issues from one world into another. It wasn't instant, by any means, but the big difference, the big thing for me was the DEEP network, peer support, peer groups, because we just encourage each other, we just have ideas, we just talk about things, I mean sometimes depressing but often not.

Jennifer Bute

Included in the family

As I wrote earlier, Rosemary and I have not been on holiday since the initial COVID-19 lockdown in March 2020. However, in February 2023 our daughter, son-in law and grandson did arrange for us, and then accompanied us on, a four-night mini break to the Brecon Beacons, which was fabulous and so much appreciated by both Rosemary and I. When we spoke in August 2021, Jennifer had not been so fortunate.

I can't go on holiday because no one will take responsibility. My family aren't available to do that. I've even offered to pay for friends to travel with me. I've said let's rent somewhere with a garden because you can get these rented cottages with beautiful gardens. I'll be safe, I can't get lost, you can do exactly what you like, but they won't because I've got dementia, and they're frightened. But no, they don't want the responsibility even though they've been well educated and I just have to accept that but it is tough.

In a nutshell

Knowing how important walking and talking with a companion is to me, and indeed it has been a part of my care and support plan with students taking on this role for the past 4 years, it deeply saddens me to hear Jennifer conclude this part of the conversation with this heartfelt statement:

Now no one will go for a walk with me anymore.

Julie Hayden

Included with others living with dementia

Being included with other people who have dementia has allowed me to be out and meeting such a wide range of people that I wouldn't of otherwise have ever come in contact with.

Frustrations around being included

Sometimes people identified relationship issues as being barriers, but on other occasions it is, as Julie commented, the impact that dementia has upon the person that creates the barrier to inclusion.

Overall, the last 18 months, there certainly has been increased brain fogging and I've had an increase in problems related to the balance issue. I seem to get really strange headaches that are like a tight band being around my head, so I have to go and have a lie down and that happens more and more. My speech has slurred and word-finding is more of an issue than it was. I don't know how much of that is progression in the dementia or how much that is from not being out and about among people because I know quite a few friends who've said that they've recognised that their own speech has deteriorated during lockdown. Whether that'll improve as I get out among people a bit more I don't know, I'll just have to wait and see.

Included in the community

I think it comes down to how people see me. Many just see me as Julie is her dementia now. Julie's interests are her dementia, so I wouldn't be invited around to someone's house for a meal or for a party, and not be invited to just go along to the theatre or to the cinema with someone. It's like I don't think I'm really even considered as part of the equation really now.

Included by professionals

If you want to know about our dementia, speak to us. I always try to speak openly. To get people instead of speaking to people around us to speak directly

*to us and ask us, especially when you're putting yourself out there and mak-
ing people know that you're willing to talk about any aspect. So, if you have
got any questions, ask me. But people still tend not to do that. I remember
being at a community event. It was the annual general meeting of our clinical commissioning group, and they were having an opportunity beforehand
for local groups to set up a stall and to give information. One of the professionals there stood next to me and he didn't ask me any questions but every
single question he prefaced with. 'Excuse me, I hope you don't mind my asking'. It's okay if you don't want to answer, but he was asking me a question
and I repeated each time, 'it's okay, ask me anything – I don't mind'. I'd
answer his question fully.*

In a nutshell

I think it is a sad part of human nature that many people struggle to overcome
embarrassment or uncertainty when speaking with someone who has dementia. Indeed, the same could be said for including someone with cancer or any
other serious, life-changing health challenges that people in the community live
with. Hopefully, as they get to know the person, everyone can feel more relaxed
and engaged in a conversation.

*People are very nervous about asking us or talking with us, and it might be
around issues such as they don't want to upset us or perhaps they feel embarrassed asking something.*

Keith Day (Cam)

Included in the family

Often one person with dementia in a relationship requires all parties in the relationship to make some adjustments to enable everyone to feel included, and
there are times when our usual nature seems to desert us.

*My wife's sister accepted it you know, and my family from up in Yorkshire –
they again accept that I have dementia. Yeah, and to me that day it was as
though the shutters came down you know because to them it was completely
new to them, same as it was to me. I think sometimes again I get frustrated
because I know I can do something but I'm not allowed to do it, silly little
things like we had we bought new light fittings and I've always done them.
Then no you can't do it, you might do something wrong. You know I'm fine but
it was still no, and that frustrated me.*
    *I won't isolate myself really you know. We went on holiday to Egypt for 16
days and the first 10 days I never even spoke to anybody, which was ridiculous you know and that was completely out of my character you know because
I'd talk to anybody.*

Included with others living with dementia

Cam's experience here is in line with that of many others who have, after a diagnosis, found inclusion from a service user group to be so positive in aiding their wellbeing.

Having joined the Pathfinders group in Sittingbourne, it was the best thing I did. I then started to get interested in things again, and this year I joined the 3 Nations Dementia Working Group. I do feel very accepted by people that have dementia.

Included by professionals

Prior to and since joining our little band of five Dementia Envoys in Kent, Cam has been included and supported to help even more the local mental health trust improve its services for people affected by dementia. Included in this he has spoken on numerous occasions to post-diagnostic groups where people need to feel included in life after their diagnosis.

I do a lot of voluntary work now with the NHS.

Included within their faith

There's about six people that preach. At one time I could read something in the Bible and I could preach on it as it meant something to me. What they've done now is they've gone book by book and it goes on and on and on and has lost me, so I don't feel as included, but I have learnt to cope and it doesn't bother me too much now. If I've got something to say, I'm quite happy to say to Paul the pastor, 'right, look, I'd rather say something' and I'm quite happy to do it.

    In fact, I would say some of the things that have happened over the last 2 years with people in church ... I'd say my faith has gotten stronger.

In a nutshell

As we have read elsewhere, Cam's religious faith is very important to him and nowhere does his sense of inclusion come over as stronger than when he is talking about this. So, it seems apt to conclude his contribution here with the following words:

Sometimes I think now is like with the stroke, when I lost the capability to speak. It knocked me down, and sometimes I feel as though I'll embarrass myself. As Christians they should accept me for who I am, and they do.

Masood Ahmed Qureshi (Maq)

Included in the community

People only know the last stage of it or somebody further down the line, and if you mention dementia automatically you're going to lose some friends. I've seen people and heard people on Zoom sessions where they have actually lost friends.

I am looked upon as an elder, as a mature person and I have found that people in my community listen to me. If I advise something they actually take that on board and appreciate it. I think within a whole community I've spoken to around 3,000 people in the last couple of years.

Nigel Hullah

Included in the community

In the following paragraph, Nigel disproves the notion that people with dementia cannot be reflective about themselves. I know personally this can be difficult but with encouragement is certainly as possible as it is for someone who does not have dementia. In the second paragraph, he touches on an area where I know he is passionate, which is around the human rights of an individual in order that they can be included in our society.

Because, you know, it's one thing being outspoken, it's another thing to be rude. I have my moments, but the friendships are different, they're quite empathetic now, whereas before they were just based around what we were doing. There were people I didn't think I would get on with, I now do very well indeed, simply because I made the change, and people respond to the change. I'm a different person than my first year of diagnosis. I'm a different person now.

I think human rights are important – they're vital and they form the framework of our society. Society can only be valued on the way it treats its most vulnerable. I think we have to understand that when you start talking about Article 3 of the United Nations Convention on the Rights of Persons with Disabilities, most people's eyes roll into the back of their head, but if we talk about kindness, dignity, fulfilment, choice, then people know what those words mean.

Included by professionals

Although most of us who are activists in the dementia world usually respond to opportunities provided by professionals to be included, Nigel has taken the initiative and formed a group which reversed the pattern and model and invited professionals to be included.

I think if you're having your voice heard, you know, I formed a group called Lleisiau Dementia, it's … Lleisiau is Welsh for voices, because I felt that there weren't enough people independent of organisations like the Alzheimer's Society and the Welsh Government. Groups like Improvement Cymru was always done through the framework of an organisation. So, I put together this group of people, and now we're on every strategic level of dimension in Wales with a member of a group in there. We've been asked to give our view, so we're there, and we're getting feedback and affecting change. In a small country like Wales, that's easier to do.

Included with others living with dementia

It was immensely humbling to hear Nigel talk modestly and honestly in this way about his sense of self and being included in the important activist movement. I relate to what he says about being a leader but also a follower, we need this within the world we move in today, but it is rare to witness it expressed and then lived as Nigel describes.

It's great to be a part of the movement which is the 3 Nations Steering Group. I can't believe the figures about the fortnightly webinars that people keep telling us … [109,000 views at the time of writing this – 17 April 2023 – and increasing weekly]. *Absolutely stunning, and it's a clear example of when people like us get together.*

But I think in the dementia world, there are people who are household names, and this has drifted outside the dementia world to other people who may have a sort of fragmented attachment to all things. It's inevitable that people like you Keith, Chris Roberts and Wendy Mitchell, the pioneers really who, you know, we wouldn't have a voice if the work that you guys hadn't been done, and you have to acknowledge that people like yourselves have led the way. It's so important, so that's it, that's the legacy that we leave on, is the people who go before us. It's like standing on the shoulder of giants.

In a nutshell

Being included is sometimes very exhausting, and it is important that we all seek ways to 'recharge our batteries and refill the reservoir' in order that our ability to be included in things we value can be sustained.

Getting a diagnosis of dementia has given me a period of self-reflection and in the past my days were so full. Now, I need that space, and without it I don't function. You can't put a bubble around yourself. You can switch off the phone, switch off Twitter, switch off everything else, and just don't respond and go off and do something totally aimless but which gives you pleasure.

Tracey Shorthouse

Included in the family

Tracey's honest, pragmatic approach is one mirrored by others where she outlines a difficulty she faces but shows an element of resignation to offset increased frustration and a negative impact upon a cherished relationship.

The family forget I have dementia a lot of the time, which is good because … *but then it's not good in aspects if I forget something, 'Well, why did you forget?' my mom said to me, 'don't you remember that conversation last year?'*

'Well, no, mum, I don't remember'. Sometimes I remember some things, but not other things, and I never know how that works. But it's just the way things are, isn't it?

Included with others living with dementia

Tracey outlines both the benefits and what she sees as potential risks about just being included in groups of people with dementia using the DEEP network as the example. We got the impression that Tracey felt best included in the local SUNshiners group where she is a founder member and recognises the activist function of the group in the Shepway area of Kent. When I asked her what it is about the SUNshiners group that really makes her feel included, she gave a swift and direct response:

You have a voice. We all have a voice. I love the SUNshiners, I think it's because it's not like a peer support, it's like an activist group.

I do feel a different part of DEEP community, but then sometimes I don't always as well because I'm trying to strive away to be not always part of that, does it make sense? I want to be part of other communities as well … to have a happy medium.

In a nutshell

Dementia does tend to narrow our physical but also mental horizons and shrink our worlds, and for many it seems to make the person a little more self-centred or egocentric at times. Tracey kicks against this in her final comment in this part of our conversation:

I think I miss talking to complete strangers and finding out about them, that's why I like social media like Twitter, for example. You can chat to different people and just have a good old chinwag without really knowing each other.

So what learning can we take from the Fifteen?

These interviews provided a rich and varied account of how dementia impacts on a person's sense of inclusion. We reflect here on what we can generalise for others living with dementia and those who support them.

From the point of view of someone living with dementia:

- Always try to be realistic in one's expectations on being included by maximising opportunities while taking the time to establish and then build connections and relationships
- Don't be frightened to try new things and if you feel it works for you and that you feel included, then great; if not, then at least you've given it a try and can walk away with no regrets.

There are also implications for those who provide professional support and care for persons living with dementia. For them, the main takeaway messages are:

- Use inclusive language by always avoiding the use of jargon and acronyms without explanation, which tend to exclude people affected by dementia in the conversation or piece of work.
- When planning a piece of work, always seek to include the voice of people with dementia at all stages of the work, not just at the end.
- Think about pacing and be aware of the risks of malignant social psychology which stop people with dementia from feeling and being included.
- Be mindful of the amount and length of meetings to which people with dementia are invited and usefully expected to actively contribute. Similarly, in order to include them be wary of long emails and trails which are lengthened by unnecessary 'reply all' emails, which really do stop people with dementia being included.
- As with all the petals in this model, putting the person at the centre by getting to know them as an individual is crucial in dementia care. For some, apanthropy is key as they seek solitude by getting away from crowds and busy places and not being included in activities and conversations at times. Others will feel lonely and isolated if treated in the same way. Within the fifteen conversations, we find examples of both.

10 Attachment

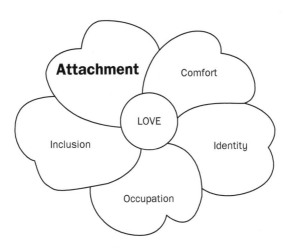

Walking this road with you by my side
Holding my hand my consistent guide
Leaving the shadows, lit by your smile
Departing the storms to rest for a while
Unrolling a safety net for us both to share
Banishing challenges, anxiety and fear
Welcoming security of time spent together
Stopping to admire one last gayfeather
Bonding like glue, stuck in a moment in time
Going uphill, the mountains to climb
Lifting me up, whenever I fall
Departing the scene, the play's curtain call

– Keith Oliver

The Fifteen on Attachment – narrated by Reinhard Guss

The concept of attachment in psychology (Bowlby 1969) was relatively new during my time at university and was mainly concerned with infants and child behaviour. However, it has since been developed and is much better understood across the life span, including in old age. Richard Cheston summarises attachment-based research and approaches in the later stages of dementia in his commentary in *Dementia Reconsidered, Revisited* (Kitwood and Brooker 2019) and in his book *Dementia and Psychotherapy Reconsidered* (2022). It is clear how an I-Thou informed way of relating can help to build connection and foster the sense of safety in relationship that lies at the heart of the need for attachment.

However, attachment needs and attachment styles also feature in my clinical work with older people generally and in people in much earlier stages of dementia. Influenced by personality, attachment styles are often based on very early life experience and are frequently a subject of reflection in therapy. A fortunate person with a secure attachment style, a sound sense of themselves and a life story that has helped to deepen rather than to undermine these notions may well be able to navigate the experience of living with dementia without excessive anxiety, and without the need to retreat into denial. On the other hand, anxious, insecure attachment styles, and avoidant attachment styles, can be the result of a history where important attachment figures are absent, unreliable, unavailable or vanish and are likely to make this more challenging. With her history of early and repeated losses of key relationships, it is no wonder that my grandmother had a bit of both: anxious attachments where she felt never quite good enough and that she needed to work hard to ensure the relationship was retained, and avoidant of attachment with a sense that since relationships are unreliable, it is best to be self-sufficient and fiercely independent. Each of these attachment styles causes its own difficulties in the course of adjusting to living with dementia. If independence and self-sufficiency are vital, then accepting help and support are problematic, even if objectively they may be sorely needed. If much effort and energy have to be invested in maintaining relationships and feeling they are secure, then dementia also makes that increasingly difficult and stressful, adding to the sense of loss and insecurity.

Talking with the Fifteen, a wealth of stories and experiences emerged of the strengths and the challenges in family relationships, those with friends, acquaintances and neighbours, and in the activism world with peers, services and professionals. Of course, the Fifteen are a special group of people, and all have made new relationships with other people with dementia since their diagnosis, and are in a habit of speaking openly about their experiences as part of their activism. However, I was particularly touched by their willingness to share the more difficult sides of adjusting to changes in family and marital relationships as a result of living with dementia.

In what follows, the words of the Fifteen are italicised to help distinguish them from Reinhard's commentary.

Agnes Houston

Changing family relationships

Rather than be the butt of the jokes – we're the west of Scotland, there's a joke about everything, you know. They see me as strange, and we thought that it was like, dementia had stopped me being able to enjoy myself. And they didn't understand. And now there's more of an understanding that there's a certain place I need to sit for the noise. And the fact that it's in a corner with a back. So that makes you an observer, you know, and certain places where I sit at a table, so I can hear conversation, but I don't hear all the conversation, only the wee bit round about it. So yes, I think a great way of putting it is 'passive observer' – where you're getting great enjoyment out of watching the interaction of what people are doing. But it's almost as if you're above, looking down on it, and you're not in there doing the hype and doing all of this stuff. So yes, a passive observer is a very good way of putting it.

Losing community connections

And the people who knew me, sadly, have died and people have moved on, they're retired. And it's new people in the community. And they do not know me. And you know ... and I find it quite sad. And sometimes sit and think, 'Oh God', you know, when you hear people and I think, 'Well, and it was me that instigated that getting changed', you know. But it is what it is, and we just do that. I don't have a local community. I live in a place, and I chat and what to people, but I'm not known. Yeah.

Finding a community online

I have a strong attachment to a virtual community. Some people I've never met, other than on the virtual screen. And you know, you can chat to someone any time of night. So, depending on where they are in the world, you're never alone. And I think it's a much more inclusive community.

So, I never feel alone now because of the virtual window to the world, as I call my iPad.

A need for solitude

Sometimes I need solitude. That is a need for me – I search it out and will seek it. You know, that 'a-ha' moment where it's getting into your wee comfort solitude area, and you go, 'Aaah ... [breathes a sigh of relief] ... This is great'. And that's good, too. But I am quite a social butterfly when I'm out at events. So, I'll pop from table to table and things like that, but it can be quite tiring for me. So, I'm happy with the both sides of 'Agnes' now, whether it's solitude and seeking 'Agnes' time you know, that little thing in Scotland we call it 'get your head peace'.

Impact of the pandemic

COVID-19 has played a big part, you know, I only recently went to the shop I haven't been to now much over the last 18 months, 2 years, and you don't know whether you can touch anybody even, you know, that comforting touch on the shoulder. You think, 'Oh don't do that'. So, I think I'm going to have to learn a new etiquette going out, especially maybe in conferences and events. What is the etiquette now, and expressing yourself? You know, I think I've lost that.

As a person who used to be very involved in the local community, Agnes describes the sense of loss when describing her relationship with her local community today, following years of national activism in the dementia world. In her own family, she now feels more like a passive observer than the active participant she used to be – and arriving at this place required some negotiation, education and rearranging of family expectations.

As one of the pre-pandemic pioneers of using Zoom to connect with people with dementia in remote areas of Scotland and Alzheimer's Disease International, Agnes was well positioned to build on this when COVID-19 arrived. She describes the vital relationships that have been built online, and the comfort of having contacts, friends to communicate with at any time of the day through her i-Pad 'window to the world' to keep her connected.

At the same time, Agnes describes the need for solitude and disengagement from business and demands, and her efforts to balance these, especially as the pace of life increases post-pandemic. She also gives us a particularly insightful description of the difficulty navigating the changed landscape of social conventions after the restrictions imposed during the pandemic.

Chris Maddocks

Reaction of family to dementia

My dad had Alzheimer's disease, and so my brother, my sister, myself saw dad's journey with that and also my grandmother had Alzheimer's disease. When I had my diagnosis at the age of 60, I had an actual leaflet about vascular dementia which I gave to my brother and my sister because it explained it better than I could explain it. They never told me that they read it, they never discussed the dementia with me.

Heather was living in Eastbourne and I used to come back and forth, back and forth. My brother and sister said that they couldn't look after me. So, Heather said come to me, come to Eastbourne. At first, I kept saying 'no' because I thought it's not fair to impose my dementia on Heather. And she kept insisting, so I moved to Eastbourne in July 2017.

Social activities

I do some exercise, with the Parkinson's group.

And I've got a friend who's a personal trainer so I'm starting to do exercising with her now.

And Heather and I like to go and visit friends, we go for walks and meals out.

Friendships

There are social situations and I'll give you an example. We've got one friend and she's 80 ... she's 80 but she doesn't, she doesn't stop talking. And when we are in her company, I just find that a bit of a brain overload. Heather said to me, 'Chris, you're going to the bathroom an awful lot'. But I was doing it just to try and clear my head a little bit. So I said to Heather, 'I can't cope, she talks over people, didn't you know, didn't answer you, and was just talking so quickly, it felt like a big, huge ... like my head was going to explode.

I lost some friends after my diagnosis. And I thought, 'but why? You know what, why have I lost friends?' They just don't want me to talk about dementia. But I've made loads of new friends who have dementia.

Previous experience of a dementia in a family often has a profound impact on how a family copes with its arrival one or two generations later, and Chris describes the experience of her father's dementia as related to the reaction of her siblings when she tried to speak to them about her own diagnosis. The focus of the brother and sister seem to have been on the spectre of needing to provide increasing amounts of care, which they could not envisage.

Instead, Chris describes a rare example of relocating a long distance away, with encouragement from her partner to come and live with her at the opposite end of the country, and gives several examples of her partner's support, of shared times and activities.

Chris describes the sensory and cognitive overload of a particular interaction, and it reminded me of how Agnes describes how she manages large family gatherings, and her need for solitude in between social activities. Like others, she mentions the loss of some friends, and the many new friends gained in peer support and activism.

Chris Norris

Reaction of family to activism

The diagnosis has changed the family dynamic in a number of ways. With my family, when I first became involved in activism around dementia, they were amazed at the things that I was involved in, because I am, oddly enough, despite being a police officer, my go-to personality is introvert rather than extrovert.

So, initially, they were very impressed, and they were following it. But now, because it's been 8 years on since diagnosis, I just feel there is that element that I don't seem to have, in their eyes, changed as drastically as they would expect you to change

And so, I feel sometimes my family are thinking, 'Well, yeah, but have you really got dementia?', which can be a challenge. So, I don't actually argue with them. I just accept that. Because there's no point.

Relationship changes

And some of my friends have moved further away in contact to me, and it's not because they don't want to speak to me anymore, it's because they don't know what to say to me, I guess.

You're kind of ... well, you don't know how to ask the question in the first place, because you don't know where that person is, how they feel about it. Which is why I'm very upfront with everybody that I speak to. Very early on, I let them know that I'm living with dementia. And so, it gets rid of the elephant in the room.

So, relationships have changed, I guess, a bit there. But other relationships have come more on-board now.

It's funny inside my head, sometimes when the words come out, and to other people that doesn't seem so funny to them, but some things I just find so hilarious, and I will find myself chuckling because there's this conversation that's going on inside my head sometimes. And I mean, sometimes, it's not just in the home, but in the family, I will start a conversation halfway through. And then people won't know what I'm talking about, because I've already had half the conversation with them. When I start to actually say the words out loud, they're like, 'What are you talking about? Where are you coming from? What's that about?' But generally, everybody I find that people have been accepting and very helpful, as helpful as they can. So, I've not felt alienated in any way.

Developing online friendships

I've met loads and loads of new people that I didn't know before online, who I now regard as friends online, who I would have never met before – or maybe just in passing. And certainly not have the in-depth conversations that we now have. When you go to conferences, you have a brief chat, but it's only on the very surface. But now, particularly with these Zoom meetings, you can really get to know the people – you get under the skin, and you understand what they're all about.

I might have lost some friends, but I've gained a whole wealth of new people who I don't regard just as acquaintances, but I regard them as friends. There's differences and there's people who are acquaintances, and people who are friends. At the end of the day, if they disappear off into the horizon when you tell them about the challenges you're having with dementia, then they're not really a true friend anyway. Because if they were, then they'd care about what you have to say.

Using humour

So now, when I'm joining new groups or whatever, I'm very reliant on what I think is my good sense of humour, like I do constantly try and raise and lighten things up. If you know, things are getting too heavy, I try and lighten them up.

But again, I do use my humour when we have tremendous fun – an awful lot of laughter around the subject within the family of dementia. When I say things or do things which are slightly off the wall, and we can – right from where my children were born, I've always taught them to look on the funny side, particularly with their medical challenges to look on the funny side of it. And we all take the mickey out of each other. Then sometimes it does get to a point where you're thinking, 'Yeah, I don't feel that that's quite so funny today'. But I push that away, because once you put a block up for people, then they stop feeling free to be able to talk to you in a normal way.

In a nutshell

Generally, they still do treat me the same. And because I don't wear a big badge that says, 'I have dementia'. It's very easy for them, in the general run of life, because of the way that I still am. It's very easy to forget the extra challenges that I may well be having.

My family are now very good, they do little things subtly to make my life easier. So that I perhaps don't have to face that challenge quite so much. And it is only little things – but it's the little things that count, so I can concentrate on the major things of getting on with getting on with life.

That's how I want to be treated; in a normal way for everybody, or as normal as possible.

When Chris speaks about lost friendships, he ascribes this to their helplessness in knowing what to say to him, a difficulty also often described in relation to bereavement or a cancer diagnosis, and perhaps avoiding 'wearing a big dementia badge' is one way of managing this outside the dementia friends world, especially since it is very important to him to be treated as normally as possible. At the same time, he talks about a way of being very upfront with people about his diagnosis in order to avoid there being unspoken issues that he or they would then need to worry about avoiding, or addressing later. This also seems important given his awareness of frontotemporal dementia symptoms and the challenges that can arise in reading social situations or responding in interactions.

Chris, as others, describes the benefits of the many new contacts and acquiring friendships through his activism. The forced move to online conversations and meetings is described in a positive way by Chris, who sees it as a way to deepen relationships with people he would otherwise not have had the opportunity to speak with at length.

The reactions Chris mentioned to his activism from within his circle of family and friends seemed to me to mirror what can be seen in the wider world of dementia policy and service development or on Twitter. On the one hand, there is admiration, encouragement and perhaps surprise in the case of people who are seen as more reserved or shy. On the other, when people seem remarkably able or remain surprisingly well for much longer than expected, questions are raised as to whether they have 'proper' dementia at all, leading to added pressure and distress.

Chris Roberts

Changing family relationships

It's also changed my relationship with Jayne, with my daughters, my sons. I'm not the patriarch anymore … is that right? I was the one that everyone looked to, you know, I was the one that fixed things … I'm not being big headed but rightly so. I would go beat up my daughter's boyfriend, you know, things like that.

Jayne: 'Yeah, he'd frighten them but he wouldn't hit them'.

> *But they always felt they can look to me and that changed. I don't think any of us were aware of it but now looking back, it really changed, you know. We did drift apart in that way, that they wouldn't ask for help anymore, that they wouldn't ask my opinion, because my opinion was not trusted – I know that, you know. It really brings you down to the ground when you realise that that relationship side has almost disappeared.*

Jayne: 'But he doesn't feel it. He doesn't know the feeling. Chris has expressed to me that he's disappointed in himself because he doesn't know what to do about it, and he would've had more of an idea pre-dementia. We know that definitely. And he'd be able to give more advice or more practical advice you know'.

Marital relationship

We're still close, we're very, very good friends and always probably will be. We have a great time, but dementia does stop you emotionally, it stopped me emotionally anyway. Sometimes I can't stand being near someone and it's also stopped the closeness sexually as well because if you're not performing very well mentally and cognitively in everything else you do, then you're a bit worried about performing in bed. So I've pushed Jane away a lot before the benefits. But now like … now, I can blame her. Win-win!

Relationships with peers

When you can't ride a motorcycle any more, what is the point of having one? I don't have one now. I've had motorbikes forever. And then you don't see all your motorcycle buddies or your friends. You know, your brothers.

   Meeting peers has helped, and people like yourself. Yourselves, both of you.

   You go on a campsite, people are so much more amicable. You know, they wouldn't give you the time of day in the street. Because that's what people are like these days. But on a campsite, they just suddenly change and everyone is your friend. And because I'd come out and I would explain to people about my dementia and try and educate them. I used to say, 'I'm not bragging, I'm educating you', and a lot of people were quite thankful for that. But then it also took the pressure off Jayne because 30 or 40 people at the campsite knew about my dementia and they'd keep an eye out for me.

Relationship with the dog

It changed my relationship with my dog. Absolutely it did. You know, I used to love my dog. I trained him so well, but I don't even know where he is now. I took a lot of pleasure in training him didn't I? We understood each other. I can't stand the dog now.

Jayne: 'The dog became the whipping boy because Chris used to shout at the dog and I took offence at that because it's not the dog's fault and he did say to me once 'I'm shouting at the dog instead of shouting at you', so I stepped back. He's never hit or hurt the dog but the dog takes the brunt of Chris' anger'.

And little things like, you know, it's so frustrating when you're sat very quiet on your own and you're chilling or you're trying to concentrate on my iPad to do something. I can hear the tapping of the dog's claws every time he moves on the laminate flooring. It drives me mad. I wouldn't hear that before but now I can hear it. So, that relationship has totally changed and it's, you know, he was my boy, you know. I could rely on him. I don't think I could now.

Keith: 'Did it happen gradually or was it quite an abrupt change?'

Oh no, very gradually and a lot of it happened without us even knowing it had happened.

Impact of the pandemic

But that's all, I'm less of that person now. I really can't be bothered being bolshy and forceful. You know, I just … I've just gone so lethargic. I really can't be bothered. Yeah, I don't know. So … and I felt very disappointed with the Alzheimer's Society. Yeah and Dementia Voice and DEEP. No support. Apparently, in this life, you have to ask for support. Like you don't ask, you don't get.

In his usual outspoken manner, Chris spoke in detail and very freely about relationship changes brought about by dementia itself and by the social perceptions around it. His turn of phrase, 'who wants to sit with a load of people with dementia?' is contrasted with his many new contacts, activism and extensive time spent with people with dementia.

I think Chris' honesty and expressiveness about his emotional struggles very much speak for themselves and resist summarising. With Jayne's assistance, Chris gave us a particularly detailed description of the losses experienced due to changing roles, and the challenges in adjusting to these, perhaps most vividly described in the changing relationship with the dog. Here the impact of dementia symptoms come together with the emotional challenges that encapsulate the issues in a compressed form.

Moving from the position of 'the patriarch', 'the man in the house' and the go-to person for DIY and practical advice is an adjustment that often has to be made along the ageing journey, but is forced in an accelerated and untimely fashion on younger people who develop dementia. Chris describes the anger and self-criticism as well as the reprieve from it found in 'dementia-friendly communities' such as the peer support movement, but also on campsites.

Here is also a detailed account of the impact of COVID-19 and lockdowns, which have curbed social activities to a point where it seems an inordinate effort to re-start. There is anger at 'being retired without having a choice', a sense of the dementia having deteriorated and social contact becoming more of an effort. Alongside the sense that others may be disappointed by him, there is also disappointment with the organisations that he spent many years and much energy supporting not being more proactive in providing support during these difficult times.

Dianne Campbell

Family

Well, my family are just exquisite. They just are. So, I think I've mentioned that as the only thing about them, because they're just the best.

Relating to peers who do not understand dementia

The way I kind of communicate with people is a bit different, because, especially those around me, if they don't know much about the dementia or Alzheimer's or if you have memory problems. Then they would ask things like, 'Okay, did you remember that? I did tell you so and so?' or, 'Did you remember that I asked you to do so and so?' And I go, 'Yes'. Well, when did they ask? I don't know, of course! So, I like to make a bit of a fool of them and myself.

Relating to carers of group members

We have got some people in our group that have really gone far. Really, really, gone far. And so, to me, having a go at it to say to them [staff and carers], 'Listen, it can happen to you. You need to know what to do and how to take care of yourself'. But we still let them come out. I just said to the family, 'Just let them come out'.

Dianne underlined her sense of support from her family by the brevity of her statement. As organiser of dementia peer groups, she describes her ongoing efforts to educate: by ensuring that people in the later stages of dementia can continue to attend and be included, and by her teasing and sense of humour when faced with people around her who do not take memory issues into account when interacting with her.

Frances Isaacs

Overcoming family tragedy

My father went off with the last of a long line of bimbos and ended up married to her. And then it was a complete nightmare, but my mother couldn't cope. And on our first wedding anniversary, she killed herself …

Keith: 'Oh dear'.

> *I know, it's sort of ruined our wedding anniversaries. It kind of ruined my life for quite a long time. In fact, it ruined my life until I reached 48, that's how old she was when she died. From then on, I started to pull myself together. But I mean, it was a terrible, terrible experience, which I'm able to talk about quite glibly now, whereas until a few years ago, I couldn't talk about it.*

Marital relationship

My husband has turned from … he hasn't changed his personality, but he has been so caring. He's never been a great one for saying, 'I love you' or any of that slushy stuff. But we have been friends and everything else for 54 years now. Which is the longest I've ever been out with one bloke, definitely!

And he's just become incredibly wonderful. He's doing things that he's always loathed, like cooking and cleaning. He now knows how to do both those things. We do tend to cook together, because it does prevent the household fires that have been when I'm left here alone. Not too many food disasters either. Yes, so he's been absolutely wonderful.

Relationship with the dog

You know, and my son will tell you that the dog has made a massive difference to how I cope with things. I know it sounds absolutely potty, because it's just a little dog. You know, but she and I have really … well, we just love each other. Dogs give you back with knobs on, they're just so giving, and sometimes it actually overwhelms me. It really does. But I love her, and we go out together.

Having found a way of talking about the impact of disrupted attachments and relationships in her family of origin, Frances goes on to describe two central attachments that sustain her now. The difficulty in adjusting to new roles is described by her more in terms of her husband taking up activities he used to loathe than in terms of her loss of independence, morphing into sharing rather than wholesale handing over. Besides a declaration of love for her husband, there is an evocative one for her dog, and the emotional support and strength this very positive attachment provides.

Gail Gregory

Relationship with children

Yeah, my family, my children were very, very supportive. I suppose they hid the fact that they were devastated by the diagnosis, but they've been brilliant. They've supported me. and there have been odd times where they've said, 'should you be doing that', and I just said, 'yes I should'.

Relationship with parents

But for me, when I got the diagnosis, my parents were the biggest obstacle because most people, when they get the diagnosis, the parents aren't still alive. For me, both of my parents are very much alive, and they didn't want to believe that the diagnosis was real. They said that I was too young, that I couldn't possibly have dementia. The first thing that my mum said to me was, 'how long have you got to live?' I said to my mum, 'please don't look at things negatively, because there's lots of people out there that are living really well with a diagnosis, so don't think that I'm going to be put into a home in 12 months' time because this is just the start of it, and nobody knows how long it's going to be'. There's the beginning, and there's an end, but there's all the in-between things that come as well, so we make the most of what we've got. They're accepting it now, and because of the things I have done, they're sort of really proud of me because of what I've achieved through this journey.

Relationship with wider family

Another thing was when I got the diagnosis, one family member, whom we don't speak to now, took it upon themselves to judge what I should look like with dementia, and on several visits stared at me, which made me feel very uncomfortable. So I did eventually pluck up the courage to ask and say, 'why do you stare at me?' They said, 'well, I've never ever met anybody with dementia at your age', and she just couldn't accept it. And later on, it was about 6 months later, there was a mistake I had made on a Christmas card, and we got a terrible message saying that I was using my dementia as an excuse for missing a name off the Christmas card. I think, we all come across hurdles, and that was a family member. We don't speak to them anymore because of that which caused me a lot of upset. I was upset that I had missed the name off, and I was also upset to think that I had upset that person, so it upset me. I still think about that.

Relationship with friends and neighbours

Friends, I've lost every single friend apart from one. The difference is she treats me as me. She treats me as Gail. She rings me up. She sometimes asks how I am, but sometimes she doesn't, and I think that it's just a normal way of speaking to somebody. Nothing's changed, you know, it's the same friendship we've always had. She doesn't treat me any differently.

Yeah friends, it's very strange … one friend in particular that I'd been friends with for over 20, 30 years, suddenly stopped calling me and when I rang to ask why, she just said, 'well, I don't know what to say to you really. What do I say?' And I say, 'you talk to me like you did before, because I'm no different. I don't know if it's embarrassment or I don't know what it is, but yeah, there's been no phone calls for months.

Neighbours, they used to go back into the houses because they didn't know what to say to me. That is getting better, and they are starting to realise that I'm still me, at the end of the day, I'm still the same person that I was the day I got my diagnosis.

Relationship with peers who have dementia

But you make new friends. And I've made lots of new friends now, and the friends that accept me for who I am and for my diagnosis, which is brilliant.

Yeah, I think I've had a problem with this [being put on a pedestal] *because obviously since I've joined the groups and done lots of things, it's like people, I don't know, it's the pedestal thing. I am not very good at accepting lots of praise. I'm very quiet, so then I withdraw because I don't want to be classed as some fantastic person, because I'm just me. This is how I've always been, you know, and don't put me on that pedestal because I don't like it.*

Talking with Gail showed the multigenerational aspects of family relationships that people with dementia often face, since increasingly not only people under the age of 65 (and therefore with young-onset dementia) have parents who are still alive. While imparting the news of a dementia diagnosis to (usually adult) children, rethinking the relationships and attachments may be more expected, it can raise particular challenges when considering parents. Gail describes her assertive approach to negotiating these intergenerational relationships in both directions in a family that responds well and is proud of her way of managing.

This is in contrast to most of her previous friendships. Like others, Gail describes the reactions of helplessness and embarrassment of friends and neighbours at not knowing what to say to a person who has had a dementia diagnosis. This is reminiscent of the experience of people who have had a bereavement or a cancer diagnosis, and leads to significant losses and breaches in the lives of people with dementia. It makes awareness-raising and education all the more important. Like Chris Norris, Gail appreciates being treated the same as before the diagnosis, which helps in maintaining continuity in relationships.

The losses in friendships are mediated by the new friends found through activism and by a supportive family. A downside of activism that Gail describes as *'being put on a pedestal'* would also make it difficult to maintain a sense of continuity with relationships in the way that they were before dementia arrived and activism was developed.

George Rook

Marital relationship

In terms of family there's been little change. I mean my wife, who is a health professional herself, although she's working nowadays in organisational change and leadership with a trust in Stoke, she was very matter-of-fact about it but, in a sense, didn't really want to talk about it early on. She sort of watched as I declined very slowly, and things were quite tense at times about the fact that I couldn't work out ... well my hearing's not good anyway ... but I couldn't work out what she was saying. I still can't a lot of the time, and she doesn't like repeating stuff and the rest of it. But that's improved actually in the last year. I think lockdown has helped us.

I was thinking about this one, certainly earlier, the big change is how we've adjusted our roles. So I've given up doing things like trying to look after money, I was never very good at it anyway. I'm really pleased to have given up that stress. I just have a little bit of money that comes into my account each month. The rest goes straight into hers and she does the bills. And she's very good at it. She's stopped asking me to do jobs which involve going up a ladder, because my balance is such that I've got a damn good chance of falling off nowadays. Indeed, I have had to recognise I can't do that, so we have to pay someone to do things like decorating where she can't do it. The status quo has changed but it is actually, for me at least, pros. I think my interpretation would be for her it is better, more positive, as we just settle into different roles. She likes being in charge and I like not being in charge, so that's fine. I've always had someone to look after me, and now she is that person. Great!

Relationship with children

Children-wise, I have a son who is married with two children who live just 10 miles down the road, so I see them quite a lot, which is nice. And he doesn't do talking about feelings and things – well, none of them do. I suppose my daughter does a bit. I think none of them, none of the three children want particularly to talk about it unless I particularly want to raise something, and I've learnt really not to. It would be if we did, I think, but we don't, because I don't see them often and the last thing I want to do is make them feel or think that all I ever do is moan about having dementia. I do think about it a lot. Every day, I'm thinking about something, but if someone visits I rather like to talk about something else, if I can talk about anything.

Relationship with friends and acquaintances

I wouldn't say I have really close friends from before dementia, I just don't, I haven't found any. I had a very, very close friend when I was in my 20s, when I lived in Birmingham, and I've never had another one since. He disappeared off the face of the Earth, I don't know if he died or if he had a breakdown but he just disappeared. Breakdowns are the story of my bloody life, I tell you. Anyway, I haven't met anybody who I've really clicked with up here [George touches his head].

I've got lots of acquaintances and few neighbours but we don't have any neighbours where I live. Um, relationships with acquaintances, I mean they are in a sense different because I don't socialise with them very much at all. I may have joined in in the past but I don't now because I don't do socialising. I can't do the noise and the talking and stuff, I just don't want to. And also the fact that there's this thing, this sort of screen between me and everybody else, which is actually dementia. They don't want to talk about it because they don't know what to say or ask. And I'm not going to, well unless people ask me, talk about dementia. I'm happy to, very happy to, but it doesn't tend to be a great conversation starter.

New relationships through activism

DEEP stuff really is incredibly important. From one world into another! It wasn't instant, by any means, but the big difference, the big thing for me was the DEEP network, peer support, peer groups. Because we just encourage each other, we just have ideas, we just talk about things, I mean sometimes depressing, but often not.

Dementia, certainly through speaking and campaigning and conferencing and whatever else, has introduced me to a lot more people, not just people with dementia, but professionals as well. Some lovely people who I wish I could meet more often.

I mean my attachment feels strongest, other than to my wife and dog, my attachment is closest to DEEP people.

I think we tend to judge even without knowing we're judging, so there are people in any group that you will hone in on because they look as if they are people who you'll be interested in or you might enjoy talking to. And dementia takes that away, in a sense, because you don't know who the hell you're going to meet on these zooms sometimes, and there are people who I would have never ever met, and if I had met, I might well have walked straight past. Just because that's what you do.

George shared some detailed thoughts on the way that his marital relationship has changed over time, and the process of adjustment from his difficulties initially being somewhat ignored to a redistribution of tasks that suits him, and possibly his wife also. He also gives us an example of the forced joint isolation leading to a better understanding and having been helpful for the relationship. When it comes to children and grandchildren, he seems to want to protect them – and perhaps himself – from the subject of dementia, preferring to talk about other things.

George describes himself as not having any close friendships, not spending much time with acquaintances and, living in an isolated area, not having any neighbours. He also talks about himself as somewhat quiet and reserved in social situations, which has intensified with the arrival of dementia. Like Agnes, he enjoys watching and listening and following his own thoughts, and all the more so now as it is becoming difficult to follow the multiple strands of complex social gatherings.

This contrasts somewhat with his enthusiasm for his DEEP groups and the friends and contacts he has made through activism, people he wishes he could spend more time with, and who he describes as his 'social group', where he experiences the closest attachment other than to his wife and to his dog.

Jennifer Bute

Relationship with friends

I've been very blessed. People have complained about losing friends. I haven't lost any, I've gained a tremendous number because I have an obstinate spirit, as you can probably gather. So if my friends will say, 'well, I don't want anything to do with you', I would say, 'why not' and I would educate them because often its fear, it's not understanding. If people run away from me, which they did at the beginning, I would run after them and say 'here's a leaflet', and they've understood. My neighbours from years back still come and visit me here. I can't believe it, I mean it's wonderful! The relationship is different, of course, but they rightly feel they are supporting me, which they are. But it was hard work and I'm glad that I made that effort. I think it's sad when people let people kind of disappear.

I was quite open about the fact that I had dementia, quite open about my hallucinations, and slowly people understood, didn't they, because they found they didn't need to be frightened – because it's always fear.

While not discussed directly, Jennifer's relationship with her Christian faith is central to her approach to her life and relationships, and forms a thread throughout our conversations with her. Perhaps it is faith alongside her 'obstinate spirit' that helps her to maintain such a positive approach to relationships despite the changes she acknowledges.

Contrary to most of the Fifteen, Jennifer told us that she did not lose any friends when first sharing her diagnosis of dementia, hallucinations included, although there was distancing and fear on the part of some. She puts this down to her tenacity in educating about dementia, although on meeting Jennifer, her indomitable spirit and kindness shine through and will have helped with the educational endeavours as well as the maintenance of her relationships.

Despite all the positives, Jennifer describes the lack of anyone who could support her to go on a holiday, which given my own love of travel was quite affecting, and made me wonder about holiday offers for people with dementia who do not have a carer to accompany them.

Julie Hayden

Dementia in the family

There's been quite a lot of dementia in the family. I have a sister, but when my dad got dementia, she started to move away from the family, and actually cut herself off entirely from the family. She didn't even bother coming to dad's funeral. Not long after dad died, mum started developing dementia symptoms, and so for those reasons there was estrangement.

Relationship with children

The only kind of close family involvement is that I have two daughters and a grandson and a son-in-law. When I first got diagnosed, because my daughters live a long way from me, I knew that I wouldn't be seeing them for quite a while, so I put off telling them about my diagnosis. Not because I didn't want to talk to them, but I knew that that conversation would have to be by telephone, and that made it more difficult. I live in Halifax in Yorkshire, and they live right down in Bracknell in Berkshire. Because they haven't been around they don't get to see me very often and so they think because they have seen dementia in their grandparents, that they sort of know what dementia is about. They've been quite dismissive of it, but actually when we do meet, they get quite irritated really by my disabilities, they get quite, what's the word, they're very impatient. So that causes difficulties, they don't understand.

I once had a row with my oldest daughter over the phone because I tried to share some of my work with them, and send things down that I've been doing, things I've written or bits of film or webinars that I've been involved in to keep them up to date with what I'm doing. But, of course, you're protective of your kids and you're only sending them positive stuff down, and my daughter said something to me and I kind of shot back with her and said something to the effect of 'you don't understand'. And she said, 'well, no mum, all we ever hear is positive things from you, so how can I possibly understand?' I thought well, she's got a point actually, you're protective of your kids so you don't want to tell them the really bad stuff, especially when you have only a little chance to sit down and talk with them. But then you're kind of shooting yourself in the foot, because they don't fully appreciate the dementia.

Relationship with friends

My best friend, who've I've known from when I started grammar school at the age of 11, she's still my best friend now and she's incredible, she always has been, right the way through the good and the bad in my life. Actually, she's now full-time carer for her dad who is living with dementia, and so although we don't get to see each other very often, even outside of COVID-19, we do speak every week together. Yeah, she's been wonderful.

I have another friend outside of dementia who not always around because she's with her family living down south. She's a retired nurse and really her full-time home is over in Spain, but she can't get there for the time being [due to COVID-19], but whenever she is around locally, she's always a very great help.

From work there has been no contact ongoing from former colleagues.

My friends really are dementia friends now, the rest of my friends have kind of all faded back or taken back steps and I don't hear from those now. The reaction I got from the friends I had at the time I was diagnosed was that kind of 'you sure, you don't look like you've got dementia', and then kind of 'well, what kind of symptoms are you having' and then whatever I told them was the kind of 'oh yeah, I get that all the time'. And then the inevitable 'well if you need anything, just let me know' and then from that point onwards I never heard from them again.

Peer support and activism relationships

It comes back to the beauty of getting involved in peer support and in the activism. Neither of us would've ever liked to have met through dementia and it would've been wonderful if we could've got to know each other, Keith, without having had dementia, but nevertheless this has happened, and our paths would never have crossed if it wasn't for dementia. In a way, it's kind of been a boon, the range of people that I now have in my life as friends is just incredible. Dementia is a great leveller because of the fact it can apply to anybody, whatever your background or wherever you are from. So, if I'm talking to someone in this country or abroad, or if I'm talking to someone who's come from a very different upbringing, it doesn't matter when it comes down to it, we kind of have that common ground to start from. Within the peer support network, it's very much a non-judgemental arena and people understand what you're going through, what you're about, and kind of just accept you for what you are. And what I love about peer support is that you can talk very openly about things, whether you're talking about the good stuff or you're coming into a group and you say, 'gosh, I've had a really awful week'. You can have a good old moan and everybody is going to accept that, but they're not going to think 'oh my God, Julie's about to slash her wrists because she's had a really bad week'. Chances are by the time you get to the end of that period of time with your friends you can be back laughing again, because you can kind of help each other look on the bright side and look at the positives and find a way out of that mood.

Like Chris Maddox, Julie talked about the experience of dementia in the generation above hers leading to estrangements that have continued. Julie then described the difficulty of children living a long way away, and the protectiveness in sharing what life with dementia is like only when the moment seems to be right, and then only the parts that seem more positive.

There is often a disconnect between what families see activists with dementia achieve, to the point that at times they may doubt the diagnosis, and being affected by difficulties in seemingly trivial areas, where the person might be seen as not making a sufficient effort and is met with irritation or impatience. Julie had particularly insightful thoughts about how she may be contributing to this dynamic by mainly sharing the positive achievements rather than the downsides.

While work colleagues and acquaintances have all but disappeared from Julie's life, she describes two different enduring long-term friendships that have continued. As others among the Fifteen, she finds peer support invaluable and is amazed at the number of friendships that have developed from this alongside activism. She describes dementia as 'a great leveller' that has opened the possibility of meeting people from many different walks of life who nevertheless understand the ups and downs of living with dementia and are supportive in a non-judgemental way, without overreacting to occasional expressions of frustration or despair.

Keith Day (Cam)

Changes in family relationships

What my wife and daughter noticed was the change in my manner.

It only happens gradually, like you said. We have a sign at home: 'it is what it is', and that's it, you know. Obviously, it's like my wife in a way – she is the breadwinner now, so therefore I understand I have to respect her work privacy and stuff, so, you know, that's what I do; because my wife, she's 8 years younger than me, so she hasn't even got to the retirement yet.

Losing and maintaining relationships

Our best friend, when she found out that I had dementia, she changed completely. She said, 'oh no, I can't give this to you, because if you have it [dementia], you'll forget where it is'. So, you know, that really upset me, because we'd been good friends for so many years!

My wife's sister, they again accepted it, you know, and that's it. And the week before that I was up in Yorkshire, with my family, and they again accepted that I have dementia.

Relationship with DEEP group

I am a member of Pathfinders, and we are very limited, I want to spread and grow it.

If it doesn't work, I'd admit it and just say sorry. I need help, as simple as that – rather than just saying 'you can't have it'. Just give me a chance!

Relationships in the church

The pastor's wife, her mum had dementia, so she accepts it, and that's more helpful, you know, so it really was just that one person that shut us off.

To me the church is a lot of comfort, and to my wife as well, and I really think sometimes it's our faith that's taken us through all the things that happened to us, and we believe it's there for a reason.

Cam described one example of losing a very good friend after the diagnosis, but had many examples of relationships being maintained, albeit sometimes with adjustments in the roles. In contrast to older, retired people who develop a dementia, Cam's partner continues to work, reducing the time that can be spent together.

Cam relayed one of very few expressions of frustration with a peer/activism group, as he would like it to do more and expand, and seems to be meeting with some resistance.

Cam spoke about the importance of his church affiliations, and the helpful presence of someone with experience of dementia in their own family. He shared an example of how good dementia awareness in a faith community can help to strengthen the relationship as well as spirituality.

Masood Ahmed Qureshi (Maq)

Relationship with family members

I have got three sisters, one of whom is a medic. My sister in Stoke-on-Trent works for the National Health Service, and her daughter is a nurse at a local hospital. My other two sisters are school teachers. I have got five children from my first marriage and they all [together with] my parents lived with me until [my parents] passed away. I have got three children that live with me now. Two are married with their own places. My daughter who lives with me has got a child that lives with me, too. So you know, going back to 2010 and when I was diagnosed they had only just started their jobs, they all had responsibilities and their own concerns and worries. I didn't really want to bring this on them as well because they're already looking after a dad who had just gone through a major heart surgery and he's having to be led to the bathroom and everywhere. I didn't want to throw that on them at all, so I did not tell my children about my dementia diagnosis. But I did tell my sisters because they were older and they obviously live at their own homes. I asked them not to mention it to my children yet, so it was quite some time, and even then I couldn't find a way of actually being able to talk to them. Because you know, we as parents are there for them, it's a duty to look after our kids and care for them, and I didn't want them to feel 'oh no, dad's heart has got a problem, and now he's losing his mind'.

I don't think it has changed in a negative sort of way but I feel sometimes that they might be thinking, 'oh, it's not dad, its dad's dementia', do you know what I mean. I might have agitation and stress and anger and all these emotional things connected with this condition, and you know there might be times when I say things that I ordinarily wouldn't have said. But what I think is, because they understand it, they're quite happy with it.

Relationship with friends

So the next thing was friends. I excluded myself and limited my best of friends for two main reasons: one is that I didn't want them to know that I have dementia, and the second is that I didn't know what their reaction was going to be when I did tell them. Instead of them saying goodbye to me or not know-

ing, like I have learnt now that a lot of people have gone through that when they've told their friends, they've lost them. I will sort of stay away for a bit till I am fully in a position to accept the situation, research on it, know a little bit more about it, and then maybe discuss it with them and tell them. So that was the reason for me to stay away from friends and eventually I did tell them and now all my friends know it.

Relationship with friends who have dementia

I think that people living with dementia have not only accepted me as part of their family, I feel ... and I think you'll be able to probably relate to this because of the 3 Nations. I feel that not only am I part of that organisation or that group of people, but I am also looked upon as an elder, as a mature person.

Would you believe that I've got nearly 5,000 people on Facebook, 400 and something on LinkedIn and over 400 on Twitter, and 90 per cent of them are people living with dementia or connected with dementia.

We made some films, I don't know whether you've had the chance to see them. Well, within DEEP we made some films, and on one of the films I put my hands up like this, and I said, 'thank you dementia, I have gained so many friends!'

Maq expressed the need to protect his children who at the time of his diagnosis were relatively young, and how difficult it was to have deep conversations about it even with his sisters. Over time, the children have adjusted and are more understanding of his emotional reactions, which can seem disproportionate.

Maq took a cautious approach to letting his friends know about the diagnosis, only telling people after some time of isolating himself in order to avoid what he thought might be negative reactions. Being active on social media, Maq is astounded at how many people follow him. He expresses what it means to him to feel accepted as an 'elder' in the dementia community, his 'dementia family', an attachment that now sits equally alongside that with the South Asian community.

Nigel Hullah

Keeping and losing friends post-diagnosis

I think it's inevitable it [a dementia diagnosis] does [change relationships], and anybody that says it hasn't either isn't taking note of what's going on around them or is probably fooling themselves that they have the same cadre of friends as they had previously. Your true friends stay with you. You know, the people who are invested in you stay with you, and you quickly find out who that is. Oh, it's not all cases, I'm just saying generally; once it's known that somebody has something like dementia, people become embarrassed to meet you. They say, looking at their shoes thing ... I go, 'I've got dementia'. 'Oh, do you? Oh dear'. And they have a perception of what life with you is going to be like. A lot of them say, 'I didn't sign up for this' and I get it. You know, I get it. But your true friends will stay with you, and if you can count them on the fingers of both hands, you're doing well. And I can. So, I'm doing okay in that regard. But these are people who I had strong relationships with prior to the dementia coming along.

Relationship with services / professionals

In a way, what we're talking about here is attachment also with ourselves in a sense, and with professionals who are seeking to help us. We have these attachments with our family and with our friends, but also we have attachments with professionals who are helping us with advanced care directives, or should do, or helping us with day-to-day living.

Why do we have this medical model issue? We're always going to have a deficit agenda because the medical model concentrates on what's missing, or what's going, or what's gone. They don't look at what's still there, and that then gives rise to an ageist rhetoric and a hostility towards disabled people, because they continually judge you on what you can't do, not what's there, what's to be built on. Give an example. I forgot how to do my shoelaces up. I woke up one day, just couldn't do my shoelaces. And it so happened that I had a home visit from the Young Onset Team, there was a young registrar there and he said, 'Oh, don't worry about that. Just go Velcro-sided shoes.' And the O.T. said, 'Oh no, no. I'm going to build a little frame so he can learn how to do his shoelaces up' – that's the difference. That is the difference.

Yeah, I mean, some of the tactics I learnt from the allied health care professionals, there was a particular doctor, Helen Barker, she is a psychologist, she took a particular interest in some of my tics. You know, she taught me lots of relaxation techniques and how to focus and stuff like that. Whereas if I went to my GP without that, you know, for me, it would be haloperidol or something.

Advance decisions

These decisions are made when you've got capacity, sometimes these decisions come when people haven't got capacity. What worries me above all else is that I have not been given a space to make advanced, well maybe not Advance Care Directives, but I'm going to require residential care at some stage, and nobody's talking to me about it. This is something they say, 'we'll face that when we have to know' – no you don't. That's not the way you run your life.

New friendships post-diagnosis

I look for different things in people who are around me, but my friendships have changed. I still have my core friendships with people I had knowledge of prior, but I've got new friends as well – like yourself, Keith, who I consider a friend. Like Reinhard, who I consider a friend. Who, I wouldn't have met either one of you, had it not been for dementia, and I'm a better person for meeting you. I'm a better person for meeting people such as Chris Roberts and all the people who make up the 3 Nations. I've had to adapt, I've had to readjust, because dementia is isolating. It's very isolating, and if you don't adjust to your dementia, other people won't join you in your journey. You know, you have to adjust.

The friendships are different, they're quite empathetic now, whereas before they were just based around what we were doing. You know, what environment? Many people I didn't think I would get on with, I now do very well indeed with, simply because I made the change and people respond to the change. I'm a different person than my first year of diagnosis. I'm a different person.

New relationships through activism

Most of my friends, right, they're quite right, you know, it's one thing you being outspoken, it's another thing to be damned bloody rude, and I think some people overlap that, and I've had to sort of adjust that. I'm like a nuclear tomcat, 'meow', quite happy to say, like most of my old friends, and I have my moments, I do have my moments, you know.

You form friendships because of either professional similarities or because you share the same ideology in what you're doing. I mean, you bring, the shared mechanism of it. Sharing the values of the organisation you find yourself in leads to strong friendships. You know, we have a saying, 'if you're lying in the dirt with somebody, they'll always be your friend'. Of course, it's like living with dementia, but the friendship is about facing the challenges together.

You know, it's nice to know people are caring about you, but I hate patronising. I was at a meeting yesterday, it was the therapies group in my local health board, I chair that meeting. And we were working on a memory assessment. One of the therapists said, 'Are we asking too many questions?' I said, 'You never ask too many questions. It's asking the right question, the problem is that you're not asking the right questions!' And all of a sudden they develop this patronising attitude, 'oh there, there, I hope we don't bring out a stroke', you know?

What I can do is make relationships in my own little world, which are a balance, and which I call supportive, and to move forwards through having the ability to value other people's opinions and have the joy of my own opinions valued as well.

Without a close family, Nigel focuses on his relationships with friends, in activism and with professionals. His one close relative lives on another continent, and he would not want him to change his life due to Nigel's dementia diagnosis.

Like others, he describes the reactions of embarrassment and the inability to relate from some former friends, but has also experienced help and support from friends whom he had not considered particularly close previously.

Nigel speaks about the isolating effect of dementia and the need to adapt in order to take advantage of the possibilities of new significant relationships through activism and the shared experience of living with dementia, some of which develop into deeper friendships.

The relationships with professionals are mixed, both as a service user himself and as an activist and expert by experience. There is an echo of previous conversations I have had with Nigel about the negative effects of a medical model in the approach to dementia and a positive example of making use of occupational therapy, aids and adaptations.

It was sobering to hear Nigel's recollection of a meeting he was meant to be chairing and experienced as being patronised by professionals. I wondered whether in the face of one of Nigel's typically outspoken challenges the professionals felt as helpless and lost for words as some of the less enlightened friends, and resorted to the safe position of a professional / patient dynamic rather than relating as equals.

Tracey Shorthouse

Relationship with friends

I have friends who have nothing to do with dementia. So they're there for me, being me, and because of my age, being quite young I try to get away from the label of dementia. I mean, people don't really quite understand that, and it's very hard. You know, it's difficult, I'm lucky to have friends in all aspects of life because I've always been that way.

I lost about five friends when I was diagnosed. They didn't believe I had dementia, they didn't believe that dementia affected young people, they didn't understand. I think, 'their loss'. I've still met loads of new people in my life who just accept me for who I am. My friends, I can say, most of my friends are long term, 30 years, 10 years, and they just accept me for who I am, and they still see me as being me without dementia.

Relationship with friends who have dementia

I have a lot of friends who have got dementia, maybe that I speak to online or, you know, through Zoom.

You know, that with dementia, and on Zoom, there's always someone you can call back, if you had a bad day or somebody is going through the same things you're going through, because dementia, although there are different kinds of dementia, you all have similar problems, too.

But it's people, sometimes people who have dementia, they'll always understand my ethos of how I feel, and it's – I feel like I get lost in the labour of dementia, if that makes sense.

At the SUNshiners, we do support each other as well in a different way, it's just – you know, you're always there for each other.

Relationship with the cats

And I love them dearly and they sort of keep me going as well … But having cats, having any animal in the house, THAT is what really keeps me going.

It's not easy. I think when you haven't got any animals and you haven't anybody in your life to say, 'Come on, get up' and jolly you up a bit. Because sometimes, when you feel low, that's what you need sometimes.

Tracey, like some others of the Fifteen, describes the difficulty often experienced by younger people with dementia in not being believed that they have developed dementia at such a young age. Also, that when a diagnosis is obtained relatively early, that they do not fulfil the stereotype of the helpless person requiring care in a nursing home.

Very important to Tracey are long-term relationships developed over decades, and newly acquired friends, among whom Tracey feels she can be herself and is treated in the way most people we spoke with would like to be treated: as herself, as the person she has been and is now. The shared experience adds to this and Zoom has opened new avenues for support any time of the day and from anywhere – although, for Tracey, the relationship with her cats remains equally important.

So what learning can we take from the Fifteen?

These interviews provided a rich and varied account of how dementia impacts on a person's sense of inclusion. We reflect here on what we can generalise for others living with dementia and those who support them.

From the point of view of someone living with dementia:

- Sharing the diagnosis of dementia with family and friends is an important step in adjusting and living well with the condition and in maintaining open relationships with those around us.
- People describe great support from some of their friends and family, but it would be wise to be prepared to meet some challenges: people keeping their distance, not knowing what to say or how to act, and some relationships coming to an end.
- There are inevitably changes in close family and marital relationships, with responsibilities being redistributed and roles redefined, and it can take time and effort to navigate these changes successfully.
- There can also be challenges when others cannot see the struggles dementia is causing, and refusing to believe that the person has been correctly diagnosed, as they do not conform to the stereotype of helplessness.
- Activism and peer support offer a wide range of new relationships and friendships with others who are experiencing similar issues, and this can be a great source of comfort and support.

There are also implications for those who provide professional support and care for persons living with dementia. For them, the main takeaway messages are:

- Past family experiences with dementia can have a profound impact on how a new diagnosis is shared and affects the family and relationship systems around the person.
- Relationships change following a diagnosis due to attitudes and beliefs about dementia, as well as the disabilities and challenges presented by dementia. Good post-diagnosis support ought to be relationship-focused and support the person with the diagnosis in navigating these changes and losses.
- Ensuring access to peer support can help people with dementia in building new support networks and relationships.
- Paradoxically, people who manage their lives well with dementia, in particular activists, are exposed to relationship difficulties in families and further afield when doubts are expressed over their diagnosis, as they do not confirm to the stereotypical views held about people with dementia.
- Continuity of relationships becomes more important in dementia, while support services are often fragmented, with a lack of continuity in the professionals encountered. Professionals working with activists are often the most consistent contact within service settings and need to pay attention to the nature of the relationships they are building over time.

11 Comfort

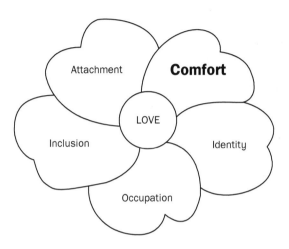

Comfort brings calm
Such a wonderful stillness
A soft melodic sound
Soothing the brain
Ending the confusion that surrounds.

– Gail Gregory

The Fifteen on Comfort – narrated by Keith Oliver

Kitwood places comfort first when writing about the petals in his flower model. For him, comfort means tenderness, kindness, closeness, soothing, calming and giving the person a sense of security. He then rightly suggests that comfort is important to people with dementia in enabling them to deal with loss, whether that be through bereavement or losing one's cognitive abilities. Furthermore, he talks about the need for comfort when partings occur, and I know from personal experience that this was a post-diagnosis challenge which previously would not have been the case.

In essence, what we were seeking to encourage in this part of our conversations with the Fifteen was for them to tell us what provides them comfort, how they feel when they experience comfort and, conversely, what impact a lack of comfort has on their life and wellbeing. Then, having spoken about this, we hoped to gain a sense of how contentment contributes to their feeling of comfort, as well as their physical and emotional safety.

While sensing that the petals of inclusion, occupation, identity and attachment might be easier for people to speak about than comfort, this largely proved not to be the case as most opened up to us readily and at ease. I believe this was due in part to me knowing each of the Fifteen, alongside placing comfort towards the end of the conversations when people felt more relaxed and engaged, and dare I say, more comfortable.

I don't recall any of the Fifteen talking about their financial situation in relation to comfort. In a way this surprised me, although in another way it did not. I recall being at a meeting held at the Alzheimer's Society towards the close of the IDEAL One project [https://www.idealproject.org.uk/] where research findings presented suggested that over a thousand people with dementia, when asked about what contributed to their wellbeing did not rank money as high as one might expect. Does money contribute towards a person's comfort? – I'm not sure it does. However, as a person's dementia progresses, they are expected to pay towards their care, unlike the NHS, which is free at the point of access to all according to need.

Without the conversation morphing into a kind of psychotherapy session (although George did once suggest this was more or less the case, although he did speak positively of it), we were interested to hear if any negative experiences associated with a lack of comfort were a result of something rooted in their childhood. Unquestionably, living with dementia causes anxiety, stress and uncertainty and for me, the single, most accurate word to describe having dementia is frustration. I wondered whether having witnessed that some people with dementia are reticent to embrace an activity that I believe they would derive comfort from, but with encouragement they find works well for them, might be reflected in our conversations.

I think that what Kitwood and I felt is likely to be the experiences of two people with dementia from very different perspectives, as this chapter shows to be the case.

In what follows, the words of the Fifteen are italicised to help distinguish them from Keith's commentary.

Agnes Houston

What provides comfort?

When speaking about what gave her comfort, Agnes felt able to reflect at some length, and shared with us a range of approaches which she had utilised in the time since being diagnosed. She not only touched on the 'what' but went into great detail about 'how this helped her'. Unusually for those we spoke with, at times Agnes spoke in the first person before switching to the second person and doing what I also often do, which is to draw upon the use of metaphors to help explain oneself.

Well, if I'm feeling uncomfortable with myself, I will use mindfulness because that gives me comfort, and my yoga twice a week gives me comfort. Meditation gives me comfort. My art gives me comfort. Do you know I feel as if I'm a bit like 'Mary Poppins'? You know, the way she used to open up her bag and she pull out lights and all sorts? Well, I open up my Mary Poppins bag and I will bring out a tool. If I'm feeling uncomfortable, I go in and say, 'Well, what am I going to do to remove that feeling and make me feel more comfortable?' Then I'll make a choice. Isn't it lovely that now I have a choice, you know, am I going to dabble with acrylics? Is it going to be watercolour? Am I going to crochet? Sometimes if I'm feeling uncomfortable, I will look and say, 'What part did you play in this? Is it something about that you to need change?' So that if you weren't comfortable in, maybe, company? Right? So, what part can 'Agnes' play in this? Do you want to change to feel comfortable? Is it important enough for you to go in and make that a comfortable situation for you? I have to look at it like that and say, 'Well, no, it takes too much of my brain and too much effort for what I am gonna benefit out of it'. You know, so I kind of look at these kinds of strategies about comfort. So it's a bit like walking in uncomfortable shoes, you bought them, you spent your money on them – I've done it loads of times, it might be a woman thing ... [laughs] ... you wear them once and you're uncomfortable, and then you throw them aside. And then you try it again. Then you think you know; I need to give them to a charity shop because I don't want sore feet. They don't suit me. That doesn't mean to say that pair of shoes in the shop wouldn't suit other people. It's just we're all different. But what part do I play in this situation? And is it something I need to change about me? So that's the way I look at it. Even in DEEP ... even in activism, you know, there's some spaces that I don't feel comfortable in, and I think, 'Well what part do I play in this?' And look at it very closely, you know, I do a wee bit of inward looking and reflection, and then say, 'Well, is it important to me?' If it is 'no', then I would rather not participate.

I think there's a time for everything. Sometimes you want a savoury packet of crisps, and that gives you comfort. Then at other times it's a big gooey cake. Do you know what I mean? Sometimes comfort for me is like that, I need solitude. There is a need for me. I search it out, and will seek it. I'm happy with both sides of 'Agnes' now, whether it's solitude or seeking – I don't see anything wrong with any of that. If someone said to me, 'I need to go back into my room or I'm going for a walk'. And you'd say, 'Oh do you want to come in?' And they say, 'no'. I think 'well good', they're having some you know, I call it 'Agnes' time you know, that little – for their space and their time.

Chris Maddocks

What provides comfort?

Knowing Chris as I do, I am aware of her love of walking along the seafront near where she lives and capturing the comfort she derives from it in photographs posted on Facebook, often of glorious sunrises and sunsets. She has also spoken on 3 Nations Dementia Working Group webinars about her love of the outdoors and how it encourages her creativity. What Chris revealed is one of a number of examples of how people with dementia can gain comfort from a wide range of activities, many of which have a creative aspect to them.

Best of all being out in nature gives me huge comfort and I live by the sea so I love the sea and the sunrises, So yeah, I think nature probably and the sea and things like that is what gives me the greatest comfort. I am very keen on 'wellness' in nature.

Listening to music sometimes brings me comfort, or maybe doing some cooking.

Experiencing a lack of comfort

Alarmingly, but maybe not surprisingly given the pressures that NHS hospitals face, both Chris and George challenged the notion that stays in hospital can and should be occasions when a person with dementia feels comforted.

I found in the hospital situation sometimes that during lockdown, I was unfortunate enough to be an inpatient twice for a week at a time. There was very little understanding of my dementia, or my Parkinson's, and not having my Parkinson's medications on time caused me to hallucinate and ... and with my dementia, not one person asked me how my dementia affected me. Before I was discharged, I asked to speak to the doctor. And I said, during my time here, for example, they moved me from Eastbourne to Hastings at 4 o'clock in the morning, and put me into a ward which was a mixed ward. There was a man snoring really loudly next to me, and all the machines are beeping, and it had a bad effect on me. I said to one of the nurses, 'I can't stay here because of the noise', but nobody ever spoke to me about it.

Seeking comfort from challenges

Whether it is the COVID-19 pandemic and lockdown or confrontations with other people, Chris navigates these challenges with a compass based upon kindness which directs her to a place of comfort either physically, emotionally or psychologically.

I didn't leave my house for 3 months; I was suffering with anxiety and depression. And I became a bit of a prisoner in my own home. Initially, I started doing the singing lessons via Zoom … And I've really enjoyed that.

Yeah, I think I've built up resilience. I think that's a big thing. And that's important. And I tried to find ways around things as opposed to it totally knocking me flat.

I think kindness is a big thing to me, that's me being kind to people, but also them being kind to me as well. I don't like confrontational issues. Although if I'm faced with one, I will deal with it. So it gives me comfort to think that people can be nice to one another and be kind to one another. During lockdown last year, I enjoyed painting the fence in the garden. I enjoy doing things in the garden and jet washing the patio. Things that most people don't like to do, you know, I quite enjoy doing those. So I find comfort in doing practical things.

In a nutshell

So it gives me comfort to think that people can be nice to one another and be kind to one another.

Often, I am one of those people, who people say I do things always for other people and I don't do much for myself.

What I'm finding is that I need more reassurance now. Yeah, as I don't know if the things I'm doing are right, whether it is a talk or … or anything else. I'm looking for reassurance that's right for me, as well as right for other people. I doubt my own abilities. I think reassurance is good and helps give me comfort.

Chris Norris

What provides comfort?

It is often said that professionals need to get to know the person who has *the* dementia rather than *their* dementia, and this applies even more so to those closest to us by way of family and friends. It is usually to our family that we turn and rely for comfort and tolerance, and this comes from having an understanding of the person. I think Chris is absolutely right in the way he describes his thoughts on this.

Firstly, the family, but it's definitely the 'family around me'. The support they give me makes me more comfortable and even more so if I make a mistake. They know that it's not me making that mistake, but the mistake has come as a result of my dementia, and that gives me comfort. It doesn't give me carte blanche to then just go off. Because some people, you know, there'd be a temptation to say to whatever you do, 'I'm sorry it's because of my dementia'. I don't allow it to give me carte blanche but at the same time, there's a reason behind it.

Seeking comfort from challenges

Lockdown featured in many of the conversations, often when we were focusing on comfort. I think Chris' thoughts on this time reflect those of many people with or without dementia and form a useful record not only for now but also for posterity, as experience and memory of the lockdowns begins to fade.

On the Zoom virtual meetings, there's that element that I still feel very safe. A lot of people said that the 18 months of lockdown have been very difficult but I actually found that quite comfortable in a way. Because I'm in my home environment and even when I'm doing things outside that environment, around dementia or whatever, I'm still within my home environment, still in my own comfortable chair, still got my four walls around me, still got my dog to lick my hand, those are the things that give you comfort, isn't it?

In a nutshell

My comfort zone is that I'm safe in my own house in what I'm saying or doing.

Chris Roberts

Seeking comfort after being diagnosed with dementia

Chris dived straight in when asked about how he achieved comfort after his dementia diagnosis by describing the heavy sense of loss he felt about something which previously was a major source of comfort. We then felt after he reflected further that while peer support from his friends with dementia helped a little, it was deep within himself that he turned for comfort.

Yeah, absolutely, anyone that tells you that it doesn't affect your ability to feel comfort, have been diagnosed far too early. It interfered with my driving, it interfered with my biggest interests which was motorcycles. If you can't ride a motorcycle, what is the point of having one? I haven't got one and now there's a massive hole in my life and I've lost all my motorcycle buddies. You know, your brothers.

What provides comfort?

I was keen to give Chris the opportunity to talk about how his and Jayne's campervan is an important part of their lives as they look to enjoy the current and next chapters in their lives, and also in what ways does it give him comfort.

I relax by enjoying the nice newish motorhome that we now have. It's the best motorhome we've ever had, you know, I want to spend time in it. I sort of enjoy it. It's a very beautiful space. I love the space. I love sitting outside.

I love watching people. I don't want to engage with them. But it's great watching them in the campsites. I get to spend a lot of quality time with Jayne, which I know we were always together before, but it's different. It's different now. Yeah, and I know that at the moment, Jayne also needs that support.

Our campervan is so dementia-friendly I can immediately sit in my chair which looks at the whole van, this little one room and I can see anything I need. You know and its great, and when you go on a campsite, people are so much more amicable and everyone is your friend.

In a nutshell

When I struggle to feel comfort, I think I'm going round and round. I do feel it's a vicious circle. I do feel like my life is going round and round. I seem to be coming to the same point all the time, which is dementia. I've just gone so lethargic. I really can't be bothered.

During this part of the conversation Chris became very animated and was clearly beginning to tire but knowing Chris as I do, I was interested and surprised by the above extract, so I asked him what had disappointed him in the context of us thinking about his comfort. His response was instant:

No support. Apparently, in this life, you have to ask for support.

Dianne Campbell

What provides comfort?

Dianne is one of the Fifteen we spoke with who lives on their own, and we were interested to hear how she achieved comfort. Overcoming pain is a challenge for anyone but for a person with dementia, this is further compounded if there is no one at home to help care for you. For Dianne, travel, going for a walk and watching TV are clearly her main sources of comfort.

I'm very passionate about things, and when I travel I'm not in pain, that's my comfort. I tell people I live on my own and I make myself comfortable. I can make myself really comfortable. I would laugh at the TV watching any silly things. Because I think that at times if you just overwork your brain, it kind of puts you down in a depression and because I know I've got my spinal problem, that can really send me into depression, and I really tried to stay away from that. I really do. When my pain is really overpowering, it's like I just want to get out of my house. I just walk. I know I cannot walk like how I used to walk because I can slip if I make the wrong step. Then it affects me up in my thinking. So, I would just go out or I would just chill out indoors.

I love being cared for by myself. Because I think one of the things I like and enjoy is a holiday. It's taking myself away from everything. I always say that to people when I'm going on holiday.

Experiencing a lack of comfort

Being able to live within one's challenges and difficulties can be immensely comforting for some people, as described here by Dianne:

I don't get enough sleep. My memory bothers me. I had to shrug it off. Because for so long. I can deal with it. I know how to deal with it. I always said I'm not gonna let it overrule me. So, I put it aside. I had to look after myself and just leave the memory.

In a nutshell

I close my door, turn the key and that's it. I don't think about anything else until I'm ready to get back up on that plane, wherever I'm coming from. I make sure that I take care of myself, I try and eat well and sometimes I treat myself to something nice.

Frances Isaacs

The person's home was often cited as their sanctuary and a place where they felt comfort. I think this surprised no one and adds weight to the notion that people with dementia need to feel supported for as long as possible to live in their own home rather than to move into a residential setting.

What provides comfort?

It's being at home, being in this environment here where I feel totally safe.

Experiencing a lack of comfort

I know from other conversations with Frances that she was formerly a very outgoing and gregarious person. Whether it is her dementia or COVID-19, or maybe a combination of the two, but she was very clear in explaining that beyond being comfortable in her own home, the experience of going outside this safe space was very difficult for her.

Things don't go really badly wrong until I go out. With COVID-19 around I haven't had to go out, perfect, it suited me exceedingly well. Now that I'm starting to have to go out, it's very challenging for me.

Seeking comfort from challenges

I have spoken publicly many times about how for people with dementia creativity fosters resilience, and Frances is a great example of this in practice as there can be no one with dementia who better illustrates a creative mind able to comfort oneself. Often our conversations focused on comfort arising from other people or activities; in the case of Frances, she offered the thought that comfort can come from within oneself.

I've always been quite a resilient person. I have managed to keep my feelings inside to the extent that I probably drove myself crazy. You know, I managed to suppress everything when my mother died. I also for the sake of peace and quiet in the family kept a lot of my feelings hidden.

Gail Gregory

What provides comfort?

Gail immediately identified her love of the natural world as her source of comfort and it was after a little gentle prompting that she then moved on to tell us about how she does or doesn't derive comfort from other people.

Just getting away from the house, walking either by the sea and just listening to the sound of the sea, because that's very relaxing, or just going somewhere where there's nature. We have a nature reserve very close to us, so I'll just go and sit on the grass and listen to the birds. Usually, I take my camera with me and take photos and it's just absolutely wonderful.

No, I prefer to be on my own. I prefer to be outside walking on my own, just with my dog, because he doesn't say anything to me, he just looks at me. Sometimes I do need the comfort of others and it's normally my hubby that comforts me if I'm having a really bad day. But normally I do like to be on my own, just to get my own thoughts together.

Sometimes I get comfort from others – it depends, I'm not sure who I get support from if I'm a little confused on which way to go, or I need some advice, as we all do sometimes. Just somebody to talk to, especially the people that's going through what you're going through because they understand what it is like. Whereas, my hubby is unfortunately still learning. So, yes peer support, just to talk to somebody if you're having a really bad fuzzy day and something's a little bit different, it just makes you realise you're not alone.

George Rook

As I recorded earlier, George had prepared notes for our conversation, so the breadth and depth of his comments are not surprising. I was especially interested by his statement about obtaining comfort from knowing himself, before projecting forward to when what currently gives him comfort may be less easily accessible to him.

What provides comfort?

If I go for a walk, I don't want to walk with someone else because I do not want to talk at the same time that I am walking. I want to look around and see whatever there is and listen. I think a sense of comfort also comes from George Rook knowing George Rook, and knowing that actually I'm accomplishing stuff. I'm doing alright now. I may have struggled in the past, but actually this is something I can do.

I intend to continue to carve and paint and garden as long as I physically can. Where will I get comfort when I can't do that, I haven't a clue.

Impact of the pandemic on comfort

What George says here really follows on from his previous response to what provides him comfort:

I enjoyed lockdown for two reasons: one reason is because I live in a lovely place with a big garden, and I have no desire to go anywhere else. The other thing is that it's taken away stress. The stress of people, the stress of noise, and that for me has been huge, because you know even just going on a train down to London has its stresses for those of us who don't enjoy doing it. It is important to concentrate on being quite comfortable in your own skin and with George Rook.

Experiencing a lack of comfort

George was the second person to talk about a time spent in hospital, highlighting why it was a far from comfortable experience for him.

I would always want to remain at home unless I absolutely had to be looked after with nursing care somewhere. I can't stand it when I've been in hospital, which is several times. I can't stand it because I can't stand all the noise and the ... and the people around me. I found the fact that the staff were wearing masks difficult as I didn't know whether they were smiling or not. You know they don't treat you as a person, they just, oh I don't know. It's just full of raw anxiety.

In a nutshell

I get a great source of comfort from carving and painting as they are such intense processes that take me to another place. It's not just the satisfaction of what I'd done, it's actually just being where I cannot think about anything other than what I'm doing with my hands or what something's going to look like when I have finished the creative piece.

Jennifer Bute

Being able to listen to music of her own choice is so important to Jennifer and gives her great comfort, and in this age of artificial intelligence the aid of a gadget like Alexa comes to the fore for her.

What provides comfort?

Music is wonderful isn't it? Music is just amazing. I think people don't realise the power of music in bringing back memories to tie up the loose ends in our brain which enables people who have difficulty doing things. It can ease the corners ... and it's wonderful because I don't have to remember the name of the piece or if I want a song I just say play the song to Alexa. It's wonderful that music cheers me up, gives me comfort or calms me down.

Gaining comfort from a religious faith

When I give some of my lectures to Christian groups I say, 'well, look how Jesus dealt with someone who entered a meltdown in crisis'. They are exactly the same principles that we need to use with someone with dementia, because we believe and share with those with faith that everything Jesus went through, we also go through. Jesus went through meltdowns too and how did he behave?

In a nutshell

Jennifer took her comments about the comfort she gains from her religious faith to conclude this section of the conversation with a deep philosophical statement:

My faith is very important to me and gives me great comfort, and with this everyone has equal worth and value.

Julie Hayden

Seeking comfort from challenges

The first two sections described by Julie illustrate what many people experienced and felt before, during and after the COVID-19 pandemic, and show how important home is but also the realisation that while it gives us comfort, it can also prohibit the comfort that comes from socialising with other people.

Comfort for me has always been being in my own home. Comfort is more now about being with other people, with my friends whom I feel comfortable. I'm really looking forward to getting to a point where we can actually be meeting in person again because during lockdown apart from Zoom, I've pretty much lived like a hermit, and that is no fun when it goes on for months and months. I've now had enough of being on my own. I just can't wait to be out and among other people now.

Impact of the pandemic on comfort

Now, after the COVID-19 pandemic, I'm struggling with pushing myself to get out from home more, so maybe it's become too much of a place of comfort and I need to push those comfort boundaries.

Gaining comfort from a religious faith

I can't remember the last time I went to church, as I was seeing myself as less sure about my beliefs. I suppose I like to believe that there is something more to life than just the time we have on Earth, maybe there is something after my life on Earth, and if I'm frustrated about something or I'm worried about something, then in my own mind will speak to God even though I won't actually be saying prayers.

Keith Day (Cam)

What provides comfort?

Cam captures here three ways of achieving comfort which are common to many others we spoke with – family and friends, music and peer support.

My family and my friends help me to relax. I love to listen to music and when I'm a bit stressed, I love to listen to the pan pipes. I love them so much because I can sit there and everything just goes and that's it, you know, so I feel comfortable just sitting there.
    Peer support to me has been a lifeline and great comfort to me.

Seeking comfort from challenges

Much is often said and written about the benefits to society of people giving up their time, energy and expertise as volunteers, but it is also important not to overlook the benefits to the person who volunteers.

I'm always helping people. It's like with dementia I think it's too late for me now, but I might be able to do something for people who develop dementia later and I feel by doing that role I'm giving back something into society.

Changes in gaining comfort since being diagnosed

I asked Cam whether he felt that his sources of comfort had stayed the same or similar, or had changed since being diagnosed.

Yeah, pretty much the same, because after work I used to play a CD in the car because when I had finished a shift I was often quite stressed. I realised then this was something which helped me, and it's something I've managed to keep doing since.

Gaining comfort from a religious faith

Picking up on Cam's earlier comments about his faith when talking about identity, attachment and inclusion, Reinhard was interested to ask him about how much comfort he took his religious faith.

I have my faith, and I'm not gonna knock other people because they have a different faith to me as that's up to them. To me, I don't think I'd be able to go through all that's happened such as having had a heart attack, as well that the people from the church were there giving comfort to me and my family. God won't give me more than I can handle whatever happens.

The church is a lot of comfort to me, and to my wife as well, and I really think sometimes it's our faith that's taken us all through all the things that's happened to us, and we believe it's there for a reason. Over the last 2 years with people in our church, I'd say my faith has gotten stronger. God never changes, but I think we do sometimes.

Masood Ahmed Qureshi (Maq)

Seeking comfort from challenges

While I am sure that Maq has foggy, difficult days, it was uplifting to hear his positivity around his views on life with dementia, and how he has been able to seek comfort from others to support his own positive attitude.

Well personally, I am a lot happier now that I know I have dementia, and also I'm quite content with the fact that I'm handling it reasonably well.

The thing that cushioned the blow for me was actually DEEP in the first instance. When your confidence goes, which is the first thing that happens when you're diagnosed, you need to be around people that you can trust and that you can bond with now apart from your family and friends.

What provides comfort?

At this point in our conversation, Maq broadened his views from just expressing thoughts on his own situation and experience to reflecting on what he had seen in other people. Often those of us who occupy what is regarded as an activist role speak solely from our own perspective but sometimes it is helpful if the person is able to use their experience in a broader sense so that more people can relate to, and hopefully learn from this.

Well, of course, at the top of the list are my kids obviously. They're at home, and they've been looking after me. I have found through these meetings that some families are not providing as much comfort as they could or they should. The thing is we have been comforted by people that are not trained to comfort, you know, that is important because I've been in a field where you have to be trained to do certain things. The family could all mean well but because they don't know how to care, they don't understand the condition 100 per cent. They don't understand your needs and they can't assess what your needs are, so the family can't provide that sort of comfort.

To a certain extent, I get comfort from friends. While you try not to tell them everything because you don't want to worry them, or they don't understand what it is like with dementia, but with DEEP you've got these people that you don't really know or see as friends, but they are professionals at what they do and they do a really good job. That gave me an opportunity or a platform if you like to be able to say what I want to say because these people listened. Later, I started a peer support group in Stoke-on-Trent. Members all come after me because I'm the founding member, and it includes nine people now. We've lost a couple sadly, but it's grown and that peer support has been the backbone to my recovery. They were my advocates. They gave me a voice. When you volunteer together, I feel a much stronger feeling of comfort.

In a nutshell

Peer support we always say is close to top of the comfort list simply because these people are all going through the same situation, and they know and understand everybody's needs and that bond is far stronger.

Nigel Hullah

What provides comfort?

Nigel was one of those people who related one of his current sources of comfort back to how he sourced it many years previously, which is something that many of us do both consciously and sub-consciously. I was also very interested by the way he expressed himself in the second paragraph here where the reflective Nigel was very evident.

I get comfort and pleasure from the old radio plays on Radio Four. You know they take me back to my younger days. Indeed, there are two reasons, they take me back to another place and another time which I enjoyed. Also, they're damn entertaining, you know?

I get comfort from a sense of achievement. I like achieving things. I like getting things done. I'm not afraid of confrontation, although I don't do it as much, or as often as I used to. I loved 'Time and Place', the poetry project. My only regret about that was I never joined it soon enough.

As I was heavily involved in the 'Time and Place' poetry project myself, I was aware that Nigel sat on the fringes for much of the time and only really joined in fully towards the end. Consequently, I asked him why he hadn't joined sooner, and what he had taken from the project once he contributed a poem and attended the virtual Zoom celebration to conclude the project.

I don't know. I can't answer that, I can't actually find you an answer for that, other than the fact that I think I felt a bit nervous. If 15 years ago I had said to my friend, 'you know, I'll have a poem published one day', then we both would have thought I was insane.

While we all to varying degrees advocate the importance of peer support in giving and receiving comfort, no one does more to facilitate this for others living with dementia than Nigel. This can be close to his home in South Wales or on a national platform with the 3 Nations Dementia Working Group where he suggested, planned and then tirelessly led weekend online socials so that people could connect and chat through Zoom with others. He has even led such socials on Christmas Day and Boxing Day, realising that these can be very challenging times for some, especially those who do not have family or friends close by.

Peer support is where you can happily forget where you are, seeing how other people deal with things and bring you hints and tips. It's more than this though, it's having this really empathetic, safe space, where you can go, be yourself, and take your dementia with you, and not worry too much about it. That gives me a great deal of comfort.

Seeking comfort from challenges

Nigel told us a story of how challenging he found the period soon after being diagnosed and how he sought comfort in a bottle or on a plate. I suspect this was influenced by earlier challenges in his life. Nigel will only occasionally open up to friends about the challenges he had confronted prior to being diagnosed with dementia but I know some of these still affect him today. As an active soldier, I am sure he saw things which remain with him to this day, and while these are immensely challenging, they also I suspect have given him an inner strength and an approach to life which better enables him to seek comfort. As always with Nigel, I was left with a feeling of admiration for the humility and wisdom he shared with us in talking about how he is able to gain a sense of comfort.

I have very active post-traumatic stress disorder, and that needs me to manage it. I can't manage that unless I take a long period of self-reflection, and that self-reflection and rest could either be sat in the garden hearing the birds, or looking at the flowers, or indoors listening to a nice piece of music, or trash television depending on what mood takes me. I don't think there's any sort of ... formula to it, other than stop what you're doing, do something you like and regroup.

The other thing is that I get some comfort and reassurance from my dementia journey being pretty good up to now, in terms of cognitive stuff. However, my perception issues have gone to pot, you know. I can't judge distances anymore, all the rest of it. But the one great thing is the fact that the cognitive issues kind of plateaued. I haven't done anything about that, I've just been lucky. I had a review just before the COVID-19 pandemic started. I was told to expect that when the shoe is about to drop because the holes in my parietal lobe are getting bigger, and he said, when it goes, it can go quickly or not.

Impact of the diagnosis of dementia on comfort

Getting a diagnosis of dementia has given me a period of self-reflection. In the past, my days were so full. Now I need that space. I need that space, and without it, I don't function and don't feel at all comfortable.

I stopped doing things for a while and then reassessed them when I started gaining a bit more confidence because, you know, my weight ballooned up to 32 stone. I mean, I was conscious that I was having four food deliveries a week from the online supermarket, and they were all usually bourbon, single malt whisky, fillet steaks and baguette bread. I felt I could live on that. Of course, I wasn't going anywhere. I went through two La-Z-Boy armchairs. I mean, I'd get up in the morning. I'd switch on the TV. I'd have a steak baguette for breakfast, and I'd have my first drink at about 11 o'clock and that would continue until midnight and I wouldn't do anything, I wouldn't go anywhere, and I wouldn't talk to anyone. I think looking back on it, it was probably an unconscious way of killing myself, you know, without all the rigmarole of, you know, will it all work out? I knew what was going on and I got up to 32 stone and, of course, I became totally immobile.

All of this stuff meant that I was able to sort of forget the dementia because I was drunk most of the time, and eating steak sandwiches and thinking that I was coping. I wasn't, I mean ... I couldn't walk 10 yards. I'd sit it down and my back would ache. Then came these two very annoying ladies who said to me, 'Oh, we're going to make you better, you know, we're going to get you better'.

Of course, because of what they did, the weight fell away. I think I lost 10 stone very rapidly, and you know, I was eating green stuff and what people and I would have normally ate. As I got better physically, everything else got better as well.

Then I was introduced to what I think is the most important source of comfort I've supported the whole of my dementia journey, which is peer support and it's invaluable. Just to talk to people who you know. There's this story about the guy coming over from the pub in Ireland and he falls down a big hole that he can't get out of. It's too deep. So the priest comes up, looks down and says, 'What are you doing down there?'. [The guy] says, 'I've fallen down the hole, I can't get out'. 'Oh', he said, so then the priest jumps in the hole and the guy says to the priest, 'What have you done? You can't get out now'. He says, 'I know, but at least we're both in the hole, and we'll work together on getting out'. That's sort of what a peer support group is if it's done properly.

In a nutshell

I believe that the great joy of dementia is saying every day – this is a personal view –but every day, there may or may not be challenges, but every day is another day. It's so important to remember that every day is another day. It's another day where you might feel a bit low, you might feel a bit high, you might feel a bit calm. You might need to sit down and smell the roses or you might need to go shopping, but it's another day. Seek comfort in all of this and don't waste that day is my mantra.

All so true Nigel!

Tracey Shorthouse

What provides comfort?

Tracey made it very clear when describing to us her sources of comfort – in fact, one of her cats made a brief but notable appearance during our Zoom conversation, so I suspect they knew we were talking about them and wanted to show the relationship they have with Tracey! Tracey is one of the Fifteen who lives on her own near the Kent coast, and this came through in the way she described her comfort-giving strategies.

Just being on my own with my cats. That brings me so much comfort because I don't have to try to do anything.

This house is my castle. So being at home brings me comfort. Going on walks and being in the field on my own. That brings me comfort too because there's no people about.

I feel comfort when I go out walking or when I go into the sea to swim. It's not everyone's cup of tea, going into a cold sea, but actually going down, and then just, going out and being away from people reminds me how strong I am then. You see you have to be strong to tread water, which not many people can do, and then be safe. It is also very peaceful, I feel at peace when I'm in the sea. It's what I said to somebody the other day, it's freeing, and it's calming as well.

Seeking comfort from challenges

I have known Tracey for 7 years and it is clear that she strives to contend with the difficulties posterior cortical atrophy presents her with when speaking. Consequently, I was interested to ask her about expressing herself through her poetry.

I wrote poems in a way to deal with my diagnosis of dementia. I couldn't really talk about the dementia and I didn't have anyone to talk to after my diagnosis and I had all these things in my head all the time because my dementia was quite bad when I was first diagnosed. Later, I used the poems when I wrote a poetry book.

I can understand being ill from a nursing point of view, and I know it's quite stressful. I think I deal with stress much better now because I put things in place. If I feel a bit stressed with my dementia, I can go for a walk or do something to stop that stress. I could never do that in nursing, as I just have to get on with the job and then collapse at home.

Brigitta, who's part of our SUNshiner's group, wanted to go on the bus. I said, 'I'll come with you, we'll do it together'. She's not used to going on public transport at all and I thought when there's two of us, it's easier. She got the bus first and then I joined her on it, because it came to me last and then we went together. Didn't know where we were going, so again, two heads were better than one. We got off where we thought we had to go and then had to walk the rest of the way but that's fine because it wasn't raining.

My response to this was to relate to the challenge of using public transport and to suggest that Tracey, and maybe also Brigitta, had derived comfort and companionship from travelling together and this had overcome some of Tracey's fears and apprehensions. Approximately a year after this conversation, I reminded Tracey and Brigitta of this when I met them at the 'Picture This' photography and writing workshop in Canterbury, to which they both very happily attended together by bus!

Experiencing a lack of comfort

I do sometimes feel stressed like when I am using public transport. I do not feel comfort when lots of people are around me, that is stressful.

In a nutshell

Every day they make me laugh and every day my cats bring me great comfort. I know how hard it must be when you haven't got any animals and you haven't anybody in your life to say, 'Come on, get up' and jolly you up a bit. Because sometimes, when you feel low, that's what you need sometimes – a pet or another friendly person to lift your spirits and give you comfort.

So what learning can we take from the Fifteen?

These interviews provided a rich and varied account of how dementia impacts on a person's sense of comfort. We reflect here on what we can generalise for others living with dementia and those who support them.

From the point of view of someone living with dementia:

- Take time and space to enjoy the things which give you comfort without any sense of guilt or misgiving.
- Live in the day but think to the near future and something pleasant that you can look forward to and then do all you can to make it happen.
- Hang on to those positive emotional memories of activities and people which gave you comfort without worrying about what you can or cannot remember by way of events and places.
- Manage your time by taking rests and seeking a balance of activities.

There are also implications for those who provide professional support and care for persons living with dementia. For them, the main takeaway messages are:

- Seek comfort for yourself in order to better help people with dementia to find it.
- Encourage, support and celebrate when you witness someone with dementia gaining comfort from something you are doing with them.

12 Love

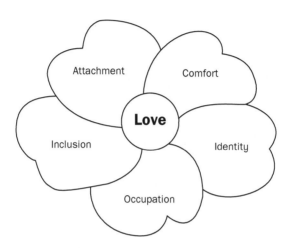

What is this simple but complicated thing called Love
A mystery to the soul conjuring up joy & deepest affection
The facets of love are many a kaleidoscope of how you see the world
I love the sky whether light or deep blue & how I have butterflies
  thinking of you
I love frosty mornings & indigo nights, the fells, the views, distant
  twinkling lights
I love seas that crash then fall away leaving glistening rocks on a warm
  sunny day
I love watching my dog as we race on the sand laughing
I tumble he stops & lays his head on my hand
As I lie on the beach watching clouds high up above I smile wondering
What is this simple but complicated thing called Love?

– Martina Kane

The Fifteen on Love – narrated by Keith Oliver

Like many poets before her, I feel Martina has beautifully captured what love means to her, and like all the other poems in this book that are written by people with dementia, she clearly shows what people with dementia can achieve, when love is given and accepted. I do think poetry lends itself to writing about love better than prose, and in our conversations with the Fifteen it was a little uncomfortable at times for some, which required both Reinhard and myself to be extra sensitive to this, and to give more time and space for the conversation to flow naturally. It seems paradoxical that love is the foundation stone of poetry and we sing about it endlessly, such as in the Beatles classic *All You Need Is Love*, yet so many people are embarrassed when asked to talk about it.

We deliberately placed love after comfort in our conversations as this seemed to make sense, and while there were of course overlaps, as indeed there were with all the petals, it is possible from what people said to detect the distinctions.

Agnes Houston

Love and intimacy

I have spoken with psychiatrists, psychologists and nurses about how people with dementia can continue a healthy and happy intimate relationship with their spouses and partners, and it was this that Agnes began talking to us about.

I think it's uncomfortable talking about love. I don't know if it's a British thing, you know, certainly a Western Scotland one, and nobody talks about sexual love. They talk about it in … what is it? I had a word there for it. You know, the nasty way, the sleazy way, you know? Then there's intimacy. Reinhard, you could talk about this better than me. Intimacy comes along for young adults and then as maturity comes, you get the comfort of knowing the person. It's just a comfortable love that I'm going to talk about – that was taken away from me by dementia because my husband's got dementia. His dementia is different. We lost the sexual side and almost the intimacy side as well. Then we're left with the 'comfort'. You know, and I don't know if that's a brotherly or sisterly love, I don't know, but there's a comfort built upon love within a long-standing relationship which we still have. I love my brother in the same way … [laughs] … do you know what I mean?

Our consultant was horrified when he said, 'What do you mean? You're going on holiday with your husband, and you share the same bed?' I said we've always shared the bed. We always cuddle up. So, there is that side of it. I think in a way, it's not today, that Alan and I don't have a safe place to be able to say that. There are not many places I would talk about that, you know, and feel comfortable with you as you know what dementia is like. I think it's a shame that there's no place where you could come to terms with the changing in your relationships, in the sexual side as well as every other way. We've got our own expression of love. We've come to terms with it. You have to give your love to your family, your love of what's right about you, but sometimes I doubt myself. Am I overly friendly in my expressions and feelings of love for others? You know, I often see someone, and you think we were long lost lovers. 'Oh! It's lovely to see you!' Then people are looking at you strangely. COVID-19 has played a big part, you know.

Feeling a healthy sense of love for oneself

We were both concerned to explore how each person maintained a sense of self-worth and self-soothing to help them cope with their dementia and life in general. There is no question that Agnes, like many others, has a sense of con-felicity in taking pleasure from seeing the happiness of others, which in turn makes her happier.

I will tell you that my love of myself has certainly improved. In my meditation I practise meta meditation, which is a love meditation, and you send it to someone that maybe you've had a wee incident with or you're not as comfortable with and that. You send love to the whole wide universe, but you don't do a lot on love of yourself. That's something I wasn't brought up to be comfortable with. I don't think anybody would say, 'You should love yourself', you know.

Influence of religious faith on love

Moving on from talking about how she tries to maintain a sense of love of herself, Agnes then related this to the influence her religious upbringing had upon her.

I can remember as a child being brought up a Catholic there were three things they said that you should definitely love – God, others, but I can't remember the third thing. It was like a ...

Keith: '... hierarchy of love almost'.

Yeah, it was three things that we just repeated all the time. I thought I'd never forget it, and here I've forgotten it then ... [all laugh].

In a nutshell

What I definitely believe is that if anyone shows me any affection or love, tears come in my eyes, because it seems so unusual. You know, so maybe it's because there is not a lot that is around about me. So, that's where I am with love. There are certain people that always have a part in my heart ... [laughs] ... and you're definitely one of them Reinhard, and so is Keith!

Chris Maddocks

Love for her partner

I was living in Cardiff on my own at that time and I was struggling a bit. And ... erm, Heather was living in Eastbourne and I used to come back and forth, back and forth. My brother and sister said that they couldn't look after me. So, Heather said come to me in Eastbourne. At first, I kept saying 'no' because I thought it's not fair to impose my dementia on Heather and I knew it would get worse. Well, she kept insisting, so I moved to Eastbourne in July 2017. I had known Heather since 2006 and then we were in a relationship from 2010.

I mean we both find the dementia difficult. It's certainly affected the future that we had planned because I've got a touring caravan, and we were going to tour all around Europe. Erm, I can't see that happening now. Heather says sometimes when she goes out or if I'm not able to go ... she goes on her own and she finds that difficult. I think that sometimes I can't go with her even though we've made plans to go somewhere or do something, I'm too tired to go, but we try to understand one another, and I always try to explain what's happening and how I'm feeling. But that's not always easy.

Loving and liking

I was very pleased that Chris spoke so clearly about this aspect of love as I have in the past related closely to this. My experience has been that the love is constant and more long-lasting whereas liking the person may fluctuate more according to what they do, say, don't do, don't say – in other words, how they interact. Usually, thankfully, my experience is that love wins through!

But you can love people, but you may not like them, always like them. I've found that out recently because of some things they do that affected me. Yes, I love them. But there are times when I don't actually like them.

Love and kindness

There were a number of times in the hour-long conversation when Chris mentioned the word kindness and the importance it has in her life, and this was never clearer than when talking about love.

And I love it when other people show kindness.

We've got a friend who used to do massage, and during lockdown she couldn't do it. So she did something else. She used to go into a dementia day centre and she used to massage people's hands. She did it all in her own time, alongside talking to people while massaging their hands. She said that the smile that came onto somebody's face when she was showing kindness meant so much to her. That contact is a form of love. Also sometimes people who are living with dementia don't have any family, so what's wrong in just holding somebody's hand and touching them. She said there was one lady who wouldn't have her hands massaged. But over weeks, she held her hand out one day to Sandy to show she wanted a massage. She also wasn't verbal. Over a couple of weeks, this lady started talking again. And that was all down to kindness and love shown through touch.

I think I get satisfaction and fulfilment from helping others. So maybe that's how I show love to myself. You know, what goes around comes around, I suppose, doesn't it?

In a nutshell

Rather than love, sometimes I think probably people might show more sympathy, feeling sorry for somebody and empathy. I genuinely loved people, you know, my friends, and even some of my work colleagues, and my nieces and nephews, I loved them to bits. That love hasn't changed. What has probably changed for me since the diagnosis is that I don't really want people to feel sorry for me.

Chris Norris

Although Chris only spoke quite briefly about love, and it is recorded in one paragraph, there is a lot within this extract which spotlights aspects of love that I know many will readily relate to, and is in places almost poetic in imagery and metaphor.

I think it [the dementia diagnosis] *has to a degree changed it. I've never been – I say never, I guess when I was really young and in love, I've always found it difficult to express love. I built a shield around myself when I was in my early teens, to stop myself being hurt by anything. But unfortunately, by building that shield, it excludes other people; feeling that they can't come in. But that's something that my wife accepted when she met me. She found ways to wriggle in behind the shield. She found my Achilles' heels really. But I've always been that way, I was brought up that way. You know, 'Men don't cry' and all of this. Very stiff upper-lippy. That was my background. My dad went to private school and that was his upbringing, so he passed that on – not inflicted but that was there in my life. Even now, I still find it hard to express that love and let people in sometimes. I fear if I let them in, what will happen? But with the dementia being there, that has changed things to a degree. Because I now allow people to connect with me at a much deeper level than I ever would before. The person before dementia was very much on the surface. A bit like in a farmyard where the silage goes ... [Reinhard laughs] ... It looks solid on the surface but underneath there's all sorts of things that's going on. And that, to a degree, is how I viewed myself and my life really. There are all sorts of things going on, and it looked pretty safe as well and secure, but now I allow people in more.*

Chris Roberts

Reinhard and I usually alternated leading the conversation with each of the Fifteen, although after I had led the conversation with Chris about comfort and we moved to talk about love, I left this aspect entirely to Reinhard. I think it is interesting to read this conversation between Chris, Jayne and Reinhard as it was recorded and then transcribed.

I'm not very empathetic anymore. You know my daughter started crying, I'd say 'here's a tissue' whereas before I would've given a hug. You know I don't understand … erm, feelings and things anymore. Jane says do you still love me and I'm like 'of course I do, I married you didn't I?'

Jayne: 'But he doesn't feel it. He doesn't know the feeling. But going back to the song, Chris has expressed to me that he's disappointed in himself and he would've had more of an idea pre-dementia. We know that definitely. He'd be able to give more advice or more practical advice you know'.

And the dementia has also affected my balance and walking and things. I can't drive my kids around, well I know they're not really kids now. You know I can't give them lifts, I can't go and babysit for them. I'm not to be trusted with young kids, with babies because I might drop them. So, it's … that's a whole thing that I was looking forward to being a grandad and you know and … erm, that's gone out the window as well. I just have to be a grandad from a distance, I can't hold the babies you know.

Jayne: 'You also don't want to. He doesn't have that you know "let me hold the baby", he doesn't have that … you know, "why would I hold a baby, for what purpose?"'

Yeah, very nice.

Reinhard: 'Yes. I think there are more blokes that feel a bit like that'.

I used to be.

Jayne: 'He was always a better mother than I was'.
Reinhard: 'And how about … how about receiving or feeling love from other people?'

Not bothered.

Reinhard: 'Not bothered either way?'
Jayne: 'You haven't seen it for a while, but he does say he misses having hugs from me. But this, this is where dementia has impacted our relationship

because we are not as touchy feely as we were pre-dementia – that has created a physical distance that was never there before'.

Exactly. Most of my friends, as you can imagine my personal friends have got dementia. But as you can imagine, I don't see many of them anymore because out of sight, out of mind – you know it's nothing to do with the dementia. It's COVID-19 and me not being there anymore. People can blame the dementia too much.

Jayne: 'It's the dementia. The dementia stopped you going to the places'.

Yeah, I suppose. But I don't blame the dementia.

Jayne: 'No, it's not the dementia itself'.

It's my lifestyle has changed. It's not their fault. It's not my fault, I suppose. But one close friend, a local friend used to come around all the time and COVID-19 stopped that now. Yeah, but since COVID-19, that hasn't restarted again either because it's out of sight, out of mind. You know, we tend to blame this 'out of sight, out of mind' on dementia a lot. I hear it a lot. I see it a lot. I've said it a lot. A lot of the problem isn't just the dementia.

Reinhard: 'Yeah. The last aspect is love toward yourself, and liking and loving yourself'.

I have … I have no emotion about either. I've stopped looking after myself. At present I have no pride in myself, but it doesn't bother me. I used to have a lot of pride in myself – in my dressing and showering and being clean and I don't do any of that without being reminded. Luckily I don't smell!

Jayne: 'I would disagree when he said he has no pride. He does. He does have pride, but not to the degree that it was before'.

It's not something I do anymore. I don't feel the urge to do it. You know, I used to love having a hug, who doesn't? I don't care now. Emotion just doesn't enter my life anymore.

Reinhard: 'Somehow Chris, you also have a way of being alright with yourself. You're not going around being constantly upset with yourself and annoyed at yourself for how things are'.

I get very … I get very annoyed, not with myself but with the situation I'm in. I also get very annoyed when I'm trying to do something that I could do so easily before dementia. I suppose this is natural, but I don't get upset about it.

Dianne Campbell

It's not a matter of that I don't want to show love, but sometimes I don't remember. My love is for people – it's just there. Sometimes my mind just takes me away and I don't bother. But love's always been there.

Frances Isaacs

Love within the family

When asked about showing, giving and receiving love to and from others and to herself, Frances responded by merging her views on self-love with love within her close family.

I don't know. I'll tell you one thing, I should really try very hard not to be self-centred, because it'd be very easy just to think me, me, me, me, me all the time. But the world isn't all about me, because I still need both my sons occasionally to draw on, and to give and receive a bit of parental advice. We're very aware of each other as a family of great friends together. I suppose you could call it love but we are all great friends, and we all talk to each other all the time. I think to have that kind of relationship with your children ... and my husband is important, and we still spend hours talking to each other. Having said that, afterwards I have no idea what we have said to each other!

Gail Gregory

Love towards and from other people

Within this short paragraph, Gail tells us a lot about her thoughts on love, starting from moving on from the restrictions COVID-19 placed upon us and not only her thoughts on giving and receiving love but also a sense of how she feels some of this has changed since her diagnosis.

It's great now that I can hug again and I obviously love my children to bits and my hubby and my mum and dad. But I do now tend to push people away, including sometimes with my husband, yeah I tend to distance myself. Whether that's because I don't want to get too close because I know that I'm not going to be here forever, and in a way, am I sort of preparing him? I don't know. It just happens. Then at other times I want to be loved and I can get the love, but it's strange that giving and receiving love has definitely changed since the diagnosis.

George Rook

Love within marriage and the family

As it is true that each person with dementia is unique and different, the same could be said about the marriages, families and close relationships that people with dementia share. George shed some light upon his relationship with his wife and his children.

It follows from my childhood and baggage that I seem to carry, that I find it hard to feel or express love. Um, and it's probably no coincidence my wife probably has the same sort of issues, stemming from her parents and upbringing. We suit each other. We're sort of in a sense companions. I mean what I've written down is, essentially, as I said earlier my wife with her support and increasing understanding of what's going on in me and of the power balance between us. I suppose you could say this is certainly a really important part of our love and comfort towards each other.

I often think that I don't love my children as much as I should. I like seeing them, I love seeing them, I do. Um ... and I don't know whether it's because it's like having a school holiday. When at school, someone comes and stays for a day, or a few days and when they leave, the world can be crashing down around you because you think 'oh no, not again, I was just enjoying that'. Then you get a bit tearful and stuff.

Challenging emotions connected to love

George moved seamlessly on from talking about the emotional pain sometimes felt about goodbyes and here we get a sense of how he seeks to protect himself from being hurt.

I don't know, maybe I think I probably 'shut that out so I'm not getting too close', you know? I think that's probably what I do generally with people, and with life in general.

Love of activities

George spoke eloquently elsewhere in the conversation about some of his hobbies and interests, which he clearly felt passionate about and loved being engaged with.

I am content when I do get close into something I really believe passionately about. I can't say much more about love really.

Jennifer Bute

Effect of diagnosis on loving relationships

I began by asking Jennifer if her loving relationship with family and friends has changed since her diagnosis of dementia. In the following extract, she also reveals how different members of her family treat her differently and how she responds to this knowing that they share a love for each other, a love which can overcome our weaknesses, mistakes and foibles!

Well of course it has. I mean it would be ridiculous to say it didn't. Of course it has changed but I think in many ways for the better, because they're closer. They are different of course but they're more real. I am very blessed for having a very supportive family. They're not the family that go, 'oh poor dear, poor mum' you know. My son says, 'you can't hide behind your diagnosis, pull yourself together, find a way round it' and for me that works. He doesn't ever sympathise, and sometimes I might like sympathy but it's because he loves me. I made him some rock buns when he came to visit me from where he lives in Ukraine. I hadn't seen him for 2 years, and he put them all in the bin saying you forgot to put sugar in them. Because I know he loves me and I love him, I'm gonna do something about that next time. So I have to work out a strategy to make sure next time I do not forget the sugar! He pushes me all the time and I'm very grateful for that but everyone is different. I have another son who doesn't think like that, so you know I am very privileged to have a great variety of love.

Influence of religious faith on love

I'm loved and accepted by God and I know my family love me, so caring for oneself can be difficult. I think that is probably something I find difficult but my family are good because I like to put myself out for other people. I do this now with all the talks and lectures I was doing. I was doing so many at one stage that my family put a limit on the number I was allowed to do before COVID-19 because I was being asked to do talks up and down the country.

The meaning of love

It is widely accepted that there are no synonyms for the word love, so one can safely say that no other single word adequately expresses, captures or can replace love in the context of the range of emotions, feelings and experiences that love generates. When concluding this part of our conversation, Jennifer told us what the word love means to her and how she sees it viewed in our society today.

I think the word love has got a bit mixed up and confused, hasn't it, because love encompasses care and acceptance and doing the best for the other person, doesn't it? Sadly, so often in today's culture love is what I can get out of it with my particular version of whatever it is. Love and dementia is a different kind of thing, and perhaps it's not the best word because of all the other connotations but I think one of the benefits of dementia is that we lose our social inhibitions and we find it easier to express things. I mean we don't go around telling people we love them for goodness sake of course, but we show it more easily in how we do things for other people more willingly or with more enthusiasm. That's why people show emotion here in this place where I live – they get cross with me at times or they're more appreciative. This is because our emotions are higher and the inhibitions have one haven't they? So yes, it has changed. Touch is so important in showing concern and care and love, and of course we haven't been able to do that recently. In COVID-19 days, it has really just been a hand on someone's shoulder. I'm not talking about going around hugging everybody but physical touch is so important. I think there have been people with dementia who have been ill in hospital who haven't been allowed touch, which I think is outrageous. If they're going to die anyway, why can't they have the risk of getting COVID-19 but don't start me on that ... but you know touch is so important and I think especially so for people with dementia.

Jim McNee

Jim was very clear that while a little uncomfortable talking about love, he immediately directed the conversation to speak solely about his wife Kathy and his daughters, and connected this to his view on love and a fear of not being a burden as his dementia progresses.

The important thing to me is that I'm not a burden.

We've got two daughters and we're proud of both daughters. We're very fortunate. We've now got two grandchildren. I think I've been very lucky.

Julie Hayden

The love of friends

Friends can play such an important part in all of our lives, and when asked who she loves and who she thinks loves her, Julie was unequivocal in her response.

It's fair to say friends become my family that I've chosen by surrounding myself with those special friends, that's where I get the majority of the love coming back to me. I feel that I can talk with them about anything because of a kind of acceptance and freedom of expression between us. With these special friends, I know when we eventually do meet up it'll be like we met only last week.

The people that I get love from are my friends rather than anyone else because my family doesn't understand. They say 'I love you' but there isn't that understanding that should go hand in hand with love. So at times I do feel quite tolerated and so essentially it's love from my friends that makes a positive difference, and sometimes ... you may know the phrase, 'you can choose your friends but you can't choose your family'.

Feeling a healthy sense of love for oneself

Whether one has dementia or not, I think most people as they age can relate to the wisdom and the balanced way Julie expressed herself when asked about her love of self.

The love for self is very difficult because sometimes when you look at yourself and the way your body changes you can't help but see yourself in a negative light. This is much worse when you see yourself as not being able to do as many things as you want or could previously do and are now struggling to do things, that does change self-perception or self-love.

Yeah, it's about how you accept yourself, how you are now and each time you get to a new difficulty accepting that about yourself but that can take so much adaptation. Translating that into love means I tend to be very over-critical of myself and this does vary from day to day depending on how I feel.

Keith Day (Cam)

Love within the family

Without it being necessary for Cam to use the words tolerance and patience, these two words shine through when he spoke about the love within his family, and how those close to him love and support him, especially when he is seeking to explain something verbally.

I say they can give me the time so I can explain to my wife and my family about dementia and for me that's showing me love because they aren't rushing me. I can certainly give love to other people such as my daughters. With everything we've got going on with my daughter at the moment there's an awful lot of love going into there.

Feeling a healthy sense of love for oneself

It was interesting that Cam related this to his professional experience of when he was working with vulnerable children. I could relate to this myself as I find that dementia threatens my self-esteem and consequently it is often hard to self-love or self-soothe, and one strategy is to think back to when one was in a caring profession.

I think loving myself is hard for me and a lot of people to do. I think sometimes I wouldn't say to me that I love myself but I have got some capabilities and I know that I can still do things. The thing is I have dementia right, but in a way I still like myself.

When I worked with the children, usually they had lost their self-esteem, their self-worth, and to me when I first got the diagnosis that's how I felt you know. I had nothing to give back or anything to give me purpose, and so I started to look back to what I used to do with the children and that helped me to regain my self-confidence and self-esteem.

Influence of religious faith on love

Reading all of Cam's insightful contributions, it is evident that his religious faith means a lot to him and for how he navigates his life with dementia. He clearly sees his faith as a key guiding light helping him along the way, through the love of God and those who attend the church with Cam.

The thing is I have my faith, and I'm not gonna knock other people because they have a different faith to me as that's up to them, but to me I don't think I'd be able to go through all that's happened, such as having had a heart attack, without the people from the church being there for me. All through my diagnosis and since, the church has been the main thing to me you know, because God loves me, and I know that God won't give me more than I can handle whatever happens.

Masood Ahmed Qureshi (Maq)

Ways of expressing love to others

What you have to think about love is that people with a condition of this nature find it difficult to express their love. They try to make people understand how much they love them because we are at that stage where we can actually talk about this but there are some that can't express it. They can't express it verbally. They have to hug or touch or show it in that manner but love is the route of communication. Obviously, it needs to be done, and from the other side they need to be patient and they need to use more body language as opposed to verbal. They need to look at the person so it has a little bit of an impact. I don't see myself at the moment at this stage and for me everything is okay now because we can talk to each other and we can express our feelings.

Feeling a healthy sense of love for oneself

Two things caught my attention when Maq spoke about love for himself. The first was how he equated it to his physical appearance, personal hygiene and the clothes he would wear. In a sense, he like others is placing himself to an extent in a former professional role in order to maintain his self-respect. Secondly, I was interested that the issue of stigma is intrinsic in his comment about not wanting to look like he has dementia in order to 'love himself' or to maintain his self-esteem.

I think dementia has changed me in the manner that I look after myself more than I did before. For instance, I might have taken daily showers because as a part of my job I needed to be really nice and presentable with a suit and tie. Then when I stopped work and went through the heart surgery and all the rest of it, I cut down to two showers a week. When I started this campaign and going out before the lockdown because I visited people at home with dementia, I started looking after myself more because again you're going to see somebody. They're good enough to allow you into their home, so you need to be presentable. I started dressing smartly and looking after myself again. I think it's changed me for the better in a sense. How long I can keep this up? I don't know but as long as I can I want to still be able to look like I've not got dementia.

Nigel Hullah

The love of friends

Nigel and I have shared many conversations over the years about our shared passion for watching football and the two very different teams we love to support and cheer on. There are many people like us who feel a very strong bond of attachment to a favourite team, which sometimes goes back to our childhood and is a relationship that, like a human one, has many ups and downs along the way but that love remains constant, often for life. In Nigel's case, the love of his team is also a catalyst to show the love for a friend who enables Nigel to support the team he loves.

For me it was going to football. Because of problems with my depth perception due to my PCA [posterior cortical atrophy], which of course does affect your perception, and gives problems negotiating steps. My friend Alan said, 'we'll take you now'. Well, he has no real interest in football, you know, he likes drinking, and he likes me but that's it! Alan and his son guided me down to my seats in Cardiff City Stadium, and they stood behind me and it chokes me up when I think about it. He said, 'don't worry, I've got your back'. What he meant was I wouldn't fall backwards. But I interpreted it totally different of him saying, 'Whenever you want to come to the match, we'll be there with you'. They are too! I think that's what we need.

Love within the family

Before speaking personally, Nigel chose to explain his views on love within the family in the second person, which might be due in part to the position he holds nationally on various groups where he has some sense of responsibility for speaking on behalf not only of himself, but also of others affected by dementia.

I think dementia puts an untoward pressure on loved ones – wives, sons, daughters, husbands. You know, they suddenly come from being a part of a family group to being a carer, and I think that's a difficult transition. I also think sometimes people living with dementia hide a lot away from their loved ones because they don't want their loved ones to worry. My stepbrother, who I love dearly, and he's my only living relative ... he has got a life of his own in the United States. Immediately he wanted to drop everything and come across and I told him if he did that, I would step off. Because I don't want this horrible thing, and it is horrible, ruining both our lives. Now that's not a sacrifice on my part because my dementia would have gone on anyway. So, him coming across at this point would just be a proximity thing. OK, I do miss him. Because of COVID-19 I've not been able to visit often, not at all really, and vice versa with him.

A loving, caring community

The Dementia Friendly Communities initiative, which originated in Japan and then spread to many countries including the UK before the pandemic, had many fine attributes but also in my view some flaws. In the case of the former, it certainly raised public awareness and the Dementia Friends campaign that accompanied it was a great success by way of numbers accessing the awareness-raising package. I guess also you have to highlight the problem to then seek ways of addressing it, and of course the problem is dementia itself. I did always feel, however, that it was a pity that we could not simply advocate and generate 'friendly communities', as I thought this was more sustainable, long-lasting and wide-reaching. *Everyone* I would hope would wish to live in a friendly community where tolerance, understanding, respect, caring – and yes, love – was given and received by all.

Social care is everywhere. It doesn't just happen in nursing homes or community centres, it happens everywhere. It's the postman that looks out for you. It's the taxi driver that knows you. It's the guy at the train station that helps you. That's all social care, and we all occupy the same space, and we are all going to come into contact with people with different needs. I really don't understand why that's so hard for the policymakers to understand.

Now there is a different kind of love, that is a love of – or an appreciation of – people and a willingness to want to do the best for them. It's not the physical and emotional or sexual side of love, it's a different kind, it's a regard or empowerment or attachment kind of love for people who you would go out of your way to do things for, who in some cases you never met, and never will. But you've done something, and it's impacted their lives and you move on, and I feel that's great.

The love of dedicated professionals

As Nigel twice waxed lyrical about the role the occupational therapists (OTs) played in bringing him back from the 'cliff edge' or abyss, I felt it right to include this second version of his story in this chapter on love, as I do feel that was a key motivator for those professionals he described.

I have this theory with OTs, you know, I always think of the cheery cockney prisoner of war in those black-and-white war films, you know? The optimist saying, 'I will be home next year, this war won't last'. I have got this feeling that they're all built with that mould. You know, there is nothing to be miserable about because we're going to get you out of this. The OTs that visited me did this because before they came to see me, they spoke to my stepbrother and they colluded with the people around me and I use the word colluded because that's what it was. Then I was assaulted by these two … these two women, who just threw stuff out of my fridge and wacked the whisky bottles and everything else and said I was drinking too much and encouraged me to get my act in order.

Personal love

Love is certainly not always a smooth road for any of us, and Nigel was very reflective and contemplative when sharing with us this part of the conversation.

Ah well, I've loved two people in my life. Two people. In the traditional sense of love, in that they're the last people you think about when you go to sleep and the first thing you think about when you get up in the morning, just two people. Both are not related to me. I mean, close related family and I always found loving relationships, in the early days, very perplexing because I didn't think I deserved anyone to love me back. To a certain extent, I think that was because of the sorts of things I got involved with as a young man, and again I didn't think that I was sort of deserving of it.

In a nutshell

I have looked at Kitwood's flower, and I know the overarching thing is love and empathy and all the rest of it, and I get it. I never used to, but I get it now. If you don't understand people and if you don't care about people, you're not going to do the best for them either. You must have this intrinsic notion that, yeah, together we can make the world a better place. I mean, that sounds grand. But why not?

I could not agree more Nigel!

Tracey Shorthouse

Tracey was one of the most comfortable among the Fifteen talking about love. Her comments here give us all a very clear picture of Tracey the person, and are very wide-ranging and direct to the point.

I just love seeing things grow.
   I love my family and I don't want to upset them.
   I love my cats dearly and they sort of keep me going.
   I think I'm more loving with myself … I think I like myself better.
   I love the fact that I have very good friends that still see me, that still spend time with me.
   So many people don't care very often these days, it's all very singular, and I hope I never turn out that way because I've never been that way.

So what learning can we take from the Fifteen?

These interviews provided a rich and varied account of how dementia impacts on a person's sense of love. We reflect here on what we can generalise for others living with dementia and those who support them.
   From the point of view of someone living with dementia:

- It is important to regularly seek ways of connecting to people, activities and places that one loves.

- Few of us are islands – when love is offered that you recognise is going to enrich your life, don't walk away.
- To maintain wellbeing it is crucial not to shy away from making time for yourself and for making your own needs a priority in order to maintain your own self-esteem.

There are also implications for those who provide professional support and care for persons living with dementia. For them, the main takeaway messages are:

- My first hope is that professionals feel able to step into the shoes of people affected by dementia as human beings rather than first and foremost professionals. I am reminded of a line in the book *Love Story* by Erich Segal and spoken by Ali MacGraw in the 1970 film of the same title: 'Love means never having to say you're sorry'. I disagree in the context of dementia. I hope that when a professional makes an error or lets a person affected by dementia down, they have the good grace and humility to say – and mean – that they are sorry. That shows 'professional love' in the best way possible.
- In getting to know the person with dementia, find out about the loves in their life – the people who mean a lot to them, their passions and interests, their pets who they care for. Get to know the loving person you are helping to care for.
- Whether it is love, caring or empathy or a mix of the three, I would wish professionals to treat those of us affected by dementia as they would wish to be spoken to, cared for, treated and regarded if they, too, had dementia. It is one thing to care and quite another better thing to show you care.
- To care for others you also need to care for, and exercise love for, yourself – the reservoir of compassion is so easily emptied and not always so easy to refill.
- I began my thinking about this chapter by writing about how widely love is used in song and poetry, yet seldom seen in conversations or the writings of professionals. Bertrand Russell wrote that 'to fear love, is to fear life' – maybe there is something that professionals and everyone else for that matter can take from this.

Give Me ... I Will

Give me myself and I will be me
Give me an ear and I will speak
Give me patience and I will relax
Give me music and my heart will dance
Give me joy and I will laugh
Give me a way and I will follow
Give me a baton and I will share
Give me inspiration and I will excel
Give me teaching and I will learn
Give me truth and I will consider
Give me compassion and I will care

Give me identity and I will shine
Give me attachment and I will engage
Give me occupation and I will be focused
Give me inclusion and I will belong
Give me comfort and I will feel warmth

Give me love and I will thrive

– Keith Oliver, *Alzheimer's Society Ambassador*

(From *Dear Alzheimer's: A Diary of Living with Dementia*. Reprinted with kind permission from Jessica Kingsley Publishers)

Part **3**

Looking to the Future

13 Societal changes towards dementia

Ruth Bartlett

Improved understanding of the lived experience of dementia

When Kitwood's classic text was first published, 30 years ago, there was very little interest in the experience of living with dementia. Research and clinical practice at that time were focused instead almost entirely on what was then called 'challenging behaviours' (later termed the 'behavioural and psychological symptoms of dementia'). Certain branches of medicine, such as biological psychiatry and neuroscience, dominated research into the condition. Take, for example, a research article published 20 years ago about 'noise-making among dementia patients'. The researchers describe and attribute the 'screaming, shrieking and muttering of 12 dementia patients' in terms of damage to the frontal lobe and chemical imbalances in the brain (Nagaratnam et al. 2003). As a social scientist and mental health nurse, I find the article disturbing to read, as the possibility that patients might have been in pain, or distressed by their environment, is not considered at all by the researchers. Furthermore, the label 'noise-maker' (like all labels) is demeaning and othering and does nothing to enhance our understanding of a person's lived experience of dementia.

In other areas, however, there has been a broadening and deepening of interest in the lived experience of dementia among researchers and practitioners in health and social sciences and the humanities. As a result, it is relatively easy nowadays to find a research article or academic text that provides a more rounded picture of a person's life with dementia. One reason for this is because there is now a journal dedicated to publishing social research of direct relevance to understanding the lived experience of dementia. Launched in 2002, *Dementia: The International Journal of Social Research and Practice* publishes high-quality research articles on the theme of 'improving the quality of life, wellbeing, and quality of care for people with dementia, their families and communities'. The journal was born out of frustration felt by researchers at the time, including the journal's first editors, John Keady and Penny Braudy Harris, that there was nowhere to publish research on lived experience. Informally known as the 'purple journal', it has since become highly influential, as evidenced by its impact factor and publication of eight issues a year. Another reason is because researchers are conducting reviews of the lived experience literature, which are then being published. For example, Norwegian researcher Siren Eriksen led on a set of review articles. She and her team identified 169 articles on the lived experience of dementia. Other researchers have conducted reviews of the local context to understand the experience of dementia (e.g. Bailey et al. 2013). Changes in the publishing world, and reviews like this, have been important not only for advancing knowledge of the lived experience of dementia, but also confirming each of the facets of Kitwood's flower.

Kitwood's concepts of identity, attachment, inclusion, occupation, comfort and love underpin much of the care research that is produced today. Researchers tend to concentrate on one or more of these concepts in their studies. For instance, Beard (2016) has focused on the impact of dementia on identity; others have examined people's attachments, such as friendships (McFadden and McFadden 2011); while social scientists, like Heather Wilkinson, have written extensively about inclusion in the context of people with dementia (Wilkinson 2001). Researchers with a background in occupational therapy have, perhaps unsurprisingly, led the way in improving understanding of occupation – the importance of a person with dementia having something meaningful to do has been the conclusion of several major studies in recent years (e.g. Kottorp et al. 2016). Comfort is a particularly important concept in palliative care studies, and there has been a rise in research on end-of-life care for people with dementia (e.g. Lawrence et al. 2011; D'Astous et al. 2019).

Then, at the centre of Kitwood's flower, there is love. This may be difficult to define in the context of dementia, but a person's need to give and receive emotional affection has certainly featured in much of the research over the last 30 years. Take, for example, work by Brendan McCormack and others on person-centredness, which emphasises emotional competence and the wellbeing of a person with dementia (e.g. McCormack et al. 2010) – this relates to love. Additionally, studies related to sexuality and couple intimacy in dementia are associated with love (e.g. Abdo, 2013; Holdsworth and McCabe 2018). We hear a lot, too, about 'loved ones' in the scientific research and practice journals, although this can be seen to negate the possibility that people may not be loved or respected by family or by partners. In sum, most of Kitwood's concepts evidently feature in the research literature; of these there is perhaps only one that we ought look to the humanities for a clearer understanding of, and that one is love.

Love is the theme for many films, books and photographic exhibitions featuring people with dementia. In fact, love for a person with dementia is often the motivation behind creative projects. Take, for instance, the short film 'Ex Memoria' directed by Josh Appignanesi, who made it because he wanted to understand what life in a care home might have been like for his Jewish grandmother who had dementia and had lived through the Second World War (Appignanesi 2018). Or, a film and photo exhibition called 'Love, Loss, and Laughter: Seeing things differently', which launched in Australia in 2013 and has since travelled the world (Greenblat 2012). It was revolutionary at the time to depict people living with dementia in this positive way. Many of Cathy Greenblat's photographs were used to illustrate *Dementia Reconsidered,*

Revisited (Kitwood and Brooker 2019), which inspired this current book series. Cathy wanted to show the very human faces of people living with dementia and she was inspired by the love for her mother. More recently, sociologist Laurel Richardson published her memoir, *A Story of a Marriage through Dementia and Beyond: Love in a Whirlwind* (2022), which is about her love and caregiving through the last period of her husband Ernest Lockridge's life – from his transient amnesia to his death from Lewy body dementia. Creative works like these centralise love in the same way that Kitwood did in his flower. In so doing, they serve as a reminder that love is the focal point of life for a person with dementia – for us all.

As well as research articles, new edited collections are being published that challenge readers to think beyond a person's life as a 'patient' to their experiences of everyday life generally. Two books come to mind here: *Living with Dementia: Relations, Responses and Agency in Everyday Life* (2017) edited by Lars-Christer Hyden and Eleanor Antelius, and *Leisure and Everyday Life with Dementia* (2023) edited by Karen Gray, Christopher Russell and Jane Twigg. These texts not only resonate with Kitwood's flower, notably the concepts of identity, inclusion and occupation, they push its boundaries by adopting a more critical perspective. For example, *Living with Dementia* is replete with chapters on the challenges facing people with dementia because of social divisions such as gender and ethnicity. While *Leisure and Everyday Life with Dementia* engages with the idea of citizenship to consider people's rights and entitlements in relation to leisure. Texts like these take us beyond the confines of a care setting to everyday life, where the concepts of identity, attachment, inclusion, occupation, comfort and love take on new meanings.

Everyday life has always been an important idea in social research, as it homes in on the background and details of social life. The idea has anthropological roots with its focus on human behaviours, cultures and linguistics including, for example, small-scale processes and events, such as sparking up a conversation with a stranger, or a person's experiences of a regular activity like shopping or exercising. Such interactions and routines are of interest to social researchers, including those working in the dementia field, because they shed a light on the barriers that people can face on a day-to-day basis. Some of the earliest work on the lived experience of dementia in people's own homes was conducted in Sweden, with Louise Nygård and her team focusing specifically on everyday occupation (Nygård and Öhman, 2002). This research documented for the first time how people with dementia use a range of strategies to adapt to the condition and to overcome occupational problems – one participant, for example, wrote down the specific steps of how to prepare the Christmas table in anticipation of forgetting the procedures the following year. Such details are useful for improving understanding of how individuals deal with the (anticipated) effects of dementia.

In the future, it would be good to see more acknowledgement of, and services aimed at, people living with multiple conditions and disabilities, including dementia. We know from Sube Banerjee's research that 90 per cent of people with dementia will have at least one other co-morbidity – that is, another health condition such as diabetes, cancer, arthritis, cataracts or age-related macular degeneration (Banerjee 2015). Such conditions can be painful, distressing and / or make it difficult if not impossible for a person with dementia to manage by themselves. Yet, researchers still tend to focus on dementia as the only condition affecting a person, while health services cannot seem to count past one (condition) (Banerjee 2015: 597). Kitwood included physical health in his enriched model of understanding dementia, and comfort is one of the petals in the flower. Moving forward, physical health should be more central in our understanding of life with dementia, and we must counter the possibility that dementia may not be the only issue causing problems for an individual and their family.

Increased visibility of (some) people with dementia in the public sphere

Another major change in recent years has been the increased visibility of people with dementia in the public sphere. Many more people with dementia are speaking out and sharing their experiences of living with dementia than they were 30 years ago – the Fifteen are a case in point. This change has been evident in many parts of the world, including Canada, the USA and Australia. Indeed, the global campaign organisation, Dementia Alliance International, was established by a group of eight younger people living with dementia from these countries in 2014. A few researchers, including myself, recognised the significance of people with dementia being in the public sphere and sought to find out what motivated people to speak out and explore the effects it had on a person (Bartlett 2014). It was around this time that I coined the term 'dementia activism' to capture the public visibility and actions of people with dementia (Bartlett 2012). Since then, researchers and campaign groups (such as DEEP) have supported the participation of people with dementia in the public sphere.

In the past, people with dementia have had very few, if any, opportunities to be visible and participate in public life. People with dementia were seen by others as incapable and voiceless and were excluded from public spheres. For example, researchers were unlikely to include people with dementia in their studies, the assumption being that people with dementia could not provide any useful information, and so family carers were approached to share their experiences of supporting someone with dementia. Perhaps understandably, family carers focused on the problems they faced, leading to the development of the Caregiver Burden Interview (Zarit et al. 1980), which is still widely used by health service researchers today. This compounded the perception that people with dementia are voiceless. Within care settings, people with dementia are often not seen as having the capacity to influence their care or make decisions; instead, we hear the perspectives of health and social care professionals. In society generally, people with dementia have been marginalised and excluded from public life, especially people with advanced dementia who are in their

80s and 90s and live with frailty. The only sign we tend to see of this subgroup of people with dementia are images of 'wrinkly hands' in magazines and news stories. Images of persons with advanced dementia are rarely seen. In part, this is because a person who is profoundly cognitively impaired will be unable to give informed consent and just gaining assent from a next of kin doesn't seem right.

In recent years, there has been a noticeable change in the propensity of people with dementia to share their diagnosis. When I first started working in the field over 25 years ago, the former US president Ronald Reagan was possibly the only famous person to make it publicly known that he had Alzheimer's disease, which he did in a letter addressed to the American people on 5 November 1994. Since then, many famous people have shared the news that they have been diagnosed with a dementia. In 2023 alone, we have learnt that the Hollywood actor Bruce Willis, former British newsreader and journalist Alistair Stewart, and former politician and mayor of London Ken Livingstone have all been diagnosed with a dementia. However, unlike the Fifteen, I imagine these people will become less visible in the public sphere following their diagnosis, rather than more so. That said, the science fiction author Terry Pratchett did become very visible in his campaign for assisted death and increased research funding following his dementia diagnosis. Maybe it comes down to personality. Nonetheless, celebrities sharing their diagnosis and the increased visibility of people with dementia in the public sphere are undoubtedly helping to erode the stigma of dementia. By speaking out, people show that there is no shame in having the condition.

The visibility of people with dementia in the public sphere has helped to bring about a major shift in public attitude, enabling more people with dementia to feel and be included in their communities. This is evidenced by the fact that today, there are many more opportunities for people living with dementia to get involved in public life, such as through research, joining a DEEP group, responding to surveys, or helping to shape their local communities and services. However, such opportunities typically require a certain level of capacity. For example, it is assumed that talking is a person's main mode of communication. If a person with dementia is non-verbal, then a family member might speak on their behalf, which is not ideal but it does help to elicit the person's perspectives. Furthermore, it is important to note that socio-economic status, gender and ethnicity will all play a part in inclusion initiatives: a Muslim woman living in a deprived neighbourhood might be more reluctant to get involved in public events than a white man living in an affluent area. Some people are unaccustomed to inclusion, and this is compounded further by dementia. We need to acknowledge this and recognise that certain people with dementia are not visible in the public sphere, and perhaps it is those people the dementia world must advocate for more.

In particular, there is very little talk of what life is like for people whose dementia is advanced, and for whom dementia is very visible as a disability, perhaps because they are unable to co-ordinate their movements, or speak and express themselves. Yet these people are living with dementia too.

Furthermore, they are by far the largest group of people living with dementia, as people now live longer with their dementia and with greater levels of dependency and co-morbidities than ever before. When a person (with dementia) is no longer able to act in a way that society expects or finds 'deviant', such as getting lost on a routine basis or knocking on neighbours' doors in the middle of the night, social exclusion is still a very real possibility. Often, of course, a person with advanced dementia will become increasingly isolated at home and / or have to move into a care home, which might be located a long way from their family and community. For these reasons, I would argue that people with dementia who are non-verbal and / or profoundly impaired are in effect 'shadow citizens', even in the dementia world. They remain unseen and unspoken of in the public sphere.

Going forward, modes of communication other than talking must be prioritised and enabled in the dementia world. In this way, people with dementia who are non-verbal could be included in the change agenda, just like those who can talk. Back when Kitwood first formulated his theory of dementia care as an interpersonal process, he argued that 'facilitation is the missing concept in dementia care' (Kitwood 1993). He said that people with severe dementia often communicate through gestures and actions (rather than words); therefore, there needs to be a facilitator – someone who can help others to understand the meaning of these gestures and actions – for a 'successful communicative act to occur'. Given that some forms of dementia affect a person's language skills, I think we need to revisit and continue Kitwood's work on facilitation, otherwise there is a risk that people with dementia who are non-verbal will continue to be marginalised and excluded from public life.

In the learning disability world, individuals with a learning disability have an advocate whose role it is to help facilitate conversations in social situations. The advocate is not a family member but someone with advanced facilitation skills who knows the person very well. I have often wondered why we do not have a similar advocacy model in the dementia world. Cost is obviously a major factor, though I am not sure that is the only reason. I think it is because family carers have always been regarded as the spokespersons in the dementia world: a family carer will often speak on behalf of a person with dementia, even if the person is able to speak for themselves. A family advocate has many advantages, of course, particularly if the family member loves and knows the person very well. Unfortunately, this is not always the case. Even when it is, there are still drawbacks: (a) a family carer often has support (and possibly health) needs of their own; (b) they may not be a skilled facilitator; and (c) family dynamics can get in the way of effective communication, especially if there has been a history of abuse or problematic relationships. For these reasons, a family carer may not always be the best advocate for a person with advanced dementia. However, if we were to move towards a model of professional advocacy in the dementia world, involving a competent facilitator trained in ableism, then the perspectives of those with more advanced dementia could be discerned.

Ableism refers to the discrimination of, and social prejudice against, people with disabilities based on the belief that typical abilities are superior. It is a term used a lot in relation to people with physical disabilities, where abilities perceived as superior, notably walking, are clearly prejudiced against people in wheel-chairs. While ableism has not been a term used extensively in relation to people with dementia, it should be because it does apply. Think back, for example, to the point that medical ethicist Stephen Post made about us living in a 'hypercognitive society' in which rational thought and coherent memory are valued. This is ableism. Likewise, Kitwood argued that the interactions and gestures of people with advanced dementia do not always make sense by the standards of everyday conversation. Like he said: 'The illusion of incapacity has been created because life was so often set up for [people with dementia] on impossible terms' (Kitwood and Brooker 2019: 112). This, too, is ableism. Competent facilitators trained in ableism could enable more people with dementia, including those who are non-verbal, to participate in everyday life. The neurodiversity world is generating a wealth of knowledge about how to engage with people with profound communication disabilities from which we could learn a lot.

As well as professional advocacy, more could be done to help individuals and families get into deeper discussions about what will be important to the person as their condition progresses. Currently, the emphasis is on advanced care planning regarding future care and treatment wishes, such as resuscitation. However, if we talked to individuals and families more broadly post-diagnosis, and documented their wishes through video or other means, it could have a real impact on the person's identity being maintained, and their personhood and citizenship status being supported. It is a very sensitive and skilled area of work but the workforce (e.g. dementia advisers, Admiral nurses and memory assessment staff) could be trained to facilitate such discussions and to manage the secure storage and communication of the information.

Despite the increased visibility of people with dementia in the public sphere, when it comes to the human abilities that are regarded as superior, some things have not changed. Post and Kitwood were both writing in the early 1990s, but what they said then still applies today. Take, for example, memory. I recall watching the televised funeral of Queen Elizabeth II on 19 September 2022 – the broadcast was one of the biggest collaborations in British television history, with a peak audience of almost 30 million viewers. At one point during the coverage, the commentator said, 'no one who is watching this will ever forget it'. My immediate reaction was 'they might!' Anyone with a progressive neurocognitive condition (like dementia) that affects memory might not remember the event the following day, let alone for the rest of their life. The comment shows how deeply held the belief is that everyone can remember significant events. This is ableism, specifically cognitive ableism.

Development and implementation of global policies and initiatives

Historically, policies related to people with dementia have been about managing the 'rising tide', as individual countries produced strategies to manage the growing numbers of people with dementia. In the UK, for example, during the 1970s and 1980s, pre-Kitwood, the main policy concern was how best to care for 'the elderly mentally infirm'. Dementia was regarded as a 'problem' for older people and those with the condition were typically seen as a homogeneous group of patients. In addition, global organisations such as the World Health Organisation had other priorities (such as HIV/Aids) to focus on and were yet to turn their attention to strategic planning regarding dementia. Furthermore, the campaigning organisation Alzheimer's Disease International, even though it was established in 1984, did not produce its first global policy-related report until 2009. The lack of global co-ordination and prioritisation may explain why the dementia world seems to have a lot of catching up to do compared with other health conditions (like cancer) and disabilities (like learning disability). That said, a lot more investment has been made in the dementia world in recent years, which is beginning to redress the imbalance. However, the starting point was low, so much more investment is still required.

In the last few decades, three major policy areas have emerged that reflect and extend Kitwood's key concepts. Each area has been developed to bring about global change and is still in the process of implementation. First is the work of the dementia-inclusive societies initiative (also known as dementia-friendly communities), which started in Japan in 2004 and has since been bolstered by organisations like Alzheimer's Disease International and the World Health Organisation calling for nation-states to establish dementia-friendly initiatives. The main aim of the initiative is 'inclusion' in society for people with dementia, and the emergence of this initiative is a recognition that dementia is both a social and health issue. Nowadays, there are hundreds of dementia-inclusive initiatives across the world aimed at improving support and everyday life for people living with dementia. The policy initiative has had its critics, arguing that it increases stigma. Nonetheless, it has led to people talking more openly about the barriers that people with dementia face in a way that they might not have done before (see, for example, ADI 2009).

A second major policy area relates to building the evidence base, and capacity for research. Such plans aim to support the global prioritisation of dementia and provide a focus for researchers working in the field. This change is best evidenced by (a) the establishment of the Global Dementia Observatory (World Health Organisation 2021), which is all about sharing dementia-related information, and (b) the recent publication of a global blueprint for scientific research for the field of dementia (WHO 2022). The blueprint is the first of its kind to set out several key global priorities for all researchers working in the field of dementia, including bench scientists, epidemiologists and care researchers. The blueprint usefully highlights where the evidence gaps are and calls for researchers and funders to redouble their efforts to find a cure, improve care and reduce health inequalities. While this is a landmark piece of guidance, bringing together for the first time cure and care research, it falls short of asserting a more holistic view of dementia that takes account of environmental and societal factors. For that, we need to look to another area of policy.

The third major policy area to have emerged in the last few decades is the United Nations Convention on the Rights of Persons with Disabilities (CRPD).

Established in 1997, the CRPD is considered by many as a powerful starting point for (re)framing disability in terms applicable to persons living with a disability – that is, with due consideration to environmental and societal factors. With this convention, disability is understood in terms of 'long-term physical, mental, intellectual or sensory impairments which in interaction with various barriers may hinder their [persons with disabilities] full and effective participation in society on an equal basis with others' (United Nations 2006: 3). It applies to everyone with a disability, including citizens living with a dementia, and has been ratified by 185 countries as of May 2022. However, it is only relatively recently, and in certain countries, that the CRPD and promotion of disability rights have been discussed in relation to people with dementia. In this sense, it is a new policy development for the dementia world.

As we look to the future, it is important that each one of these policy areas is fully implemented. Change needs to continue for at least another 30 years to ensure that no one gets left behind. The world is unstable and prejudice against those with disabilities can increase when resources are scarce. For this reason, it is important that dementia-inclusive initiatives *are* inclusive of people from all faiths and backgrounds and *not* exclusive for those with certain privileges and capacities. Similarly, the work of the 10/66 Dementia Research Group remains important, particularly with respect to those living with dementia in low- and middle-income countries and could expand to include more studies of everyday life, as well as care services (Prince 2009). Finally, and perhaps most importantly, disability rights need to be recognised and applied in relation to people with dementia. People with dementia do not necessarily need to identify as 'disabled' for this to happen, but the dementia world does need to engage with the convention for real change to occur.

Conclusion

In this chapter, discussion has focused on changes in the dementia world since the inception of Kitwood's flower 30 years ago. We have considered how much more is known about the lived experience of dementia, discussed the increased visibility of people with dementia in the public sphere, and highlighted the development and implementation of global dementia-related policies. There have, of course, been other changes in the dementia world, not mentioned in this chapter, which have been significant.

At the start of the chapter, it was suggested that a lot has changed in the dementia world since the inception of Kitwood's flower, but some things have not. One of those things, I would suggest, is the absence of people with advanced dementia from the public psyche: people with profound cognitive impairments, and distressing symptoms of dementia, are rarely seen or mentioned in the campaigning dementia world. The reasons for this are complex and no doubt relate to capacity and safeguarding concerns. When I first investigated the rise of dementia activism over a decade ago, people with dementia told me they faced a paradox: other people did not believe they had dementia because they seemed so capable. I wonder if now, we are amid another paradox: people with dementia who are visibly disabled and distressed are not seen or spoken of, and yet they are the people who most need the petals and our love. As we look to the future, we must not forget to look back. Kitwood acknowledged people with advanced dementia, and so too must the dementia world.

Hopes and concerns for the future of people living with dementia

Keith Oliver

This chapter presents reflections on my life over the past 12 years since the word Alzheimer's was first suggested by the neurologist as a possible diagnosis to my wife and I. Taking these backward-looking reflections and talking about them here after the words spoken by the Fifteen will enable me to look forward to how I wish dementia care to develop through the lens of Kitwood's flower.

When writing my contributions to this book, I often mused upon how Kitwood would feel, and what he would think about a person with dementia writing a book of this type in alliance with a clinical psychologist. On the day I received the bombshell of a 'suggested diagnosis' of Alzheimer's at the age of 54, I said to my wife Rosemary, as we tried to assimilate this startling news while walking along the beach at Broadstairs in Kent, 'one door will close, but another one will open'. I never dreamed which doors would open for me over the years since that day in May 2010.

Since that day, I have found that my hopes and concerns intermingle, which is reflected in the way I have outlined them here both for now and also when looking to the future.

My first hope is that whether you are a health or social care professional, an academic or student, a person living with dementia or that person's carer, you can take something useful from reading this book. I also hope you will connect with the fifteen people we spoke with, alongside seeing how useful the Kitwood flower model can be in dementia care. My wish is that you will then be inspired to take this learning forward in your work and connections with people who are affected by dementia. In addition, I hope that everyone with a diagnosis of dementia will have a care plan put in place, produced in consultation with them wherever possible and as soon as is achievable after diagnosis. There is so much evidence here in this book to encourage plans that provide more person-centred support to the individual, not just a prescription for medication which is then occasionally monitored by a GP or consultant.

My second hope is that peer support, which is intrinsic to this book, will develop and grow because the words of the Fifteen make it clear that it can make an enormous positive difference to those living with dementia. We often, after diagnosis, feel abandoned and left to our own devices with little or no person-centred support. Invariably, once peer support is in place, the inclination to take on the mantle of activism emerges, and in their own distinct way the Fifteen could reasonably be said to be activists to varying degrees. Looking back, a small number of people with dementia emerged between 2000 and 2010 who felt able to take on that mantle of activism. This book focuses upon 19 individuals, all of whom are part of what is termed the 'baby boomer generation' – the Fifteen, plus Wendy, Martina, Ronald and myself – and there are many more who we could have spoken with. DEEP, the Alzheimer's Society, 3 Nations Dementia Working Group, Scottish Dementia Working Group and Dementia UK (along with Young Dementia UK when it was operational) have all very much contributed to supporting other people with dementia to have an effective voice and to express our concerns alongside co-producing an agenda and actions for hope both today and in the future.

So often we hear – and I have said this myself – 'what is good for people with dementia is good for everyone', which encourages empathy, understanding and positive sustained action. I could add that at times what is 'good for everyone is essential for people with dementia'. I hope that as you read Part 2 of the book, you recognise the areas to which I am alluding to.

My next hope is that a more diverse range of voices can be heard from among those affected by dementia. Thankfully, the label 'hard to reach' is being dropped where it was widely used in the past, and the emphasis is now upon professionals making extra efforts to seek more effective ways to engage with those parts of the dementia community who have not previously had the opportunity to be heard. We wanted the Fifteen to come from a wide range of backgrounds and communities but our selection was as flawed as any other. If with justification we claim that the voices of the community which I am a part of are not being heard, how must those who are marginalised as part of the BAME or LGBTQ+ communities feel?

Wherever you live, I expect that you will share some of my hopes and concerns about your health and social care systems. In the UK, we are immensely protective of our National Health Service and, where it works well, we are justified in being proud of how since its introduction in 1948 it has sought to provide health care free at the point of access from birth to death. Consequently, what echoes throughout the words of the Fifteen is the frustration that social care remains the poor relation, presenting immense challenges. Many ought to be applauded for taking responsibility for their own care and wellbeing and then being comfortable in sharing their experiences to help inspire others. Furthermore, those of us with Alzheimer's disease, which is – as its name suggests – a disease of the brain rather than a natural result of ageing, often receive no person-centred care beyond medication, which, sadly for many, is only tentatively helpful. Too often I have witnessed care being process-centred rather than placing the person with the dementia at the centre. While the scientific world backed by pharmaceutical companies continues to search for the holy grail of a cure or disease-halting drug, those currently who have the disease deserve better by way of treatments which make living well at least a possibility now.

I also hope that we can restore some positivity and optimism in our thinking about dementia care. Since 2012, we have had strategies, plans, government commitment and a number of widespread initiatives such as Dementia Friends and Dementia Friendly Communities. It appears now that all we have from central government are broken, half thought-through promises, rhetoric and little insight. In March 2023, Nigel Ward, organiser of the annual Alzheimer's Dementia & Care Show, invited undergraduate Lara Stembridge and myself to talk about dementia care over the last 10 years. What we truly co-created and co-presented at that meeting certainly tried to show balance while having some optimism when we based our hopes for the future upon the preceding 10 years. Alongside this, although the Alzheimer's Society has tried to – and continues to – knock on the door of government, it needs some of the activists who contributed to this book to help prise those doors open to let the light shine in, and as one of my heroes Maya Angelou said, 'nothing can dim the light that shines from within'. I did try to push the door further open at the Alzheimer's Society annual conference in May 2023 when, alongside Julie, Chris Roberts and Maq, all of whom are members of the Fifteen, I added an extra line to 'Give Me … I Will', the poem reproduced on page 204. Here, after thinking about good replacing bad, positivity replacing negativity, and confidence overcoming fear, I added 'Give Me hope, then I will have a Future.'

Becoming an activist and putting one's 'head above the parapet' is not easy and takes some courage. While not usually an admirer of celebrities putting themselves in the spotlight, I do have some admiration for the work and personal beliefs of Michelle Obama and Martin Sheen. Michelle Obama wrote, 'our hurts become our fears, our fears become our limits'. And I am reminded of a story Sheen tells in his memoir, which I often use to illustrate my point:

> The Irish tell the story of a man who arrives at the gates of heaven and asks to be let in.
>
> 'Of course,' Saint Peter says. 'Just show me your scars.'
>
> 'I have no scars,' the man replies.
>
> 'What a pity,' Saint Peter says, 'Was there nothing worth fighting for?'

Very good though life clearly is for those with dementia who have contributed to this book, they too carry the scars they have picked up along the way.

So what learning can we take from the Fifteen?

From the point of view of someone living with dementia:

- While acknowledging the many challenges that living with dementia present, seek ways of retaining hope by living in the day and seek ways of achieving something positive in the near future.
- Seek the support of peers who are well placed to understand the concerns that you have because they may well share those concerns and have ways of addressing them.

- Be authentic and true to yourself as an individual with hopes and aspirations which fit comfortably within your personhood.
- Try looking at Kitwood's flower alongside the words of the Fifteen and think about what you can helpfully take from these.

There are also implications for those who provide professional support and care for persons living with dementia. For them, the main takeaway messages are:

- The flower model and the conversations with the Fifteen illustrate the need to understand and help facilitate the need for each person affected by dementia to not only retain their independence but to continue to foster and encourage their interdependence.
- Remember that each person with dementia is unique and different and comes with not only a past and a present but also a future, one that needs professional as well as personal support if it is to thrive.
- Make yourself aware of what is available to signpost people affected by dementia both in your local area and nationally and then keep up to date with this information.

15 Hopes and concerns for the future of dementia care, services and research

Reinhard Guss

Listening to, writing down, reviewing and re-reading the words of the Fifteen has been an education and reminder to me of what people with dementia can achieve, of what is possible with sheer willpower and resilience, and of how far we have come since the early days of my practice. It has also been sobering in showing how much better the lives of many more people with dementia could be with more person-centred and accessible support and services, and of how very much further there is to go in terms of care, services and research.

Research in the field of dementia remains dominated by the search for a pharmacological 'cure'. While applauding the discovery of medications that may at least partially slow down some of the forms of dementia in some people and the increased knowledge about proteins and various genes that contribute to their development, it has often struck me how disproportionate the number of projects and amount of funding is to their usefulness to people living with dementia today. Research into the application of Kitwood-based concepts is notoriously difficult due to the many variables involved, and to carry it out well would require vast amounts of funding. Nevertheless, psychological research has yielded impressive results with the small amount of funds available to it, when compared with biomedical trials, as can be seen in the increase of evidence-based interventions that we were able to include in the second edition of the BPS *Guide to Psychosocial Interventions in Early Stages of Dementia* (BPS 2022), only 8 years on from the first.

In the UK, the National Institute for Health and Care Excellence (NICE) requires 'gold standard' research trials of effectiveness before interventions can be recommended and offered by NHS services. This means that non-pharmacological interventions, therapies and support are at an immediate disadvantage, as many cannot be researched in the same way that taking a pill or a placebo can. Here, my hope would be that funding for psychological therapies and psychosocial interventions in dementia is increased to a level similar to that of biomedical research in order to produce the evidence to make these more widely available. At the same time, research ought to give more weight to the voices of people with dementia and pay closer attention to their experiences.

Much of the support and the activities which the Fifteen described as helpful and which ought to be made more widely available for people living with dementia are suitable for the programme of 'social prescribing' (NHS England 2021), wherein GPs in primary care can access programmes offered often by voluntary sector organisations and funded by grants from social services with the participation of local health trusts. There are many examples of excellent programmes and activities in the arts, museums, sport and social participation that have sprung up in this way. Unfortunately, due to the localised way of organising and funding, it is a postcode lottery for people with dementia whether this happens to be available in their local area or not. In addition, charities have to bid for short-term funding and when financial pressures increase, grants are cut and services disappear. My hope would be that guidance is developed to ensure the availability of such support across the country, and funding models are developed to make this more sustainable.

Following the 2009 National Dementia Strategy (Department of Health and Social Care 2009), there was a brief period in British politics when there was focus and attention on the improvement of dementia services and for society to become a better place for people with dementia to live with a good quality of life. Funding for local Dementia Action Alliances and Dementia Friends began to deliver on the promise of the strategy to address stigma and make the UK 'the best country in the world to live in with dementia', and impressive work was achieved by the National Dementia Action Alliance, for example, with the co-produced Dementia Statements (Dementia Action Alliance 2017), a framework for dementia-friendly hospitals and awareness-raising of dementia among ethnic minorities and in the LGBTQ+ community, work in which several of the Fifteen were instrumental. In the intervening years of neglect at a national level, and hastened by the COVID-19 pandemic, much of this work is already being forgotten, and my hope would be that it can be revived and strengthened.

Unfortunately, the strategy has long since expired and the promised renewal has never materialised. Consequently, responsibility for the maintenance of progress already made and further development has largely reverted back to the local health service systems, with the loose oversight of NHS England providing 'guidance', which is all too easily ignored. The only remaining metrics for memory assessment services that are collated nationally are the local diagnosis rate (67 per cent of the expected local incidence) and the time from referral to diagnosis. Given the increasing number of older people, and hence of expected cases of dementia, this means that an ever greater proportion of local resources is directed to achieving higher levels and quicker diagnoses. This is not necessarily a bad thing, though without additional funds for specialist memory services, staff and resources are taken from post-diagnostic support in order to achieve this. Instead, post-diagnostic support and care are provided by a patchwork of charities with the insecure and ever-changing funding issues described above, leading to yet more of the postcode lottery determining what is available locally. More specialist psychological support, such as counselling to help come to terms with a diagnosis, managing anxiety or depression resulting from newly diagnosed dementia, is also no longer seen as a specialist service and instead is supposed to be accessed through generic primary care services, where the skills to work with older people, not to mention people with dementia, is often sorely lacking.

These difficulties in the way services and support for people in the early stages of dementia are structured and funded lead to an ever-changing patchwork of local provision and a lack of enduring relationships with staff who have specialist knowledge of the person, their history, their strengths and disabilities, and who could provide the attachment and continuity that helps people with dementia function at their best. Consequently, the ways in which the Fifteen found and accessed support and services often appeared serendipitous, and much dependent on their own initiative. The role of 'dementia advisor', which many areas have developed, is meant to mediate this, but suffers from low pay, basic training, heavy caseloads and insecure employment, making it difficult to maintain this in practice.

Alzheimer Europe has published a report on dementia strategies in Europe (2020), showing a national dementia strategy in place in Scotland (Department of Health and Social Care 2023) and a national action plan in Wales (Dementia Oversight of Implementation and Impact of Group 2021), notably with contributions from some of the Fifteen. The strategy in England meanwhile has lapsed, and thus my hope would be for a new national strategy, perhaps arriving with a new government, to provide some equity of availability and access to services, and for a recognition within NHS systems that working with and supporting people with dementia is a specialist undertaking that needs high-quality training, ongoing support, and a reliable and securely funded structure. These would be the conditions in which 'Kitwood'-type appointments and the use of the flower to individualise care and develop personalised support plans might flourish.

In the latest drive for 'transformation' in the NHS, there is much talk about 'integration', which is desperately needed to improve dementia services. An early and accurate diagnosis, sensitively communicated and supported by personalised post-diagnostic support, enshrined in a regularly reviewed care plan, continuity of relationships from early to late stages, and with options for engagement and participation in communities would fulfil many of the needs identified in the Kitwood flower model, and would require the close, integrated and co-ordinated working of different professions, parts of the NHS, social services and voluntary sector organisations. This would be my hope for future services. Unfortunately, in England, dementia is now just one of many 'long-term conditions' that are meant to form a 'silver thread' throughout service planning and commissioning but, in reality, are too often relegated to an afterthought.

Some of the Fifteen have pioneered the use of the internet, social media and videoconferencing for peer support and during the pandemic made this much more commonplace. Also in the wake of the pandemic, co-produced materials like the Dementia Toolkit (IDEAL 2022) and 'My Life, My Goals' (Alzheimer's

Society 2021) have arrived, with the aim of reaching people with dementia who have poor access to post-diagnostic support or need help with strategies to manage the impact of dementia. The webinar series organised by the 3 Nations Dementia Working Group now forms a formidable library of content produced by and for people with dementia. The proportion of people with dementia who have access to technology and are able to use it is rising steadily, making it easier for people to support each other, connect and become involved, even where local services are poor or difficult to access.

When Keith and I started working together, there was no infrastructure to link individual people with dementia or groups trying to improve services and participate in planning and awareness-raising. The arrival of DEEP has changed that and has, in my view, been the single most effective factor in bringing about the community of activists and establishing participation and co-production across the UK. The support from Innovations in Dementia has ensured that the old excuse that 'we would like to involve someone with dementia, but we can't find anyone who might be interested' no longer holds, as there is a communication network and an ever growing pool of people like the Fifteen who can be contacted via the network of local groups. Support from DEEP for setting up and supporting new peer support and activism groups has been vital in this development, and essential to support people with dementia to take on new roles in the dementia activism and involvement work, much to the benefit of clinicians like myself, researchers, service planners and policy-makers. My hope is that funding for DEEP and similar organisations will continue well into the future and is increased to allow for appropriate support of this growing movement and for the next generation of the Fifteen.

One of the early DEEP projects was a guide to language use in writing and talking about dementia (DEEP 2014), which has been particularly important in my teaching and training, but also my clinical roles. Language shapes consciousness, and fostering a positive and respectful language is, alongside decent services, a prerequisite of shaping a society, where dementia is no longer so frightening that it has to be ignored and denied, and no longer so stigmatised that it attracts malignant social psychology. Perhaps the UK nations do not have to be the best, but my hope would be that they will become good counties to live in with dementia.

So what learning can we take from the Fifteen?

- Funding for research into psychological approaches needs to improve and people with dementia should be included in decision-making about the allocation of research funds.
- Even with small amounts of funding, the evidence base for the effectiveness of psychological care and interventions has grown exponentially in recent years.

- Despite the rhetoric of integration, dementia services continue to be fragmented and often an afterthought among other priorities. National dementia strategies that are funded to place the needs of people and families living with dementia as their central tenet are crucial.
- Internet-based peer support and materials to assist with living well with dementia are becoming available. Statutory services need to integrate these in their offer and support their use.
- The supportive structure provided by DEEP and similar organisations that encourage and enable activism and participation needs to be maintained and expanded.

16 Reflections and conclusions

Keith Oliver, Lara Stembridge and Ellie Warman

I have always been a curious, thoughtful person, interested in others' stories and keen to give them the time, space and encouragement to share them openly. Working in the way Reinhard and I did gave us the opportunity to invest in that curiosity. Throughout the conversations and afterwards, we kept Kitwood's flower alongside us and Kitwood's ideology and principles were very much at the front of our minds as a constant beacon guiding our way through new, unexplored territory. It is remarkable that 25 years after his death, Kitwood still occupies such a central position in the dementia landscape. His work though is not perfect, as is the flower model not perfect, nor any individual involved in this book, whether asking or answering the questions. But within his work, the model and words expressed in this book, there is a truth, an authenticity and a desire to contribute towards improving dementia care. Since Kitwood there has been a drive, which stuttered and stalled during and after the COVID-19 pandemic, to greatly improve diagnosis rates, and many of the Fifteen were diagnosed early in their pathway. Medications, though limited in their scope and effectiveness, have helped some to slow down their Alzheimer's and there is at the time of writing the promise of new drugs on the horizon. The Fifteen only touched briefly, if at all, on the drugs they were taking for their dementia, which suggested to me they recognised the immense potential benefits of the quality psychosocial interventions they were receiving or had heard about. I hope that with Reinhard and Ruth alongside me, we have aided this mission, which for both myself and others who see themselves as activists has become a sort of 'crusade for good'.

While in a reflective mood, I invited Lara and Ellie to express some thoughts as young adults on dementia care using Kitwood's flower. As two individuals aspiring to join the psychology professional workforce caring for people with dementia, Lara and Ellie are well placed to express their thoughts on what the future holds for those who share this aspiration with them. They have been closely involved in supporting me with planning, writing and speaking about this book while both on placement and as final-year undergraduate volunteers. Here are some of their youthful though wise thoughts about how person-centred care links to Kitwood's flower.

'Working on a placement with older adults, many of Kitwood's ideals are still used today, with particular focus on person-centred care, suggesting the integral importance of this in order to provide the best possible care for people with dementia. Kitwood's flower model emphasises aspects of people's lives that are often misconstrued or seen as redundant after a diagnosis of dementia. For example, as the Fifteen have demonstrated, identity can often be lost due to a diagnosis, with people seeing the diagnosis rather than the person. Working alongside people with a diagnosis of dementia, it is evidently clear that although dementia causes a great deal of change in life, this doesn't have to mean that people must stop doing things they love or attempting to try something new'.

– Lara Stembridge

'The Kitwood flower, and subsequently working with Keith, Reinhard and the Fifteen, has shown me that a dementia diagnosis is not in fact the end of a journey, but the start of a new one. One that may be more complex, frustrating and difficult at times, but is also full of rich, fulfilling life experiences, something that is often overshadowed by a dementia diagnosis. But most importantly is how unique this journey will be for each individual, which is a central premise of person-centred care and something that is very clearly reflected within the thoughts and comments made by the Fifteen. I'd like to reiterate the phrase, which has stuck with me since my placement and I believe to be a key premise of Kitwood's flower and that is, 'when you have met one person with dementia, you have met one person with dementia'.

– Ellie Warman

The key question this book seeks to address is whether Kitwood's flower still has relevance for people living with dementia. Based on the experiences of those people we spoke to, either as a member of the Fifteen or as one of the poets who joined them, there is no doubt in my mind that even if they were not aware of Kitwood's flower before our conversations, they all – in their own way – could clearly see the relevance of it to their lives and their ability to live as positive a life as well as possible. So much here within the poetry and spoken and written words of the people with dementia provides great insight, not in a morbid, depressing way but as pragmatists facing up to the reality of age and dementia's likely progression.

The most challenging aspect of the flower to discuss was without question that which is love. And what we hoped would come from this was the sense that each individual was able to be kind to themselves and accept that it is okay to not always be okay. Love definitely shone through in each of the conversations and the love that was talked about was for a wide range of things that enhanced each person's ability to live as well as possible.

In a way, the book is a bit of a timepiece in the sense that the conversations took place against the backdrop of COVID-19, which had an enormous impact on each of us during 2020 and then into 2021. A 2-metre social distancing rule, face masks and media coverage amplified the reality and instilled fear in each of us. All physical connection and contact such as hugging was treated with caution. This is still having an impact today and while time is a healer, time is not always something that people with dementia have got available to them.

I wholeheartedly encourage major research funders, alongside applicants for funds from universities and the third sector to carefully appraise Kitwood's flower in the context of this book and Kitwood's original writings when considering research proposals. For far too long, care research has been the poor relation when viewed alongside the many millions invested in seeking a successful, safe and easy-to-administer pharmacological treatment. I do believe that commissioners of services have much to gain from the detailed evidence this kind of quality research would provide.

I began the book by thanking sincerely the Fifteen who bravely agreed to speak with Reinhard and myself and did so without reservation or denial, and it seems right to close by reissuing that genuine vote of thanks. It is people like them who will continue with courage to shift mountains, climb peaks and make the world better tomorrow than it was yesterday or today for everyone living with, affected by or working with dementia. There are many times I fear that dementia care seems to be slipping down the political snake rather than climbing the political ladder, and when I do I turn to the words of the Fifteen to garner strength. When the dementia workforce who show they care and have compassion stand alongside those affected by dementia to combine, collaborate, co-produce and co-create, then we all have hope for the future, and the more we all talk about this the better.

Bibliography

Abdo, C.H. (2013) Sexuality and couple intimacy in dementia, *Current Opinion in Psychiatry*, 26 (6): 593–98 [https://doi.org/10.1097/YCO.0b013e328365a262].

Alzheimer Europe (2020) *European Dementia Monitoring 2020: Comparing and benchmarking national dementia policies and strategies*. Luxembourg: Alzheimer Europe [https://www.alzheimer-europe.org/resources/publications/european-dementia-monitor-2020-comparing-and-benchmarking-national-dementia].

Alzheimer's Disease International (2009) *Dementia Friendly Communities: Key principles*. London: Alzheimer's Disease International [https://www.alzint.org/u/dfc-principles.pdf].

Alzheimer's Society (2021) *Living with Dementia: My life, my goals* [https://www.alzheimers.org.uk/sites/default/files/2021-09/my-life-my-goals-workbook.pdf].

Appignanesi, J. (2018) Reflections on the film Ex Memoria (2006), in K. White, A. Cotter and H. Leventhal (eds.) *Dementia: An attachment approach*. London: Routledge.

Bailey, C., Clarke, C.L., Gibb, C., Haining, S., Wilkinson, H. and Tiplady, S. (2013) Risky and resilient life with dementia: review of and reflections on the literature, *Health, Risk and Society*, 15 (5): 390–401 [https://doi.org/10.1080/13698575.2013.821460].

Banerjee, S. (2015) Multimorbidity – older adults need health care that can count past one, *The Lancet*, 385 (9968): 587–89 [https://doi.org/10.1016/S0140-6736(14)61596-8].

Bartlett, R. (2012) The emergent modes of dementia activism, *Ageing and Society*, 34(4): 623–44 [https://doi.org/10.1017/S0144686X12001158].

Bartlett, R. (2014) Citizenship in action: the lived experiences of citizens with dementia who campaign for social change, *Disability and Society*, 29 (8): 1291–1304 [https://doi.org/10.1080/09687599.2014.924905].

Bartlett, R. and O'Connor, D. (2010) *Broadening the Dementia Debate: Towards social citizenship*. Bristol: Policy Press.

Bartlett, R., Windemuth-Wolfson, L., Oliver, K. and Dening, T. (2017) Suffering with dementia: the other side of 'living well', *International Psychogeriatrics*, 29 (2): 177–79 [https://doi.org/10.1017/S104161021600199X].

Beard, R.L. (2016) *Living with Alzheimer's: Managing memory loss, identity and illness*. New York: New York University Press.

Bowlby, J. (1969) *Attachment and Loss, vol. 1: Attachment*. New York: Basic Books.

British Psychological Society (BPS) (2014) *A Guide to Psychosocial Interventions in Early Stages of Dementia*. London: BPS.

British Psychological Society (BPS) (2022) *A Guide to Psychosocial Interventions in Early Stages of Dementia*, 2nd edition. London: BPS [https://doi.org/10.53841/bpsrep.2014.rep101c].

Bryden, C. (2005) *Dancing with Dementia*. London: Jessica Kingsley.

Bryden, C. (2012) *Who Will I Be When I Die?* London: Jessica Kingsley.

Bryden, C. (2018) *Will I Still Be Me?* London: Jessica Kingsley.

Buber, M. (1923) *Ich und Du*. Leipzig: Insel-Verlag.

Buber, M. (1937) *I and Thou*, trans. R.G. Smith. Edinburgh: T. & T. Clark.

Bute, J. and Morse, L. (2018) *Dementia from the Inside: A doctor's personal journey of hope*. London: Society for Promoting Christian Knowledge.

Cheston, R. (2022) *Dementia and Psychotherapy Reconsidered* (Reconsidering Dementia Series). London: Open University Press.

Clare, L., Wilson, B.A., Carter, G., Hodges, J.R. and Adams, M. (2001) Long-term maintenance of treatment gains following a cognitive rehabilitation intervention in early dementia of Alzheimer type: a single case study, *Neuropsychological Rehabilitation*, 11 (3/4): 477–94 [https://doi.org/10.1080/09602010042000213].

Clare, L., Kudlicka, A., Oyebode, J.R., Jones, R.W., Bayer, A., Leroi, I., Kopelman, M., James, I.A., Culverwell, A., Pool, J., Brand, A., Henderson, C., Hoare, Z., Knapp, M. and Woods, B. (2019) Individual goal-oriented cognitive rehabilitation to improve everyday functioning for people with early-stage dementia: a multicentre randomised controlled trial (the GREAT trial), *International Journal of Geriatric Psychiatry*, 34 (5): 709–21 [https://doi.org/10.1002/gps.5076].

D'Astous, V., Abrams, R., Vandrevala, T., Samsi, K. and Manthorpe, J. (2019) Gaps in understanding the experiences of homecare workers providing care for people with dementia up to the end of life: a systematic review, *Dementia*, 18 (3): 970–89 [https://doi.org/10.1177/1471301217699354].

Dementia Action Alliance (2017) *The Dementia Statements.* London: Dementia Action Alliance.

Dementia Action Alliance (2018) *Dementia-Friendly Hospital Charter.* London: Dementia Action Alliance.

Dementia Engagement and Empowerment Project (DEEP) (2014) *Dementia Words Matter: Guidelines on language about dementia.* Exeter: DEEP [https://dementiavoices.org.uk/wp-content/uploads/2015/03/DEEP-Guide-Language.pdf].

Denborough, D. (2014) *Retelling the Stories of Our Lives.* New York: W.W. Norton.

Department of Health and Social Care (DHSC) (2009) *Living Well with Dementia: A national dementia strategy.* GOV.UK [https://www.gov.uk/government/publications/living-well-with-dementia-a-national-dementia-strategy].

Department of Health and Social Care Scotland. Scottish Government [https://www.gov.scot/publications/new-dementia-strategy-scotland-everyones-story/].

Gray, K., Russell, C. and Twigg, J., eds. (2023) *Leisure and Everyday Life with Dementia.* London: Open University Press.

Green, G. and Lakey, L. (2013) *Building Dementia-friendly Communities: A priority for everyone.* London: Alzheimer's Society [https://actonalz.org/sites/default/files/2023-01/Dementia_friendly_communities_full_report.pdf].

Greenblat, C. (2012) *Love, Loss, and Laughter: Seeing Alzheimer's differently.* Lanham, MD: Rowman & Littlefield.

Guss, R. (2014) *Clinical Psychology in the Early Stage Dementia Care Pathway.* London: British Psychological Society [https://doi.org/10.53841/bpsrep.2014.rep101a].

Hawton, K., Salkovskis, P.M., Kirk, J. and Clark, D.M., eds. (1989) *Cognitive Behaviour Therapy for Psychiatric Problems: A practical guide.* Oxford: Oxford University Press.

Holdsworth, K. and McCabe, M. (2018) The impact of dementia on relationships, intimacy, and sexuality in later life couples: An integrative qualitative analysis of existing literature, *Clinical Gerontologist*, 41 (1): 3–19 [https://doi.org/10.1080/07317115.2017.1380102].

Hyden, L.C. and Antelius, E., eds. (2017) *Living with Dementia: Relations, responses and agency in everyday life.* London: Bloomsbury.

IDEAL Programme (2022) *Living with Dementia Toolkit.* Exeter: University of Exeter [https://livingwithdementiatoolkit.org.uk/].

Jennings, L., ed. (2014) *Welcome to Our World: A collection of life writing by people living with dementia.* Canterbury: Forget-Me-Nots.

Jennings, L., Oliver, K. and Shaw, J., eds. (2021) *Time and Place: Collected poems.* Canterbury: Lioness Writing Ltd.

Kaiser, P. and Eley, R., eds. (2017) *Life Story Work with People with Dementia: Ordinary lives, extraordinary people*. London: Jessica Kingsley.

Keady, J., ed. (2023) *Reconsidering Neighbourhoods and Living with Dementia: Spaces, places, and people*. London: Open University Press.

Kitwood, T. (1993) Towards a theory of dementia care: the interpersonal process, *Ageing and Society*, 13 (1): 51–67 [https://doi.org/10.1017/S0144686X00000647].

Kitwood, T. (1997) *Dementia Reconsidered: The person comes first*. Buckingham: Open University Press.

Kitwood, T. and Brooker, D., eds. (2019) *Dementia Reconsidered, Revisited: The person still comes first*. London: Open University Press.

Kottorp, A., Nygård, L., Hedman, A., Öhman, A., Malinowsky, C., Rosenberg, L., Lindqvist, E. and Ryd, C. (2016) Access to and use of everyday technology among older people: an occupational justice issue – but for whom? *Journal of Occupational Science*, 23 (3): 382–88 [https://doi.org/10.1080/14427591.2016.1151457].

Lawrence, V., Samsi, K., Murray, J., Harari, D. and Banerjee, S. (2011) Dying well with dementia: qualitative examination of end-of-life care, *British Journal of Psychiatry*, 199 (5): 417–22 [https://doi.org/10.1192/bjp.bp.111.093989].

Lugg, A., Oliver, K. and Stembridge, L. (2022) *The Forget Me Nots: The first ten years*. Canterbury: Lioness Writing Ltd.

Maslow, A.H. (1943) A theory of human motivation, *Psychological Review*, 50 (4): 370–96 [https://doi.org/10.1037/h0054346].

McCormack, B., Karlsson, B., Dewing, J. and Lerdal, A. (2010) Exploring person-centredness: a qualitative meta-synthesis of four studies, *Scandinavian Journal of Caring Sciences*, 24 (3): 620–34 [https://doi.org/10.1111/j.1471-6712.2010.00814.x].

McFadden, S.H. and McFadden, J.T. (2011) *Aging Together: Dementia, friendship, and flourishing communities*. Baltimore, MD: Johns Hopkins University Press.

Mitchell, W. (2018) *Somebody I Used to Know*. London: Bloomsbury.

Mitchell, W. (2022) *What I Wish People Knew About Dementia*. London: Bloomsbury.

Mitchell, W. (2023) *One Last Thing: How to live with the end in mind*. London: Bloomsbury.

Nagaratnam, N., Patel, I. and Whelan, C. (2003) Screaming, shrieking and muttering: the noise-makers amongst dementia patients, *Archives of Gerontology and Geriatrics*, 36 (3): 247–58 [https://doi.org/10.1016/s0167-4943(02)00169-3].

NHS England (2021) *Social Prescribing*. NHS.uk [https://www.england.nhs.uk/personalisedcare/social-prescribing/].

Nygård, L. and Öhman, A. (2002) Managing changes in everyday occupations: the experience of persons with Alzheimer's disease, *Occupational Therapy Journal of Research*, 22 (2). 70–81 [https://doi.org/10.1177/153944920202200204].

Oliver, K. (2016) *Walk the Walk, Talk the Talk*. Canterbury: Forget-Me-Nots.

Oliver, K. (2019) *Dear Alzheimer's: A diary of living with dementia*. London: Jessica Kingsley.

Perrin, T. (1997) Occupational need in severe dementia: a descriptive study, *Journal of Advanced Nursing*, 25 (5): 934–41 [https://doi.org/10.1046/j.1365-2648.1997.1997025934.x].

Prince, M.J. (2009) The 10/66 dementia research group – 10 years on, *Indian Journal of Psychiatry*, 51 (suppl. 1): S8–S15 [https://journals.lww.com/indianjpsychiatry/fulltext/2009/51001/the_10_66_dementia_research_group___10_years_on.4.aspx].

Richardson, L. (2022) *A Story of a Marriage through Dementia and Beyond: Love in a whirlwind*. London: Routledge.

Segal, E (1970) *Love Story*. London: Hodder and Stoughton.

Sheen, M. (2012) *Along the Way*. New York: Simon & Schuster.

Shorthouse, T. (2017) *I Am Still Me: A collection of poems*. Bloomington, IN: Author-House UK.

Stokes, G. (2017) *Watching the Leaves Dance*. London: Hawker Publications.

Swaffer, K. (2016) *What the Hell Happened to My Brain*. London: Jessica Kingsley.

3 Nations Dementia Working Group (n.d.) *3 Nations Dementia Working Group* [https://www.3ndementiawg.org/].

Thrive (n.d.) *Gardening and Dementia*. Thrive [https://www.thrive.org.uk/get-gardening/gardening-and-dementia].

United Nations (2006) *Convention on the Rights of Persons with Disabilities*, Article 1. New York: United Nations [https://www.un.org/development/desa/disabilities/convention-on-the-rights-of-persons-with-disabilities/article-1-purpose.html].

Warren, M.A. (1973) On the moral and legal status of abortion, *The Monist*, 57: 43–61.

Welsh Government (2021) *Dementia Action Plan for Wales*. Dementia Oversight of Implementation and Impact Group [https://www.gov.wales/dementia-action-plan-2018-2022].

Whitman, L. (2016) *People with Dementia Speak Out*. London: Jessica Kingsley.

Wilkinson, H. (2001) *The Perspectives of People with Dementia: Research methods and motivations*. London: Sage.

World Health Organisation (WHO) (2021) *Global Dementia Observatory*. Geneva: WHO [https://www.who.int/data/gho/data/themes/global-dementia-observatory-gdo, accessed 18 October 2023].

World Health Organisation (WHO) (2022) *A Blueprint for Dementia Research*. Geneva: WHO [https://www.who.int/publications/i/item/9789240058248].

Zarit, S., Reever, K. and Bahc-Peterson, J. (1980) Relatives of the impaired elderly: correlates of feelings of burden, *The Gerontologist*, 20 (6): 649–55 [https://doi.org/10.1093/geront/20.6.649].

Index

Printed and bound by CPI Group (UK) Ltd, Croydon, CR0 4YY

23/01/2025

01824978-0004